11.7998

e States and Their Indian Citizens

eodore W. Taylor

red in part while the author was on a Federal Executive Fellowship
he Brookings Institution, Washington, D.C., 1970–71.

States Department of the Interior   8 7
J of Indian Affairs
igton, D.C. 1972

About the cover: "Two Men Conversing," based on pictograph from an Ojibwa chant.

(Garrick Mallery, "Picture Writing of the American Indians," published in the *Tenth Annual Report of the Bureau of Ethnology* (1888–89) , Smithsonian Institution, p. 243.)

William Terrill Bradby, Pamunkey Reservation, King William County, Va.
(Photo: The Smithsonian Institution, Bureau of American Ethnology, October 1899.)

FOREWORD

This study is about the first Americans who welcomed the colonists to the shores of the New World and the relationship of their descendants to the non-Indian society around them. The very form of the American system of government, according to Alvin M. Josephy, Jr., was influenced by the Iroquois Confederacy. Over the years governmental Indian programs and Indian reactions have led to our present status of and policy toward Indians.

Although much has been written about the Indians and the Federal Government, there has been limited attention to the relationship of the Indian to local and State government. The author of this study has attempted to remedy this by special attention to Indian, local, and State governmental relationships as well as the role of Federal Government. It is clear that some American Indians have a unique relationship to the other governments in this country.

This study comes at a time of critical review of the relationships between the various governments in our Federal system and makes a significant contribution to our understanding. The conflict in the Indian community as to the desirability of special Federal services to urban Indians is explored. Indeed, the general policies and philosophies discussed in this study may significantly contribute to a greater understanding of the relationships between ethnic minorities and the general population as well as to options available for future growth of our Federal system in general. I am particularly intrigued by the study's emphasis on reservation programing and tying in the yearly budget cycles of all supporting groups to such programs.

Our democratic philosophy holds high the freedom and dignity of the individual. Dr. Taylor's suggestions on how to achieve such freedom and dignity—including a maximum degree of self-determination—will be of interest to Indian leaders; local, State, and Federal executive and legislative officials; and students of federalism in general.

Rogers CB Morton

Secretary of the Interior

PREFACE

The Bureau of Indian Affairs was fortunate in being able to recommend the nomination of Theodore W. Taylor as a Federal Executive Fellow at the Brookings Institution in Washington, D. C. for the year July 1, 1970 to June 30, 1971. He was accepted and most of this study was done in that period. Dr. Taylor had been in the Bureau of Indian Affairs from 1950 to 1956 as Management Planning Officer and again from 1966 to 1970 as Deputy Commissioner. He had also written his doctoral dissertation for Harvard University on "The Regional Organization of Indian Affairs" (1959).

In the process of this study, Dr. Taylor canvassed all of the States to obtain their statutes, executive orders, and special organizational arrangements for their Indian citizens. This resulted in the assembly of this information for the first time in the form of a draft handbook. Each State received a copy.

Dr. Taylor also obtained the attitudes of tribal chairmen towards services from the local, State, and Federal Government through circulation of a questionnaire. This material was also assembled in an informal report and sent to all respondents.

Both of the above studies provided background and information for portions of this book.

It goes without saying that Dr. Taylor approached this study as a scholar. His presentation and conclusions are the results of this study and represent his views and not necessarily those of the Bureau of Indian Affairs, the Department of the Interior, or the Brookings Institution.

"The States and Their Indian Citizens" is a stimulating and well documented book. It raises questions and issues, and offers alternatives and recommendations which should be discussed and evaluated by our future leaders. This is especially true of the discussion of the relationship of the Indian and his government to the non-Indian society. As Dr. Taylor points out, the basic decisions on these vital matters will have to be made by the Indians themselves. They will come to sounder conclusions if they probe all options.

The Bureau of Indian Affairs is pleased to make this book available to Indians and others interested in American Indians, especially those who desire to help Indians achieve their rightful place in our Nation—economically, socially, and politically.

Louis R. Bruce

Commissioner of Indian Affairs

Virginia Governor Linwood Holton receives Mattaponi Indian tribute presented by Chief Curtis L. Custalow (left) and Jacob V. Custalow at Richmond, Va.

(Photo: *The Richmond News Leader*, November 24, 1971.)

ACKNOWLEDGMENTS

Doing a thorough study on a subject as complex and fluid as "The States and Their Indian Citizens" involved the help of many people—Indian and non-Indian.

Commissioner of Indian Affairs Louis R. Bruce initially suggested the review of State Indian commissions and has supported the study from the beginning. Robert L. Bennett, former Commissioner, read portions of the manuscript and made helpful suggestions. Former Commissioner Philleo Nash gave valuable time to discuss the original outline of the study.

Assistant Secretary of the Interior for Public Land Management Harrison Loesch approved my nomination by the Department as a Federal Executive Fellow at the Brookings Institution. No Bureau or Departmental official has impinged on my complete academic freedom. I am certain that some would disagree with emphasis, interpretation, reasoning, and recommendations found in the study.

James M. Mitchell and Fordyce Luikart of the Brookings Advanced Study Program were of great assistance in counseling me on the project. Senior Fellows of the Brookings Institution David T. Stanley, Herbert Kaufman, and James L. Sundquist read all or portions of the manuscript and offered valuable suggestions. David Stanley was particularly helpful because of his interest and his previous experience with the Indian Health Service when he was in the Office of the Secretary, Department of Health, Education, and Welfare.

Dr. George A. Graham, Executive Director, National Academy of Public Administration, was very helpful in discussing the idea of this study in its germinal stage. His interest in the Indian problem had been stimulated by his experience as Chairman of the 1948 Hoover Commission Task Force on Indian Affairs.

The chairmen of Indian councils who responded to my questionnaire provided data on Indian leadership attitudes without which the study would lack a base. I am deeply grateful to them for this courtesy.

The Governors, their staffs, Indian Commission members, and executive directors with whom I have corresponded and talked to personally and over the telephone were universally helpful. Their cooperation has made this publication more useful than otherwise would have been the case.

The "Indian Desk offices" of the various Federal agencies in Washington, D.C., and officials of the National Council on Indian Opportunity, in particular Dale Wing, have reviewed manuscript materials and offered stimulating suggestions.

I was fortunate to be able to talk over the nature of the study and the construction of the proposed questionnaire to Indian leaders with Leo Vocu, Executive Secretary of the National Congress of American Indians, who himself filled out one of the questionnaires.

John C. Rainer, both as Chairman of the Governors' Interstate Indian Council and as Chief Indian Member of the National Council on Indian Opportunity, has helped the author in ways too numerous to mention. Vernon L. Ashley, when Chairman of the Governors' Interstate Indian Council, was also supportive.

Dr. John C. Ewers and Dr. Wilcomb E. Washburn of the Smithsonian Institution read portions of the manuscript. Dr. Ewers made useful suggestions concerning the later chapters, especially Chapter VIII, of the manuscript and the selected bibliography.

Dr. Frederick A. Shippey, Professor at Drew University, and Dr. S. Lyman Tyler, Dean of the Department of International Education, University of Utah, have given valuable counsel. Dr. Frederick J. Dockstader, Director, Museum of the American Indian, Heye Foundation, reviewed portions of the section on early history and made suggestions which I have adopted.

The executive staff and program specialists in the Bureau of Indian Affairs and the Indian Health Service have been subjected to numerous requests for information and many have graciously read portions of the manuscript with resultant improvement.

All suggestions could not be included and the author must bear responsibility for the statements in this study except as specified in footnotes or quotes.

Theodore W. Taylor

CONTENTS

List of Frequently Used Initials

BIA   Bureau of Indian Affairs, U. S. Department of the Interior

EDA   Economic Development Administration, U. S. Department of Commerce

GIIC   Governors' Interstate Indian Council

HCR 108   House Concurrent Resolution 108, adopted August 1, 1953, frequently referred to as the "termination policy"

HEW   U. S. Department of Health, Education and Welfare

HUD   U. S. Department of Housing and Urban Development

IHS   Indian Health Service, U. S. Department of Health, Education and Welfare

IRA   Indian Reorganization Act of 1934 (48 stat. 984). Authorized the organization of Indian tribes with a large degree of self government; stopped the allotment policy and authorized the purchase of land for Indian people

JOM   Johnson-O'Malley Act, 1934 (48 stat. 596). Authorized the Secretary of the Interior to enter into contracts with States or their subdivisions for education, medical attention, agricultural assistance and social welfare

NCAI   National Congress of American Indians

NCIO   National Council on Indian Opportunity

NTCA   National Tribal Chairmen's Association

OEO   Office of Economic Opportunity

PL 280   Statute giving consent of the United States to any State to assume civil and criminal jurisdiction over their Indian citizens, 1953 (67 stat. 588). Statute was amended to require Indian consent in 1968 (82 stat. 78)

INTRODUCTION
by ROBERT E. LEWIS,
Governor of Zuni Pueblo, New Mexico

Indian individuals and communities must work together with the local, State and Federal Governments. We at the Zuni Pueblo in New Mexico have developed a Zuni Comprehensive Development Plan with the help of local, State, Federal, and private agencies. In this development we were aided by what some refer to as the "old time bureaucrats." These so-called bureaucrats are the best hope of the Indian tribes in obtaining the progress the tribes need through new programs and new policies.

Our main problem in carrying out our reservation plan is the difficulty of tying in necessary funding to it. If a procedure could be adopted, something like that suggested by Theodore W. Taylor in this book, of tying the annual budgets and appropriations to reservation plans like ours, it would be a big help to our people and all other tribes who want to plan to reach their reservation goals.

The Zunis have also taken over most of the Bureau of Indian Affairs (BIA) functions within the Pueblo. All the other tribes are watching what we have done thus far and the progress we are making. Our progress will enable many other tribes to take over BIA and other programs with less trouble and fewer problems than we encountered. Hopefully they will have assured funding and proper budgets to support their own particular reservation plans and goals.

We are working in everything we do for the good of the Zuni people and for the good of all other Indian tribes. This book will help those who want to help themselves think through what they want to do. It presents insights into some of the complex history and problems we Indians face along with our non-Indian neighbors which I think will be helpful to Indians and non-Indians alike. We at Zuni have found a real willingness on the part of non-Indians, local, State and Federal officials to cooperate and help the best they can when they have presented to them a clear statement of our goals and plans for meeting such goals. We look forward to the future with optimism.

ROBERT E. LEWIS
GOVERNOR OF ZUNI PUEBLO, NEW MEXICO

"Where Settlers Found the Chief Tribes"—The tribes named on this map were chosen on the basis of size and importance in American history. Those shown in large type had more than 10,000 members in early times. The map location shows where each tribe lived when English-speaking settlers reached its area rather than where the tribes were at any one time. Those east of the Mississippi are placed where they lived between 1600 and 1800. Western tribes are shown in 19th-century locations. Reprinted with permission of the copyright owner, F. E. Compton Company, Division of Encyclopedia Britannica, Inc., Chicago, Illinois.

CHAPTER ONE

INDIANS ARE CITIZENS

Indians are citizens.

Yet some Indians have arrangements and special services not available to other citizens:

—some have their own tribal governments

—some have special arrangements for tax exemption, trust services, and special services with the Federal or State governments

—over a half billion dollars annually is provided directly to Indian programs by the Federal Government

—many States recently have enacted legislation or issued executive orders expressing their philosophy toward their Indian citizens

—both Presidents Johnson and Nixon thought it fitting to send special messages to the United States Congress on the status of Indians, with accompanying recommendations for legislation.

Every State has citizens descended from the original Americans. Their numbers vary widely from State to State. Some States make no distinction between Indians and other citizens; some have special programs for Indians; and in some States the Federal Government is heavily involved *directly* with Indian citizens of the State.

The "new federalism" is emphasizing moving as much government and related administrative activities as possible from the Federal to State and local levels. There is a gap in Indian literature on the Indian activities of the States and localities. This study attempts to remedy this neglect, and to develop insights into the workings of our Federal system, including the changing responsibilities of local, State, and the Federal Governments for services to Indian citizens. The education of Indian children provides an example. Although the largest program of the Bureau of Indian Affairs is Indian education, 68 percent of the Indian children of federally recognized tribes are attending State public schools. A

1

shift has occurred over the years from primarily Federal or mission schools to public schools.

Indians are mobile. Many no longer are on Indian reservations. Urban Indians have presented pleas for special assistance on the basis of Indian blood. The pros and cons of this important policy matter are being debated in Indian country, in the halls of the Congress, and at State capitols. This study outlines the difficulty of applying special services on an ethnic basis to other than members of federally recognized tribes with a trust land base. This is a crucial question. Although the 1970 census indicates a total of 827,000 Indians, there may be as many as 10 million people with some degree of Indian blood. Indians are one of the fastest growing segments of our population, with a growth rate of 2.5 percent per year as compared with about 1 percent for the total population.

The study also treats the relationship of Indian Government to our Federal system and discusses possible alternatives—especially the continuance of separate Indian governments which is apparently favored by the Indians. The Navajo Reservation is about the size of West Virginia. What is its governmental future? The Navajos and the other citizens of Arizona, New Mexico, and Utah have a big stake in the answer.

Why do we have special arrangements for our native Americans? The explanation lies in history and in law. Historically, as every child knows, the Indians were here first. The land and its resources were available for their sole use. But, as some wag put it, "The Indians had a lousy immigration policy" and now non-Indians populate the land, use its resources at a fantastic rate, and have built an astounding economy. An element in our national attitude is that many believe, Indian and non-Indian alike, that we have at least some sort of moral obligation to the natives who were literally overrun by the European invaders. Even though western legal forms were normally observed in the process, there is little doubt that the Indians' options were severely limited.

Due to the Indian's different culture and view of the use of land and nature, he was susceptible to severe loss of property and goods from predatory whites. The English Government and the Continental Congress took steps to try to protect the Indians in their occupancy of land and trade with non-Indians. The Constitution of 1789 vested in the Congress the power to regulate commerce with Indian tribes. Treaties, agreements, and statutes have followed in profusion. Most Indian-owned land in the States with the heaviest Indian population is held in trust by the Federal Government. Historically, this trust arrangement was instituted to help the Indians hold onto their land and to provide assistance in making the most productive use of it.

Land in Federal trust status cannot be taxed by the State. Where is the State, then, to obtain financing of services to Indians when those services are ordinarily funded from a real property tax?

Indian people have two kinds of relationships with the States and the Federal Government—as members of tribal entities and as individuals. Some Indian land is tribally owned while other Indian land is individually owned. Although both may be held in trust for Indians by the Government, law and regulations for the two types differ.

Self-governing Indian tribes deal as entities with the Federal Government, with the State or States within whose boundaries they are located and with the private sector as well. Indian individuals, as such, also have relationships with all three in the same manner as other citizens: for example, they are subject to Federal income tax and Selective Service laws, they are subject to exclusive jurisdiction by the Federal courts over enumerated major crimes, and they are entitled to welfare benefits under Federal statutes of general application. In the State, they are subject to its health laws, they pay real property taxes on other than trust property, and are subject to all State laws when they are not on the reservation, and privately, they can enter into contracts and purchase goods like everybody else.

Thus an Indian on a reservation with a tribal government may deal from time to time with four governments: his own tribal government, a nearby local community organized under State law, his State Government, and the Federal Government.

There are many interrelationships between the tribal governments, local communities or counties, State Governments, and the Federal Government.

History of this development and the current relationships are important to all of us, but especially to our Indian citizens. This study will endeavor to analyze Indian and State Government activities and how they relate to the Federal Government. It will also recommend basic policy for consideration by Americans generally and especially Government officials—Indian and non-Indian—involved in assuring descendants of the original Americans the "unalienable rights" of "life, liberty, and the pursuit of happiness."

CHAPTER TWO

CHALLENGE TO GOVERNMENT: REMOVAL, FORCED ASSIMILATION OR SUPPORT OF INDIAN CULTURE

EARLY HISTORY

Before the European invasions of North America, Indian tribes had their own forms of government, generally based on kinship ties. The social, political, and religious institutions of various tribes differed in both kind and degree. Some tribes were independent "states," while others joined in "complex, powerful, and well-planned confederations." Clan, village, and pueblo forms were variously involved. Different tribes had different ideas, different institutions, and different practices. What is important is that they did have their own institutions, including those exercising governmental powers.[1] The five Iroquois tribes, later joined by the Tuscaroras, formed a federal union about 1570, which ". . . attained the highest form of governmental organization reached by any people north of the valley of Mexico."[2]

Into this sparsely populated North American continent came the people of four European nations—England, Spain, France, and Holland. Not only did England, France, and Holland compete for Indian fur trade, which was lucrative, but the English colonies competed among each other for this trade. The more aggressive Europeans often took advantage of the Indians in dealing for articles of trade and land. All of the European governments mentioned above recognized this problem and tried to regulate the relations of

---

[1] Frederick Webb Hodge, *Handbook of American Indians North of Mexico* (2 vols.; Washington, D. C.: Smithsonian Institution, October 1912), Bureau of American Ethnology, Bulletin 30, pt. 2, pp. 814–819.

[2] John R. Swanton, *The Indian Tribes of North America* (Washington, D. C.: Smithsonian Institution, 1952), Bureau of American Ethnology, Bulletin 145, pp. 39–40. Dekanawida and Hiawatha provided the leadership for the initiation of this federation.

"The American Indian and His Gifts to the World" Reprinted with permission of the copyright owner, F. E. Compton Company, Division of Encyclopedia Britannica, Inc., Chicago, Illinois.

their nationals with the Indians to gain the Indians' allegiance and to protect the Indians from unscrupulous practices. To this end,

England removed control of Indian affairs from the separate colonies in 1775.[3]

In 1783, immediately after independence, the Congress prohibited settlement on Indian lands outside State jurisdiction without authority of the Congress. Treaties promising protection of Indian land, as did the Northwest Ordinance of 1787, followed, but these documents "were generally ignored by the settlers and the land speculators." [4]

A treaty with the Delawares held out the possibility of equality and statehood:[5]

> . . . The United States do engage to guarantee to the aforesaid nation of Delawares, and their heirs, all their territorial rights in the fullest and most ample manner as it hath been bound by former treaties, as long as they the said Delaware nation shall abide by and hold fast the chain of friendship now entered into. And it is further agreed on between the contracting parties should it for the future be found conducive for the mutual interest of both parties to invite any other tribes who have been friends to the interest of the United States, to join the present confederation, and to form a state whereof the Delaware nation shall be the head, and have a representation in Congress: Provided, nothing contained in this article to be considered as conclusive until it meets with the approbation of Congress.

A treaty with the Cherokees provided the option of representation in the Congress: [6]

> That the Indians may have full confidence in the justice of the United States, respecting their interest, they shall have the right to send a deputy of their choice, whenever they think fit, to Congress.

The Articles of Confederation gave the central government the responsibility of "regulating the trade and managing all affairs with the Indians, not members of any of the States, provided that the legislative right of any State within its own limits be not in-

---

[3] S. Lyman Tyler, A History of Indian Policy, unpublished manuscript, July 1969, pp. 38–39.

[4] Ibid., pp. 45–46.

[5] Delaware Treaty of September 17, 1778, Article VI.

[6] Hopewell Treaty of November 28, 1785, Article XII. Also see Vine Deloria, Jr., Custer Died for Your Sins (New York The Macmillan Co., 1969), pp. 32–34, and Worcester v. Georgia, 6 Pet. 515, 546, 548 (1832) for further discussions on this point.

fringed or violated. . . ." Thus responsibility for Indian affairs was divided between the central government and the States.

Indian governmental forms had an influence on the invaders. The structure of the League of the Iroquois ". . . had an indirect influence not only on the union of the colonies, but on the government of the United States as it was constituted in 1789." [7]

Benjamin Franklin cited the Iroquois example in his proposal for a union of the Colonies in 1754. Josephy states that ". . . in such forms and methods by which congressional Senate and House conferees work out bills in compromise sessions, for instance, one may recognize similarities to the ways in which the Iroquois League functioned." [8]

Nevertheless, the framers of the Constitution did not have equality in mind, as Indians were not considered "free Persons" for purposes of determining State population for representation, and only counted as three-fifths of a person if they paid taxes. They were not counted at all if they paid no taxes.[9]

> Representatives and Direct taxes shall be apportioned among the several States . . . , according to their respective Numbers, which shall be determined by adding to the whole Number of free persons . . . , and excluding Indians not taxed, three-fifths of all other persons.

The Constitution placed full control of trade with Indians in the Congress.[10]

The Constitution also gave the President power to make treaties with the advice and consent of the Senate and provided that such treaties would be the "Supreme law of the land." The President was to send and receive ambassadors, and the armed forces were Federal, not State. These authorities gave the Federal Government the responsibility and the tools for dealing with Indian groups.[11]

The majority view at present is that the Federal Government has full power over Indians.[12]

However, there is logic in the opposite view that the Congress

---

[7] Alvin M. Josephy, Jr., *The Indian Heritage of America* (New York: Alfred A. Knopf, 1968) , pp. 34–35.

[8] Ibid., p. 35.

[9] U. S. Constitution, Article I, Sec. 2.

[10] Ibid., Sec. 8.

[11] *Worcester* v. *Georgia*, 6 Pet. 515 (1832) .

[12] *Federal Indian Law* (Washington, D. C.: U. S. Department of the Interior, Office of the Solicitor, 1958) , p. 24.

has no constitutional power over Indians "except what is specifically conferred by the commerce clause and implied in other clauses of the Constitution." [13]

When first coming to these shores, the British along with other foreign powers claimed title to the land under the doctrine of discovery or conquest. The English soon found that the purchase of land was far cheaper and more effective than conquest. Most Indian land has been acquired through negotiation and purchase, helped, of course, by economic and military pressures.[14]

In summary, because of troubles on the frontier and the failure of the individual colonies to control matters, the central government (the Crown, the Continental Congress and the central government under the new Constitution) tried to assume control over Indian affairs. These efforts had limited success. The Government had difficulty controlling the frontiersmen and the traders.

REMOVAL POLICY: NONASSIMILATION PHILOSOPHY

During the period from initial European contact until after the Civil War, the Indians were regarded by many as strange independent groups. A dominant objective during this period was to isolate these groups that did not take kindly to becoming like white men. There was an underlying belief that there was room and sufficient resources for all. The theory of moving the Indians west to "Indian country" was based on the assumption that if the Indians were moved far enough away there would be no need for conflict with them or concern over their problems. The official relationships during this period were often in the hands of the War Department, treaty makers, and officials with trading and ambassadorial functions.

The march of events contributed to this process. In 1789, General Knox, Secretary of War, observed: [15]

As population shall increase, and approach the Indian

---

[13] Ibid., p. 24.

[14] Felix S. Cohen, "Original Indian Title," *Minnesota Law Review*, December 1947, pp 34–35. Deloria takes a different view, op. cit. pp. 30–31.

[15] Laurence F. Schmeckebier, *The Office of Indian Affairs, Its History, Activities and Organization* (Baltimore: The Johns Hopkins Press, 1927), Institute for Government Research Service, Monographs of the United States Government, No. 48, p. 18, in which *American State Papers, Indian Affairs*, vol. 1, p. 53 is cited.

boundaries, game will be diminished, and new purchases may be made for small considerations. This has been, and probably will be, the inevitable consequence of cultivation.

Alexis de Tocqueville, in his penetrating analysis, went a step further by pointing out that the European trade with Indians for furs placed a double pressure on game. The Indians not only hunted for food but to obtain sufficient furs to buy guns, ardent spirits, and iron.[16]

John Collier, former Commissioner of Indian Affairs, also points out that at the time of white arrival "these societies existed in perfect ecological balance with the forest, the plains, the desert, the waters, and the animal life." [17]

It is estimated that there may have been ten million mule deer and 40 million whitetailed deer on their original range. These numbers were reduced to an estimated total population of 500,000 between 1825 and 1915.[18]

The whites wanted more land; they wanted furs. The retreat of the furbearing animals made the land less desirable to the Indians who tended to follow the game and the whites moved in.

If the Indians did not move out fast enough for the advancing settlers, the Government would send out envoys who pointed out that the game was gone where they were, but that there was plenty of game beyond the mountains. Then they spread "firearms, woolen garments, kegs of brandy, glass necklaces" and other articles before the Indians. If the Indians still hesitated, they were informed that the Government would not have the power to protect them in their rights if they remained where they were.[19]

Half convinced and half compelled, they go to inhabit new deserts, where the importunate whites will not let them remain ten years in peace. In this manner do the Americans obtain, at a very low price, whole provinces, which the richest sovereigns of Europe could not purchase.

---

[16] Alexis de Tocqueville, *Democracy in America* (New York: Phillips Bradley ed., Vintage Books, 1956), vol. 1, pp. 349–350.

[17] John Collier, *The Indians of the Americas* (New York: W. W. Norton, Inc., 1947) , p. 173.

[18] Stanley P. Young, "The Deer, the Indians and the American Pioneers," *The Deer of North America*, ed. Walter P. Taylor (Harrisburg, Pa. and Washington, D. C.: The Stackpole Co., 1956) .

[19] de Tocqueville, op. cit., p. 354. See also North Callahan, *Henry Knox, General Washington's General* (New York: Rinehart and Company, Inc., 1958) , p. 330 for list of spirits and other persuasive devices.

Again, demonstrating the impact of environment, the Pueblo Indians in New Mexico did not suffer the same economic pressures as the eastern Indians. Having been forced by the rigors of an arid climate into tight agricultural communities along watercourses, they did not have land coveted by the invading ranchers. Further, they were not dependent on game. Thus, they were surrounded but not obliterated.[20]

Even when Indians did succeed in farming and adopted other European ways, as in the case of the Cherokees in Georgia, they were forced out by their non-Indian neighbors with the help of the State and the legislative and executive arms of the Federal Government. The members of the Five Civilized Tribes (Cherokees, Choctaws, Seminoles, Creeks, and Chickasaws) and many other tribes were removed to what is now Oklahoma.[21]

Various other smaller groups in the original 13 States such as the Penobscots in Maine and the Pamunkeys in Virginia were not affected nor were groups such as the Senecas and Onondagas in New York over which the respective States had assumed jurisdiction.

RESERVATION POLICY

Hindsight indicates that the removal policy was doomed to failure. The assumption that there was enough land and game for all

---

[20] Ross Calvin, *Sky Determines* (New York: The Macmillan Company, 1934), p. 182.

[21] The Federal Government had succeeded in obligating itself to two conflicting commitments. The compact of 1802 provided that Georgia would cede land (now part of Alabama and Mississippi) and the United States would extinguish Indian title within State limits. On the other hand, treaties with various tribes provided their exclusive use and control of land described in the treaties which included some of the same land. Georgia enacted laws "to harass and make intolerable" the life of the Eastern Cherokee. Chief Justice John Marshall held these laws unconstitutional in *Worcester* v. *Georgia* (1832) This had little effect on the State and the Federal executive. In 1830, the Congress had passed the Indian Removal Act (4 Stat. 411). Proposed amendments to this act providing respect for treaty rights and protection for Indians were defeated. This act gave the President (Jackson) authority to negotiate for removal. Indians were advised that refusal "meant the end of Federal protection and abandonment to State Laws." Thus coerced, the Cherokees signed the Treaty of New Echota in 1835 (7 Stat. 478), which ceded all land east of the Mississippi in return for $5 million and some 7 million acres west of the Mississippi which would never be included in any State or territory without the Cherokees' consent. *Federal Indian Law*, op. cit., pp. 180–199.

and that if the Indians moved west they could live unmolested proved to be an illusion.

The gold rush of 1849 spurred the adventures. They poured into South Dakota and California. In the process they invaded "Indian Territory," killed game, and were a threat to the Indians' continued existence. The Indians retaliated by attacking wagon trains and settlements. A period of sporadic Indian wars ensued. After the Civil War the railroads extended steel rails into Indian country further opening up the West and providing the logistics for the military subjugation of those Indians who were not peaceable. Hunters exterminated the buffalo in a few years.

In order to create order out of chaos, the policy developed of persuading the Indians to agree to remain on specific reservations.[22]

The establishment of reservations, as in the case of the "removal process," resulted in isolation, not assimilation, of the Indians. Many Indians, pressured by the loss of game and the superior might of the U. S. Army, agreed to stay on reservations. Others had to be subjugated, such as the followers of Crazy Horse and Geronimo. It was during this period that "Custer died for our sins."

For a hunting people the loss of game and restriction to relatively small areas of land deprived them of their main source of livelihood and their traditional way of life. Many had to be issued rations for survival.[23] This not only led to a difficult period of adjustment for Indians, which for many is still in process, but also involved the beginning of Government representatives dealing directly with individual Indians rather than with tribal officials as more and more governmental-type functions and services were taken over by the agent-in-charge.

In the early part of the reservation period tribes were considered to have a certain degree of sovereignty. This was seen as a problem by Indian administrators since the States did not regard the Indians as their responsibility. Rather, the Indians were considered as "outcasts" and "intruders" and "normal prey for anybody strong or

---

[22] Some whites agreed with General Philip Sheridan that "there are no good Indians but dead Indians." Charles A. and Mary R. Beard, *The Rise of American Civilization* (New York: The Macmillan Co., 1930), vol. 2, p. 131.

[23] Commissioner of Indian Affairs, *Annual Report*, 1872, pp. 3–9. In view of the estimated cost of military operations at $1 million an Indian (Felix S. Cohen, *Handbook of Federal Indian Law* [Washington, D. C.: U. S. Department of the Interior, Office of the Solicitor, 1942], p. 28) the policy of temporizing through issuance of rations had a strong appeal from the standpoint of economics.

cunning enough to defraud them." Commissioner Edward P. Smith stated that the "most potent and sure remedy for this evil will be found in committing the Indians at the earliest day possible to the care of the State." [24]

Thus, on the one hand, the drastic change in Indian life forced by confinement to reservations, the decimation of game, and dependence on rations in many instances led to a lessening of the potence of Indian sovereignty. Federal agents started dealing directly with individual Indians. On the other hand, the States did not regard Indians as a part of their responsibility and provided no control over unscrupulous non-Indians who defrauded the Indians. Both of these factors contributed to the development of a belief that the solution lay in the "civilization" of the Indian and incorporating him into the surrounding non-Indian society.

"CIVILIZATION" POLICY

Early Efforts at Adjustment and Education

Not all thought, even in early colonial times, was on eliminating the Indian problem by driving the Indians westward. The idea of adjustment to the invading culture was also in evidence. Education of Indian youth was included in the purposes of Harvard College (1650), William and Mary College (1691),[25] and Dartmouth (1769).[25A]

But the adjustment approach as we have seen was largely submerged by the expansionist drive, first of England and the colonists, and then of the new revolutionary government of the United States.

General Henry Knox, Secretary of War, stated to President George Washington the year the Constitution was adopted: [26]

How different would be the sensation of a philosophic mind to reflect, that, instead of exterminating a part of the human race

---

[24] Commissioner of Indian Affairs *Annual Report;* 1875, pp. 16–17. See also p. 23 for a discussion of the nature of Indian sovereignty and the need for "civilization."

[25] *Administration of the Indian Office* (New York: Bureau of Municipal Research, September 1915) , Publication No. 65, p. 12.

[25A] *Dartmouth College Bulletin,* 3rd series, vol. 35, no. 2, January 1969.

[26] Schmeckebier, op. cit., p. 18 in which he cites the *American State Papers, Indian Affairs,* vol 1, p. 53. Henry Knox's perception of the Indian problem is ably described in Callahan, op. cit., pp. 314–337.

by our modes of population, we had persevered, through all difficulties, and at last had imparted our knowledge of cultivation and the arts to the aboriginals of the country, by which the source of future life and happiness had been preserved and extended. But it has been conceived to be impracticable to civilize the Indians of North America. This opinion is probably more convenient than just.

This is an early statement of the concept, which has persevered to the present time, of educating and helping the Indians adjust to western civilization so that they could make their own way in the new environment which was engulfing them.

Jefferson, noting the effects of the overflowing European population upon the Indians, urged them to become agriculturists. However, the placing of instructors and implements with the Indian frequently met with little success.[27]   As a general rule Indian men considered working at agriculture and industry as an evil and a disgrace; war and hunting were the only pursuits worthy of a man.[28]

In 1872, Commissioner Francis A. Walker recognized two considerations for submissive Indians: (1) the continent was originally owned and occupied by them, and (2) they had lost their normal means of livelihood. As a principle of national morality, a substitute should be provided. This substitute was not "systematic gratuities of food and clothing" as was temporarily required, but by ". . . helping them over the first rough place on the 'white man's road,' and, meanwhile, supplying such subsistence as is absolutely necessary during the period of initiation and experiment."[29]

In bringing this about the Commissioner believed a rigid reformatory discipline was required for at least one generation: the Indians would be required to work in order to eat; they could not be left to their own choices as to how miserably they might live in order to escape work; they should be required to learn and practice the arts of industry. They would have to be kept on reservations during this period or they would become ". . . festering sores on the communities near where they are located; the men resorting for

[27] Saul K. Padover, *Thomas Jefferson on Democracy* (New York: A Mentor Book, published by the New American Library, D. Appleton Century Co., 1939) , pp. 104–105.

[28] de Tocqueville, op. cit., pp. 356–357.

[29] Commissioner of Indian Affairs, *Annual Report*, 1872, pp. 10–11.

a living to basket-making and hog-stealing; the women to fortune-telling and harlotry." [30]

The above is a forthright statement of proposed enforced acculturation. As Vernon D. Malan has pointed out, if friendly relationships had been possible and permissive acculturation feasible, the acculturation process would probably have been expedited. However, the force of circumstances made the achievement of an environment conducive .to permissive acculturation practically impossible. [31]

Jim Thorpe's school, Carlisle, was the first of the larger nonreservation boarding schools, established in 1789 in Carlisle, Pa. Chemawa (Salem, Ore.) was established in 1880 and Chilocco (Okla.) and Haskell (Kan.) in 1884. [32]

Religious groups were active and President Ulysses S. Grant experimented with turning over many Indian Agencies to superintendents nominated by such groups. [33]

During the "isolation'" policy period these beginning moves aimed at acculturation were subordinate. However, as the impossibility of "isolation" as a solution became increasingly evident, the emphasis shifted to "civilization" of the Indian.

Attempt to Breakup Tribes and Merge Individual Indians into the General Society: The Allotment Act

Emphasis on each Indian as an individual rather than as a member of a tribe came to a peak with the passage of the General Allotment Act in 1887, providing for individualizing Indian land. [34]

---

[30] Ibid., p. 11.

[31] Vernon D. Malan, *Acculturation of the Dakota Indians* (College Station, S. Dak.: Agricultural Experiment Station, South Dakota State College of Agriculture and Mechanic Arts, June 1956), Pamphlet No. 119, p. 13.

[32] Board of Indian Commissioners, Bulletin 242, p. 22.

[33] By 1871, 67 of the 74 Indian agencies were assigned to religious denominations who nominated superintendents and agents. Commissioner of Indian Affairs, *Annual Report*, 1871, pp. 6, 191–192. "Sectarian rivalry, narrow minded denominationalism and church jealousies provoked bickerings, recriminations, and bad feeling." Board of Indian Commissioners, Bulletin No. 242. The procedure was abandoned in the 1880's.

[34] 24 Stat. 388, sometimes referred to as the Dawes Act. Allotment of land began in the early part of the 18th Century and by 1885 over 11,000 patents had been issued to individual Indians under the authority of various treaties and laws. D. S. Otis, "History of the Allotment Policy," *House: Hearings on H. R. 7902* (Washington, D. C.: 73rd Cong., 2nd sess., U. S. House of Representatives, 1934), pt. 9, p. 428. Under the Allotment Act, the President was authorized at his discretion to have

Since the non-Indian was self-sufficient with a plot of ground (40 acres and a mule), it was believed that the Indian could learn to be self-sufficient through agriculture, too. Along with this agricultural philosophy was the belief that private ownership of property would act as a stimulus to the Indian just as it did to the non-Indian.[35]

Whenever an allotment was made, the Indian became a citizen of the United States ". . . endowed with all the civil and political privileges and subject to all the responsibilities and duties of any other citizen of the Republic." [36]

Thus, the policy was acceptance of Indians as equal members of the community, rather than considering them as aliens, dependent or otherwise, which was the basis of earlier policy. Civilization through agriculture and education would "finally enable Government to leave the Indian to stand alone." [37]

One of the underlying philosophies of the act was to break up the tribe as an entity. Supplies, rations, or payments were provided directly to individual Indians rather than to their leaders as had been the practice during the treaty period.[38]

Commissioner J. D. C. Atkins pointed out after the passage of the Act that its purpose was "ultimately to dissolve all tribal relations and to place each adult Indian upon the broad platform of American citizenship." [39]

President Theodore Roosevelt stated in 1901: [40]

---

any reservation or a portion of a reservation surveyed and allotted to individual Indians. To keep the Indian from disposing of his land, the title was to be held in trust by the United States for 25 years or longer if the President thought advisable. Surplus lands after allotments had been made could be purchased by the Government through negotiation with the tribe, subject to ratification by the Congress. The purchase price was to be held in trust at interest for the sole use of the tribe concerned, subject to appropriation by the Congress.

[35] See for example, Commissioner of Indian Affairs Edward P. Smith's statement in his *Annual Report*, for 1873, p. 4; and Commissioner T. J. Morgan's statement, *Annual Report*, 1889, pp. 3–4.

[36] Commissioner of Indian Affairs, *Annual Report*, 1887, p. viii.

[37] Ibid., p. ix. President Grover Cleveland ordered that only those reservations where the Indians were generally favorable to allotment should be allotted, Commissioner of Indian Affairs, *Annual Report*, 1887, pp. vi, vii. In this same report, the Commissioner noted the opposition of the Five Civilized Tribes to allotment and condemned them for their opposition, pp. x–xiv. The greatest percent of remaining Indian trust land today is unallotted—that is, tribally owned.

[38] See, for example, 18 Stat. 449, March 3, 1875.

[39] Commissioner of Indian Affairs, *Annual Report*, 1887, p. viii.

[40] S. Lyman Tyler, *Indian Affairs: A Work Paper on Termination* (Provo, Utah: Institute of American Indian Studies, Brigham Young University, 1964), p. 5.

In my judgment the time has arrived when we should definitely make up our minds to recognize the Indian as an individual and not as a member of a tribe. The General Allotment Act is a mighty pulverizing engine to break up the tribal mass.

Along with efforts to stamp out Indian culture and customs, the cumulative effect of action following in the wake of the Allotment Act was to largely destroy traditional tribal government. The Indian Agent and his staff were "the government" for most tribes from the cessation of treaty-making to the 1930's. The Federal Government provided employment services as early as 1905, developed programs for the increased productivity of resources, established and operated schools, and provided most other governmental services normally provided in the non-Indian world by the State and local governments.[41]

The individualization of land, where it occurred, did not achieve the results expected by its supporters. Even though Indians, for the most part, had indicated their resistance to agriculture from earliest colonial times, the non-Indians still did not realize the obstacle of Indian attitude toward this "degrading" work. Most Indians leased their land or sold it to non-Indians rather than working it themselves. Thus most Indians did not become independent farmers as was the hope of the authors of the General Allotment Act.[42]

Other Efforts to Individualize and Integrate

Two further efforts were made to disassociate Indians from their tribal governments and to integrate them with the surrounding culture. A policy of terminating the trust on allotments of Indians of less than one-half Indian blood was adopted in 1917. Competency commissions were established and issued 10,956 "forced patents" between 1917 and 1920. The Bureau abandoned this policy in 1921.[43]

Commissioner Francis E. Leupp believed education could quickly resolve the Indian problem and the Bureau of Indian Affairs rapidly liquidated. He eliminated many Indian agents and placed the Indians under school superintendents and farmers, re-

---

[41] Theodore W. Taylor, *The Regional Organization of the Bureau of Indian Affairs*, Ph.D. Thesis, Harvard University, December 1959.

[42] See Appendix I for a discussion of "Conflicting Attitudes on the Allotment Act of 1887".

[43] Schmeckebier, op. cit., p. 88.

porting directly to the Commissioner. As he analyzed it, an Indian agent was over a tribe and had been needed at the earlier stage of dealing with a tribe as a group. However, the tribes were disintegrating as the result of allotment of their lands to individuals and the education in non-Indian ways of their children. The Bureau was then dealing primarily with Indians as individuals rather than as a group. Therefore, Commissioner Leupp placed small groups of Indians "in charge of a bonded day-school teacher or farmer, who reports direct to this Office without the intervention of his former superior, the agent." This would facilitate individualization and ". . . in the course of time the Indian day schools are expected to merge into the local common school system, and then . . . they will have been absorbed into the general body politic and become like all other Americans, except as to origin and ancestry." [44]

Increased Responsibilities of Federal and State Governments

Citizenship for Indians did not begin with the Allotment Act. Citizenship had been conferred by special treaty to specific groups as early as 1817.[45] The Congress conferred citizenship on all other Indians born within the territorial limits of the United States in 1924.[46] As a result, Indians automatically become citizens of the State of their residence.[47]

The cessation of treaty-making in 1871, the Allotment Act, and the drive to make Indians like the rest of us led to the Federal and State Governments taking many more actions concerned with the internal affairs of the tribes and directly affecting individual Indians. The Indian Agent, and his staff, replaced the tribal govern-

---

[44] Commissioner of Indian Affairs, *Annual Report*, 1907, pp. 12–14, Commissioner T. J. Morgan had proposed this policy in 1892. See Commissioner of Indian Affairs, *Annual Report*, 1892, p. 9.

[45] 7 Stat. 159; Commissioner of Indian Affairs, *Annual Report*, 1891, p. 18.

[46] 43 Stat. 253.

[47] *Federal Indian Law*, op. cit., p. 523. States cannot deny Indians the right to vote if they meet the same qualifications required of other voters. The trust relationship is not considered inconsistent with citizenship in the view of the courts. Ibid., pp. 526–532. Canada, on the contrary, historically has tied voting privileges to full assumption of citizenship responsibilities and termination of the trust relationship. J. W. Pickersgill, "The Future of Canadian Indians," a speech by the Minister of Citizenship and Immigration to the Canadian Club, Ottawa, March 28, 1956. *External Affairs Supplementary Paper*, No. 56/3, p. 8.

ment in large measure. Substantive legislation reflecting this transition was adopted by the Congress in 1921.[48]

Often referred to as the Snyder Act, it indicated that the objective of the Bureau of Indian Affairs was to provide for the general support and civilization of the Indians. To carry out this intention the Bureau was responsible for: education, welfare, health, industrial assistance, improvement of irrigation, and administration of land; employment of superintendents, matrons, farmers, physicians, Indian police, Indian judges, and other employees; and necessary buildings, grounds, and incidental expenses connected with the administration of Indian affairs.

Indians not on Federal reservations became subject to State law.

Surveys of the Indian Condition

The Meriam Report of 1928 recommended, among other things, effective education to prepare Indians for taking advantage of the opportunities in the non-Indian world, preparation for making contributions in service and taxes for the maintenance of Government, preparing white communities to receive the Indian, working out systems of taxation with local and State Governments, and adopting State law and order procedures where Indians were ready.[49]

Meriam broke with the forced acculturation philosophy of the "civilization" period, and, instead recommended an acculturation program based on an understanding of the Indian point of view, recognition of the good in Indian economic, social, religious, and ethical concepts and seeking "to develop . . . and build on . . . rather than to crush out all that is Indian." [50]

The Senate Committee on Indian Affairs conducted a survey of conditions among the Indians of the United States from 1928 to 1944.[51] These hearings had an impact in the 1930's, even though a report had not been prepared. They, together with the Meriam Re-

---

[48] 42 Stat. 208. These activities had been carried out under appropriation act authority prior to the passage of this statute.

[49] Lewis Meriam and Associates, *The Problem of Indian Administration* (Baltimore: Institute for Government Research, Johns Hopkins Press, 1928), pp. 16–18, 21–22, 36–50, 462–466.

[50] Ibid., p. 22.

[51] Pursuant to Senate Resolution 79, 70th Cong., 1st sess., *Congressional Record*, U. S. Senate, February 2, 1928, p. 2368, and subsequent continuing resolutions.

port, helped prepare the way for the next reversal of Government Indian policy.

PROMOTION OF THE TRIBE AND EMPHASIS ON INDIAN CULTURE: INDIAN REORGANIZATION ACT

The Nation's reversal of the homogenization drive following the Allotment Act culminated in the adoption of the Indian Reorganization Act of 1934 (IRA).[52]

Commissioner John Collier, under the provisions of the Indian Reorganization Act of 1934, not only reversed the land policy of the Allotment Act of 1887, but also revoked the policy of trying to stamp out everything that was Indian, which was an inherent part of the philosophy behind the Allotment Act.

In fact, the IRA specifically provided authority for the purchase of additional land, the establishment of tribal organization, authorization of a loan fund for the development of individual and tribal business and extended the trust on Indian lands "until otherwise directed by Congress."

The cessation of allotments, restoration of surplus lands, and purchase of additional land, taken in historical context, seemed logical. There were 90,000 landless Indians and their opportunity to earn a living in varied activities was severely limited by the depression. Unemployment and distress were widespread among the Indians in general. Therefore, Commissioner Collier emphasized subsistence farming and animal husbandry and avoidance of competition with white industrial labor or with white commercial agriculture—both of which were in long supply at the time.[53]

There were three important factors in addition to the Meriam and Senate surveys that played important roles in the development of Indian policy in the early 30's. First, a change in national philosophy had been taking place. From the beginning of this country to the latter part of the 19th Century, Americans had abiding faith in the doctrines of expansion, exploitation, and speculation. This was reflected in their treatment of competitors, the general public, and natural resources, as well as the Indians. With the turn of the century and in more recent years, social responsibility for conservation

---

[52] 48 Stat. 984.
[53] Commissioner of Indian Affairs, *Annual Report*, 1933, pp. 69, 109.

H. R. 7902

73rd CONGRESS
2nd SESSION

Tipi Hukuya Kin El

FEBRUARY 12, 1934.

Howard-Wheeler Woope Kte

MR. HOWARD TUNKANSILAYAPI EL OSPAYE YUKANPI KIN (BILL)
WOWAPI ON YAOTANINPI WAN IKCEWICASA ON COMMITTEE YAN-
KAPI EL IYAYEYA NA HE IWANYAKAPI NA AGLIHEYAPI KTA.

Sam LaPointe yuieska

Published by
SANTEE NORMAL TRAINING SCHOOL
SANTEE, NEBRASKA

Front page of Sioux translation of the Indian Reorganization Act of 1934.

(Photo: U.S. Department of the Interior, Bureau of Indian Affairs.)

and security has become more highly valued by the American people. Social service programs such as education, health, and welfare,
as well as the development and conservation of resources were
phenomena in general as well as in Indian programs.

Secondly, the great depression starting in 1929 not only accelerated the development of the social responsibility philosophy mentioned above, but created economic distress among the Indians as well as a scarcity of jobs for everyone else.[54]

The third factor was the occupancy of the Commissioner's chair from 1929 to 1944 by individuals who were deeply concerned with the rights of minorities. Commissioner C. S. Rhoades, and his Assistant Commissioner J. Henry Scattergood, who served from 1929 to 1933, were Quakers. Commissioner John Collier (1933–44) was an anthropologist with a long history of interest in Indians.

Collier was also a reformer and interested in remaking American society. He questioned some of the values of the competitive capitalistic system. In the Pueblo Indians he found a society that blended the building of personality with social institutions. He not only thought the Indian value system had much to offer the larger white society but as Dr. Lawrence C. Kelly put it, he believed "the preservation of Indian culture was essential to the survival of western civilization." Or as Dr. Kenneth Philp stated, Collier hoped to "create a utopia where tribal communities offered a model of communal living for individualist-oriented American society." [54A]

Tribal governments established under the Indian Reorganization Act had many of the characteristics of local government.[55] They had constitutions and bylaws giving the tribe authority to: employ legal counsel; prevent sale or encumbrance of tribal land or other assets without the consent of the tribe; negotiate with Federal, State, and local governments; determine tribal membership; assign tribal land to individuals; manage economic affairs; appropriate money for salaries or other public purposes; levy taxes, license fees, or community labor in lieu thereof; control conduct of members of the reservation by enactment or ordinances, employ-

---

[54] Senator Watkins refers to the passage of the Indian Reorganization Act of 1934 as being due to the "deep social concern of the depression years" and states that it was a deviation from the accustomed policy. Arthur V. Watkins, "Termination of Federal Supervision: The Removal of Restrictions Over Indian Property and Person," *The Annals of the American Academy of Political and Social Science*, May 1957, p. 48.

[54A] Papers by Dr. Kenneth Philp, Professor of History, University of Texas, and Dr. Lawrence C. Kelly, Professor of History, North Texas State University, presented at the "National Archives Conference on Research In the History of Indian White Relations," Washington, D.C., June 16, 1972. National Archives plans to publish the proceedings of the conference.

[55] IRA, Section 16.

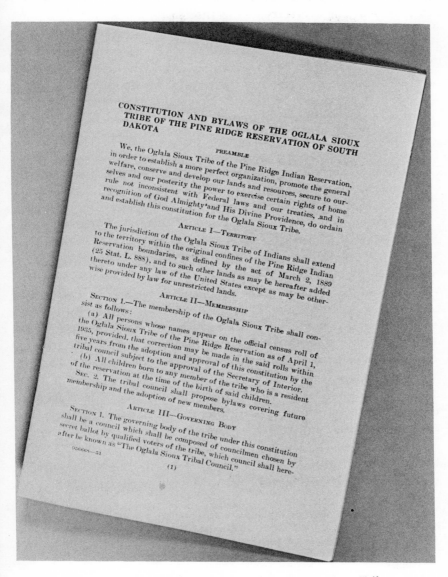

First page of Constitution and Bylaws of the Oglala Sioux Tribe.

(Photo: U.S. Department of the Interior, Bureau of Indian Affairs.)

ment of police, and operation of a court system; regulate the conduct of trade; regulate domestic relations; and enact other ordi-

nances for the general welfare. Some of these powers were subject to review by the Secretary of the Interior.[56]

Corporate charters under IRA established authority for tribal economic activity through corporations with perpetual succession. These charters generally provided that supervision over powers exercised under the charter may be terminated upon request by the Tribe and approved by the Secretary. For example, the tribal charter of the Saginaw Chippewa Indians of lower Michigan provided that [57]

> . . . transactions involving land leases or timber sales, certificates of interest in corporate property, the borrowing of money, the making of contracts calling for money payments, and other actions required approval of the Secretary of the Interior during an interim period of 5 years. Thereafter, the tribe could request the Secretary to relinquish his control over any or all of the actions, the Secretary having authority to grant the request or require the tribe to vote on the question.

The Saginaw Tribal Council made such a request in the form of a resolution and the Secretary on July 18, 1949, notified the council that he saw "no reason why this Department should continue to exercise supervision" over the items in question.[58] However, transfer of complete responsibility, including tribal trust land, requires legislation.

The assumption of responsibility by tribes under corporate procedures has been limited (only three tribes). Most tribes do not carry on business under their charters.[59]

The IRA governmental forms for the Indians were "conceived by the Indian Service" and assumed the general applicability of two principles: "(a) self-rule according to parliamentary proce-

---

[56] See, for example, the Constitution and Bylaws of the Tulalip Tribes of Washington, approved January 24, 1936; Constitution and Bylaws of the Oglala Sioux Tribe of the Pine Ridge Reservation, S. Dak., approved January 15, 1936.

[57] Commissioner of Indian Affairs, *Annual Report*, 1949, p. 339.

[58] Ibid.

[59] This is an area where tribes could exercise involvement and self-determination. The cries of militants for self-determination ring hollow. Most of the militants, however, are not tribal leaders. Many are urban Indians and they have all the options of American citizens to make the most of their opportunities. The only real restriction imposed by law is on individual and tribal trust land. If a majority of the Indians on the reservations wanted this restriction removed there is no question in the writer's judgment but that the Congress would act promptly.

dures and democratic ideals; and (b) communal enterprises as the most efficient and expedient means for economic betterment." [60] These two principles did not fit all tribes. The Makah Indians of Washington, for example, held a traditional belief "in the individual acquisition of wealth" and the Makah attitudes were an obstacle to obtaining talented leadership under IRA organizational principles.[61]

Although the IRA reversed the "total destruction of tribes" syndrome and encouraged development of tribal organization, Commissioner Collier and the Congress recognized the importance of continuing to work with other Federal agencies and with State and local governments. The eventual goal of the Indians being self-sufficient was still there.[62]

The Johnson-O'Malley Act was an integral part of the program of the 30's.[63]

> The Secretary of the Interior is authorized, in his discretion, to enter into a contract or contracts with any State or Territory, or political subdivision thereof, or with any State university, college, or school, or with any appropriate State or private corporation, agency, or institution, for the education, medical attention, agricultural assistance, and social welfare, including relief of distress, of Indians in such State or Territory, through the agencies of the State or Territory or of the corporations and organizations herein before named, and to expend under such contract or contracts, moneys appropriated by Congress for the education, medical attention, agricultural assistance, and social welfare, including relief of distress, of Indians in such State or Territory.

Although not all tribes organized under the IRA, many did. Other tribes, such as the Navajo, have developed their own governmental systems outside of the IRA structure. These tribal govern-

---

[60] Clyde K. Kluckhohn and Robert Hackenberg, "Social Science Principles and the Indian Reorganization Act," *Indian Affairs and the Indian Reorganization Act, The Twenty Year Record,* ed. William H. Kelly. From a symposium held in conjunction with the 52nd annual meeting of the American Anthropological Association, Tucson, Ariz., December 30, 1953, (Tucson, Ariz.: University of Arizona, 1954), p. 32.

[61] Ibid.

[62] See, for example, William H. Kelly, *Indian Affairs and the Indian Reorganization Act, The Twenty Year Record* (Tucson, Ariz.: University of Arizona, 1954) foreword, p. iii.

[63] 48 Stat. 596; 49 Stat. 1458.

ments constituted a "fourth government" in addition to the Federal, State, and local governments. There is a maze of relationships between these various governments.

Whereas the period following 1887 was one of pressure to break up the tribes and force rapid assimilation of Indians as citizens so that they would be self-sufficient, the period following the IRA into the 1940's sought the same objective of self-sufficiency but on a more gradual basis and through different mechanisms.

After World War II and up to the late 50's, the emphasis swung again to a more rapid assimilation of Indians with increased emphasis on the States providing the same services for Indians as for their other citizens and termination of the special Federal responsibility. Policy reversed again in the 60's with reemphasis on the Federal responsibility.

CHAPTER THREE

INCREASED STATE INVOLVEMENT IN THE 1950's

(Some of the material in this section is from Theodore W. Taylor, *The Regional Organization of the Bureau of Indian Affairs*, Ph.D. Thesis, Harvard University. December 1959.)

The destruction of the Indians' source of livelihood through the slaughter of game and the restriction of Indians to reservations, the cessation of treaty making in 1871, the Allotment Act of 1887, and the Indian Reorganization Act of 1934, along with other events developed in Chapter II, provide the historical basis for post war developments.

DEVELOPMENT OF THE CONCEPT OF STATE AND LOCAL GOVERNMENT RESPONSIBILITY FOR INDIANS

The seeds of the concept of State responsibility for Indians as citizens go back to the very beginning of the country. This concept peaked at the time of the Allotment Act. The original provisions of this act conferred citizenship on Indians receiving an allotment making them subject to the laws of the State or Territory where they resided. As the Commissioner stated in 1890: [1]

> If the Indians of South Dakota . . . are to remain forever within the limits of the state, either as a burden and a menace, or as an intelligent, self-supporting cooperative factor in the state life, no others except the Indians themselves can have so deep an interest in their practical status as the people by whom they are surrounded.

---

[1] Commissioner of Indian Affairs, *Annual Report*, 1890, p. VI. Although the above statement on the logical concern of surrounding non-Indian communities would seem to be self-evident, it is yet to be recognized in some places today.

Ever since the Allotment Act in 1887, the stated aim of the Federal Government has been to place the Indians on the same plane of citizenship as other individuals. The Citizenship Act of 1924 made it impossible for States to overlook Indians as State citizens. Most States recognized the joint problem and some of them, such as Minnesota, took a conspicuously fine attitude.[2]

ASSUMPTION OF FUNCTIONS BY STATES AND LOCALITIES

States inherit the former responsibilities of the Federal Government through three processes: migration of Indians from the reservations to the cities or other nonreservation areas in search of greater opportunity which brings them under State jurisdiction; transfer of functions from the Federal Government to the States for Indians still residing on Federal reservations; and termination of all special Federal responsibility for an Indian group.

Many nonreservation Indians, of course, were not involved in any of the above processes. These are Indians whose ancestors were absorbed as citizens by the original 13 States or who never had a treaty or an agreement with the Federal Government.

These States as colonies and later as States were accustomed to dealing directly with the Indians under the Articles of Confederation. They continued to do so, in many instances, after the adoption of the Constitution. For example, Maine, which separated from Massachusetts, assumed jurisdiction over Maine Indians. Such assumption of authority has been questioned from time to time on the premise that the Constitution places full power over the Indians in the Federal Government and that unless the Federal Government provides for State assumption by specific statute such assumption is not valid.[3]

Migration to the city brings Indians under the same governmental structure and services as other residents. Since World War II, the movement of Indians to urban centers has accelerated as is the case with other segments of our rural population and for many of the same reasons. It will not be long before there are as many Indi-

---

[2] Commissioner of Indian Affairs, *Annual Report*, 1931, p. 7.

[3] See, for example, Francis J. O'Toole and Thomas N. Tureen, "State Power and the Passamaquoddy Tribe: 'A Gross National Hypocrisy–' " *Maine Law Review*, vol. 23, no. 1, 1971.

ans in urban areas as there are on reservations. Thus, this is a process of major importance, not only because of the resultant increased responsibilities of the State, but because of the special adjustment problems of many Indian migrants to the urban scene. Some aspects of this situation are discussed in later chapters.

The termination process is discussed in Chapter IV.

Here we will portray the direct transfer of functional activities on a piecemeal basis from the Federal Government to the States for

Freddie Benally and Susie Y. Begay, Navajo students, changing classes at Central High summer school, Phoenix.

(Photo: U.S. Department of the Interior, Bureau of Indian Affairs.)

those Indians still in reservation areas, which is also a process that has had a tremendous impact on the rearrangement of responsibilities between the Federal and State Governments.

Education

The beginning efforts of applying white man's education to Indian children on Federal reservations were by mission schools or the Federal Government. In 1929, Federal legislation provided that "The Secretary (of Interior), under such rules and regulations as he may prescribe, shall permit agents and employees of any state to enter upon Indian tribal lands, reservations, or allotments" to make inspection of education conditions. These agents could also enforce the penalties of State compulsory school attendance laws if the tribal governing body adopted a resolution consenting to such application.[4]

In the past under the policy of "mutual readiness" many Federal Indian schools were transferred to public school jurisdiction whenever this could be worked out in cooperation with the Indians and the State concerned. Currently, a referendum of the Indian people concerned is required and enables them to make a clear choice of either public, Federal, or tribal (or community) operation under a contract with the Bureau of Indian Affairs (BIA). In Alaska, the Bureau and the State have an agreement for State assumption of all Native education as rapidly as the State is able to absorb the enterprise and the Natives concur. In many States, such as California and Washington, the States have taken over the education of most of their Indian children.[5]

---

[4] 45 Stat. 1185. The Secretary has issued no regulations pertaining to inspection by State officials.

[5] See Chapter VI and Table I, Appendix B, for more details on education of Indian children.

The Bureau of Indian Affairs (BIA) still operates 223 schools in 16 States. Four States, Alaska (75 BIA schools), Arizona (48 BIA schools), New Mexico (41 BIA schools), and South Dakota (24 BIA schools) account for 188 of these schools.

The other States with BIA schools are: California, 1 boarding school primarily for non-California Indians; Florida, 2 schools; Kansas, 1 boarding school for Indians from all over the country; Louisiana, 1 school; Mississippi, 6 schools; Montana, 1 school; Nevada, 2 schools; North Carolina, 1 school; North Dakota, 10 schools; Oklahoma, 6 schools, mostly Indians from other States; Oregon, 1 boarding school for Indians from other States; and Utah, 3 schools.

Social Services

The major participation by the States in this function was precipitated by the passage of the Social Security Act in 1935.[6]

The categorical aid programs under Social Security (Old Age Assistance, Aid to Blind, Aid to Families with Dependent Children, and Aid to Permanently and Totally Disabled) are administered through the States for all of their citizens including their Indian citizens both on and off Federal reservation. Over 81,000 (17 percent of the reservation total of 488,083) Indians living on reservations as of June 1971 were receiving categorical aid assistance.[7]

Many Indian families are in need of assistance who do not qualify for one of the categorical aids. Assistance provided to this group by the BIA is called General Assistance. States and localities also provide general assistance to needy persons not eligible for the categorical aids.[8]

The BIA provides foster home care for Indian children on reservations in 12 States: Alaska, Arizona, Iowa, Minnesota, Mississippi, Montana, Nevada, New Mexico, North Carolina, North Dakota, South Dakota, and Wyoming. In other States foster home care is provided by State welfare departments to Indian children needing such care, including those living on reservations, on the same basis as for non-Indian children.

It is the general position of the Bureau that insofar as possible Indians should have the same relationship to public welfare agencies as non-Indians, and that public welfare agencies should have the same responsibility for providing services and assistance as they have for non-Indians in similar circumstances. It is recognized, however, that there are certain services required by some Indians which are not provided by the State and local welfare agencies, and the tax-exempt status of Indian lands may affect the ability of some

---

[6] 49 Stat. 620, as amended.

[7] Bureau of Indian Affairs, Division of Social Services.

[8] The BIA provides General Assistance for Indians on reservations in 13 States: Alaska, Idaho, Montana, North Dakota, South Dakota, Nebraska, Minnesota (only on Red Lake Reservation), Oklahoma, North Carolina, New Mexico, Arizona, Nevada, and Mississippi. In other places, Indians on reservations receive General Assistance from State or local governments on the same basis as non-Indians. During fiscal year 1971 a monthly average of over 57,500 Indians in the above States received General Assistance from the BIA. The General Assistance caseload varies considerably on a seasonal basis and some receive assistance for short periods of time.

Bureau of Indian Affairs, Division of Social Services.

States or local governments to meet the needs of Indians, particularly if Indians constitute a considerable portion of their population.

The BIA undertakes to provide necessary assistance and social services for Indians on reservations when such assistance and services are not available through State or local public welfare agencies.[9]

Roads

During the 1950's, there was a drive to transfer Indian roads to the counties and States through "take-over" agreements. These agreements generally provided that when certain roads were built to specified standards by the Bureau, the county or State would take title to them and be responsible for their future maintenance. For example, the road work done in fiscal year 1956, "will result in turning over 500 miles of roads to county governments, thus relieving the Federal Government of future maintenance expense." [10]

Today the States and counties are responsible for the maintenance and improvement of 42 percent of the total roads in Federal Indian reservation areas. In Oklahoma, with few Indian reservations but with the greatest number of Indians of any State, most of the roads serving Indians are provided and maintained by the State and its counties.

Extension

When the BIA contracted most extension work to the States in the 1950's, it was believed "that in the interest of efficiency and

---

[9] *Social Services Program*, BIA, 1970, multilithed.

[10] Commissioner of Indian Affairs, *Annual Report*, 1956, p. 225.

National totals of reservation roads (including Oklahoma mileages) are maintained by the following units:

State	6,065	miles of road
County	19,017	miles of road
BIA	19,595	miles of road
Tribal	2,415	miles of road
Other	12,045	miles (private roads: forest, transmission line, pipe line, oil lease, etc.)
Total	59,137	miles

Special Study #60–69–8, March 1, 1970, BIA files.

economy, the Federal Extension Service of the U.S. Department of Agriculture should be utilized for providing leadership and assistance in Indian Extension work. . . ." So a memorandum of understanding was executed March 1, 1956 between Interior and Agriculture providing for leadership by Agriculture.[11]

Some States take their responsibility for their Indian citizens seriously enough to support Indian programs with State funds. For example, in fiscal year 1970, North Dakota spent $25,000 of State money in addition to Federal funds for Indian extension work.[12]

Mississippi is the only State in which BIA employs extension personnel to work directly with the Indians.

Soil and Moisture Conservation

Over the years, Indian farmers and ranchers have been encouraged by the Bureau's Land Operations personnel and the State extension workers to join with other members of the community in conservation work. Persons leasing Indian land also cooperate. At the present time, nearly all Indian lands in established soil conservation districts are covered by working agreements with them. Involved in this are 31,277,060 acres of land located in 271 districts.[13]

Health

The Bureau of Indian Affairs was working on the transfer of health functions to localities before the relocation of BIA's health activity to the Public Health Service in 1955. For example, during 1950 the Congress authorized a joint county-Indian hospital in Albuquerque to serve Bernalillo County, N. M. The hospital was built under a Federal-county contract. This hospital provided for an increase in beds available to Indians as well as a greater variety of medical services, and is used by both Indians and non-Indians. A

---

[11] BIA files.

[12] Mary Pennington, Agricultural Extension, U. S. Department of Agriculture, telephone interview July 28, 1970. Seventeen States now have BIA contracts for Indian extension work. *Hearings, Subcommittee on Appropriations* (Washington, D. C.: 91st Congress, 2nd session, U. S. House of Representatives, 1971), pt. 2, p. 1059.

[13] Consolidation of BIA area reports showing cooperation with Soil Conservation Districts as of January 1, 1970. BIA files.

formal resolution by the all-pueblo council endorsed this action of cooperation with non-Indians.[14]

As early as 1929, the Congress extended State law to Indian reservations covering inspection of health and the enforcement of "sanitation and quarantine regulations" under such rules and regulations as the Secretary of the Interior might prescribe.[15]

Neither the Interior Department nor the Indian Health Service have regulations limiting this statutory authority in any way. Most sanitation work and discovery of quarantine situations on Federal reservations is performed by the Indian Health Service. The State health offices are poorly funded and poorly staffed.

The Indian Health Service contracts with State and private organizations and individuals for some Indian health services [16] but directly provides the major portion of medical and health services for Indians in Indian country.

Law and Order

State laws of inheritance, inspection of health and educational conditions, and enforcement of sanitation and quarantine regulations have been applied in varying degree in Indian country for some time.[17] Also, a large number of offenses are punishable in Federal courts in accordance with State laws under the Assimilative

---

[14] Commissioner of Indian Affairs, *Annual Report,* 1950, p. 340.

[15] 45 Stat. 1185.

[16] In Florida the contract with the State Health Department is for the medical care for Indians on Florida reservations. The contract with the Utah Indian Affairs Board covers general medical care to Indians in Southern Utah. The California contract (with State Department of Public Health) provides for limited health services to rural Indians in California. General public health services to specified counties in Western Washington are provided for in a contract with the State of Washington Department of Public Health. The Oregon State Board of Health has contracted with the Indian Health Service (IHS) for the provision of general public health services to Indians at Burns and Warm Springs.

Contracts with some States provide for specialized care such as tuberculosis, neuropsychiatry, Public Health nursing, pathology consultation, and dental services. Contracts with some hospitals provide for care of referred cases.

(Data on State contracts provided by Edward L. Tolson, Chief, Contract Medical Care Branch, Indian Health Service, July 31, 1970.)

[17] Inheritance is discussed following this section; inspection of health and education is discussed in those respective sections. See also *Federal Indian Law,* op. cit., pp. 505–507.

Crimes Act of June 25, 1948.[18] when the offense involved is not covered under a specific Federal statute but would be punishable under State law. Exception is made for offenses by one Indian against another when punishable by tribal law.[19]

The Allotment Act in 1887 (24 Stat. 388) subjected allottees to State civil and criminal laws, but this provision was modified in 1906 to postpone the application of State law until the issuance of a patent-in-fee to the land.[20]

Federal statutes conferring some or all aspects of law and order jurisdiction for federally recognized Indians living on reservations were enacted for some States before the passage of Public Law 280 (P.L. 280) in 1953 (67 Stat. 588) dealing generally with the subject. This was true for Kansas, New York, and Iowa.[21]

Other States asserted civil and criminal jurisdiction in "Indian Country" [22] prior to P. L. 280 without Federal statutory authority. Michigan, Oklahoma, North Carolina, and Florida were foremost in this group. Also jurisdiction was asserted by some counties in Washington, Nevada, and Idaho.[23]

---

[18] 62 Stat. 686.

[19] Many tribes have responsibilities for law and order, including police and judicial institutions, under their constitutions. These programs are frequently operated in harmony with Federal assistance in this field. Some tribal programs are under procedures prescribed in the *Code of Federal Regulations*, 25 CFR 11. 25 CFR 11.1 provides that the regulations are for reservations not having adequate traditional or other law enforcement procedures. "No court of Indian Offenses will be established on reservations where justice is effectively administered under State laws and by State law enforcement agencies."

Other groups handle law and order through tribal custom. This is true for the pueblo groups in New Mexico. Of course tribal actions must be consistent with the Indian Bill of Rights provided for in the Civil Rights Act of 1968 (62 Stat 696) .

[20] 34 Stat. 182.

[21] See "Type of Court Jurisdiction" (no date but compiled in 1970) and "States Having Civil or Criminal Jurisdiction over Indians on Their Reservations as of 5-1-68," Judicial Enforcement and Prevention Services Files, BIA.

[22] Indian Country ". . . means (a) all land within the limits of any Indian reservation under the jurisdiction of the United States Government, notwithstanding the issuance of any patent, and, including rights-of-way running through the reservation, (b) all dependent Indian communities within the borders of the United States whether within the original or subsequently acquired territory thereof, and whether within or without the limits of a State, and (c) all Indian allotments, the Indian titles to which have not been extinguished, including rights-of-way running through the same. (June 25, 1958, ch. 645, 62 Stat. 757; May 24, 1949, ch. 139 & 25, 63 Stat. 94) " 18 U.S.C. 1151.

[23] Letter to Attorney General from the Secretary of the Interior, March 27, 1963. This letter also points out that following the enactment of P.L. 280 ". . . Nevada,

In 1953, P. L. 280 conferred jurisdiction on the States of California, Minnesota, Nebraska, Oregon, and Wisconsin with respect to criminal offenses, and civil causes of action committed or arising on Indian reservations within such States. The act contained the following exception: Red Lake in Minnesota; Warm Springs in Oregon; and Menominee in Wisconsin.[24]

P. L. 280 also gave the consent of the United States to any other State not having jurisdiction with respect to criminal offenses or civil causes of action on Indian reservations within the State to assume jurisdiction at such time and in such manner as their legislature prescribes.[25] The Menominees, who had requested that they be excluded from the original bill, later requested that they be included.[26]

In 1955, Nevada enacted a law (Ch. 198, Stats. of Nevada, 1955) under the authority of P.L. 280 which assumed civil and criminal jurisdiction by the State over all Indian country within the State. However, it provided that within 90 days after July 1, 1955 the county commissioners of any county could petition the Governor to exclude the Indian country in that county from operation of the act, which the Governor could do by proclamation.

Eight counties, even though the Indians therein petitioned the county to take jurisdiction, asked the governor to exclude them be-

---

Washington, and Florida passed legislation either bringing Indian country under their jurisdiction, or permitting tribes to petition for such jurisdiction, or providing local option for the assumption of jurisdiction by individual counties. The other States mentioned above did not take such action, although they have continued to assert jurisdiction. Officials of both Oklahoma and North Carolina have contended in letters to this Department that they have criminal jurisdiction over the Indians of their States irrespective of the fact that they do not have such jurisdiction under a specific Federal statute, and the States themselves have not taken positive action under the provisions of P.L. 280." In U. S. v. Wright, Circuit Court of Appeals, October 12, 1931, 53 Federal Reporter, 2nd Series, the court held that ". . . the members of the band (Eastern Cherokee), by separation from the original tribe, have become subject to the laws of the State of North Carolina; and clearly no act of Congress in their behalf would be valid which interfered with the exercise of the police power of the state." The Court held, however, that the State could not tax Indian land held in trust by the Federal Government.

[24] 67 Stat. 588. The transfer of jurisdiction in the five States involved was approved in advance by the States and by the major Indian groups concerned. Commissioner of Indian Affairs, Annual Report, 1954, p. 227.

[25] Was amended in 1968 to require consent of tribe, 82 Stat. 78.

[26] 68 Stat. 795.

cause of budget limitations. Eight other counties assumed jurisdiction over Indian land.[27]

Alaska came under the provisions of P.L. 280 in 1958.[28] Florida, Idaho, Nebraska, and Washington have initiated action under P.L. 280. Idaho has taken jurisdiction over limited subject matter and Washington's jurisdiction varies with the tribe concerned.

Florida and Nebraska took total jurisdiction but Nebraska has retroceded authority over the Omahas.

Montana enacted legislation for the Flathead Reservation covering felonies and for concurrent jurisdiction on misdemeanor offenses and certain civil matters.[29]

South Dakota provides judicial services, except for matters involving Federal law, for the Yankton Sioux and the Sisseton-Wahpeton Sioux Tribes. No services were available from the tribal or Federal governments for these two groups and the State stepped into the vacuum. An Interior Department letter of August 28, 1947 authorized State jurisdiction for the Sisseton-Wahpeton Sioux.

In some instances, as in the two tribes in South Dakota, and in states of Oklahoma and Michigan, the State assumption of these services stems in part from no tribal judiciary being available and no provision of service by the Federal Government. Maine was not considered "Indian Country" and the State assumed law and order jurisdiction for its tribes. However, there is no known authority for the exercise of this responsibility by Maine.

State jurisdiction prevails for members of federally recognized tribes in off-reservation schools or members who are not on the reservation. In the States where special Federal services to Indians through the BIA or the Indian Health Service are not provided, that is, in non-Indian country, State jurisdiction is applied in the same manner as to other State citizens.

---

[27] Memorandum to Commissioner, November 7, 1955, trom W B. Benge, Chief, Branch of Law and Order, Bureau of Indian Affairs.

[28] 72 Stat. 545.

[29] Ch. 81, Montana Session Laws, 1963. This legislation required tribal action for implementation. In 1965, the Confederated Salish and Kootenai Tribes (Flathead) by Tribal Resolution/Ordnance No. 40A (revised) requested State jurisdiction which went into effect under the 1963 legislation. However, BIA still provides two juvenile officers to Flathead. In the case of the Blackfeet, the Montana Supreme Court has ruled that the State has concurrent civil jurisdiction with the Blackfeet Tribe over cases on the reservation where a non-Indian is a party.

During the 1950's, the trend was toward increased State responsibility for law and order services.[30]

Inheritance and Devise

State law, as applied by the Secretary of the Interior, determines the descent and distribution of individually-owned restricted Indian land other than that allotted to members of the Five Civilized Tribes and the Osage Tribe.[31]

The Secretary of Interior has the authority to approve wills involving such restricted lands and State law is not applicable.[32]

The General Allotment Act [33] provided that in the event of the decease of an allottee the United States would hold the land for his heirs "according to the laws of the state or territory where such land is located" for the duration of the trust period. At the end of the trust period a patent-in-fee would be issued to the allottee or his heirs. The Secretary has authority to cause such inherited lands to be partitioned among the heirs.[34]

Industrial and Tourism Development

Industrial and tourism development must be a cooperative effort between the parties concerned for maximum results. Thus, transfer of responsibility in the sense used in other functions is not applicable. States and localities are interested in increasing payroll and frequently non-Indian portions of a State will be in competition with a reservation area for the establishment of plants and enterprises.

Beginning in the 1950's the BIA emphasized industrial development and initiated cooperation with tribes and States to this end.[35]

However, the termination activity of the 1950's slowed action in this area and the real push began in the 1960's with increasing cooperation between State industrial development people, Indian

---

[30] See Chapter VI and Table I, Appendix B, for further information and current status on law and order.

[31] 25 U.S.C. 372. 36 Stat 855; 45 Stat 161; 48 Stat 647.

[32] 25 U.S.C. 373; 36 Stat 856; 37 Stat 678. *Blanset* vs. *Cardin*, 25 U.S. 319 (1921).

[33] 25 U.S.C. 384; 24 Stat 388.

[34] 25 U.S.C. 378; 39 Stat 127.

[35] See, for example, "Navajo-Hopi Long Range Rehabilitation Act," 64 Stat. 44, April 19, 1950, which authorized $1 million for industrial development.

tribes, the National Congress of American Indians, BIA, Office of Economic Opportunity (OEO), and Economic Development Administration (EDA). The following States are actively cooperating with BIA and others in obtaining plants and establishing enterprises for Indian groups eligible for Federal services: Oklahoma, North Dakota, South Dakota, Wisconsin, New York, Arizona, New Mexico, Montana, and Minnesota. Texas is taking the initiative for its two Indian groups.[36]

Summary

The eventual result of the transfer of functions could be the assumption by the State and its local governments of all services performed by BIA and the Indian Health Service.

At the end of the 1950's, for example, California had the responsibility for the education of its Indian children (Johnson-O'Malley funds were cut off by mutual agreement in 1958), law and order had been transferred to the State, roads were being transferred to the State and counties as rapidly as they could be brought to standard, and all welfare was with the State.

The types of piecemeal transfer discussed above occurred in various ways: negotiation between representatives of the Federal Government and the State or local jurisdiction, transfer of jurisdiction by Federal statute to the State, or assumption of responsibility by the State without specific negotiation or Federal statutory authority.

STATE CONSIDERATION OF INDIAN PROGRAMS

Both the States and the Federal Government were also consider-

---

[36] As an example, the State of Oklahoma works closely with the tribes, BIA and other Federal agencies on industrial and tourism projects. The BIA's Area Industrial Development Specialists in Muskogee and Anadarko are on the State's industrial advisory committee. The Governor has made his own staff and State airplane available for Indian tribes and BIA in their contacts with private industry and himself has made personal telephone calls or visits to company executives inviting them to consider Oklahoma. Examples of results: Oktronics, Inc., located in Okemah, produces electrical equipment for General Electric and Western Electric and employs 19 Indians, 5 Negroes, and 26 Whites. Cherokee Nation Industries, Inc., wholly-owned and managed by the Cherokee Nation, is located in Stilwell and employs 51 people, mostly Indian. Others could be cited. Dewey F. Bartlett, Governor of Oklahoma, *The Okie-Type Company: An Innovation*, undated.

ing the appropriate distribution of responsibilities between their respective spheres on a much broader scale than the piecemeal approach described above.

Governors' Interstate Indian Council (G11C) [37]

In 1950, Governor Luther Youngdahl of Minnesota issued a call for a 15-State conference on Indian problems. He invited Indian leaders and officials of the Bureau of Indian Affairs, as well as the governors of the following States : Montana, Arizona, New Mexico, Wisconsin, Washington, North Dakota, New York, North Carolina, Oklahoma, South Dakota, Utah, California, Nevada, and Idaho. In his letter of invitation, the Governor stressed two main themes: (1) the desire of the States for more financial support for care of Indians, and (2) the necessity for the development of a long range program to improve the Indian and put him on a sound social and economic basis through cooperation between the Indians, the local communities where they live, the State and the Federal Government.[38]

The six main items proposed as the agenda of the meeting were:

a. Settlement of treaty claims and the consequent elimination of the uncertainty which keeps many Indians confined to reservation areas where employment is scarce.

b. Removal of needless restrictions which hamper efforts of Indians to do things for themselves and the eventual ending of wardship, so the Indian can be put on his own as an individual citizen as soon as possible.

c. Provision for improvement in the deplorable housing conditions among the Indians.

d. Organized effort to provide employment, possibly with Federal, State, and local authorities cooperating.

e. Provision for systematic training of Indians through schools and special classes for jobs in various lines, making them self-supporting.

---

[37] Also referred to as the "Governors' Interstate Council on Indian Affairs."

[38] Letter to Governor Oscar A. Rennebolm, Wisconsin, February 21, 1950, from Governor Luther Youngdahl. The governor pointed out that the county welfare boards, aided by the State, had had to assume large burdens in meeting Indian welfare needs.

f. Special effort to secure adequate and equitable law enforcement in Indian communities.

The Governor emphasized State initiative and indicated that united action by several States would be more effective than one State in presenting programs to the Congress.[39]

I feel it is imperative that state officials and other agencies having to do with Indians make a detailed study of their situation and prospects in the various states and then on the basis of the information gained, adopt a forward looking constructive program that will give the Indian opportunity to improve his social and economic condition. Minnesota alone could not give such a program the emphasis it should have to obtain the federal action desired. I am hopeful that officials of the states having a substantial population of Indians may examine the needs of Indians in their states, determine whether there are certain remedial measures that would be of advantage in all states and, if so, join in support of such a program in Congress. A *program backed by the united support of a dozen states would have much better chances of success than action requested by a single state.*

The Nation-wide interest in the Indian situation resulted in a vigorous response to Governor Youngdahl's invitation. Governors present at the May 12, 1950 meeting were: John W. Bonner, Montana; George T. Mikkelson, South Dakota; and Arthur B. Langlie, Washington. There were high State officials from ten States. There were over 100 Indian representatives. Commissioner of Indian Affairs John R. Nichols attended and reported to the Secretary of the Interior that the general tenor of the meeting was that ". . . the Indian Bureau should cease operating activities within these states, but that the Federal Government should continue present appropriations . . . " the money going directly to the States to support services to Indians.[40]

It was agreed that each governor would appoint two representatives, one an Indian selected from a panel of three chosen by the Indians of the State—to form ". . . an interstate council on Indian affairs for the consideration of problems and for making sugges-

---

[39] Letter to Governors February 21, 1950, from Governor Luther Youngdahl.

[40] Memorandum to Secretary Oscar Chapman, March 21, 1950, from Commissioner Nichols. "There seemed little inclination on the part of state officials to take over the financial burden of the problem."

tions for their solution." This action stimulated activity in the States. In Oregon, for example, Governor Douglas McKay called together a temporary committee on Indian Affairs, consisting of two Indians from each reservation chosen by the tribal councils, one representative from each of the State departments, and two representatives from the Bureau of Indian Affairs. This group met at Salem, Ore. on July 14, 1950 to discuss what could be done to establish more workable relationships between the State and Federal Government. Consideration was given to the following questions: should there be a complete transfer of responsibility from the Federal Government to the State in the fields of education, health, welfare, and law enforcement activities; should there be a Federal subsidy to help in the transition; and should the mutual objective be to abolish the reservation eventually and ". . . assimilate the Indian into our society by educational and special job placement . . . .?" [41]

At the general organization meeting (Salt Lake City, May 12, 1950, Governor J. Brecken Lee of Utah, host) of the Governors' Interstate Council on Indian Affairs, resulting from the meeting called by Governor Youngdahl, the States represented appointed committees to get "prompt and immediate action" on: education; employment opportunities; health; housing; law and order; State-Federal relations; treaties, claims and lands; and welfare. They also agreed that most States ". . . had been derelict in their duties in dealing with the Indians . . . " and had tried to push the whole responsibility on the Federal Government. The States should work closely with the Federal Government in determining future policies. They also agreed that there should be Indian participation in the formulation of any program, that segregation should be eliminated, and that there should be equal opportunities for Indians in the public schools.

---

[41] A. Harvey Wright, Director of Indian Education, State of Oregon, *Summary of the Work of the Governors' Interstate Council on Indian Affairs*, October 17, 1950. "The chips are down, the handwriting is on the wall, and the wheels of government have been started in motion. This movement is going to bring about a change in our policy of dealing with Indians. The entire trend of today is toward making every effort to assimilate the Indian into our society. This movement is upon us and we have to recognize it. It is up to the State of Oregon to face our Indian population honestly and courageously and to make every effort to see that our Indians are treated humanely and given first-class citizenship." Governor Don E. Garvey of Arizona and Governor George T. Mikkelson of South Dakota also attended this meeting.

The annual meeting of the Governors' Conference in 1950 endorsed the Governors' Interstate Council on Indian Affairs. The governors said it was "necessary and desirable" for States to join together "in cooperation with the federal government to find a solution to a widely prevalent Indian problem." They stressed the development of this initiative and self-reliance of the Indian himself, the preservation by Indian individuals of "their best traditions" as an integral part of American life, and adequate Federal aid during the transition.[42]

Thus, the governors seemed to accept their states' changing responsibilities toward their Indian citizens, but supported the idea of Federal financial assistance, at least during an interim period. The succeeding meetings of the Council stressed many of the same points mentioned in the first meeting of the Council and the 1950 Governors' Conference.

Up through 1954, the primary areas of concern were: expeditious settlement of Indian claims (as long as unsettled, many Indians wanted to wait and see the results before considering alternative activities) ; removal of needless restrictions (mentioned in Youngdahl letter) ; improved housing; improved employment opportunities; improved training; better law and order in Indian country; better welfare services; better education, including more Federal funds, more funds to States, and wider use of public schools (the 1954 meeting objected to BIA administration of Johnson O'Malley funds as being limited and with termination as goal); better health program and recommendation of transfer of the health function to the Public Health Service which was accomplished in 1955 (68 Stat. 674) ; and repeal of the prohibition against sale of alcoholic beverages to an Indian which was accomplished in 1953 (67 Stat. 586).

From 1955 on, additional items were considered, such as industrial development (1955). This topic was expanded to include economic development (1961), recreation and tourism (1964 and 1965), development both on and off the reservation in 1967, and the roles of Federal Housing Administration (FHA), EDA, Small Business Administration (SBA), and BIA loan fund were discussed in 1968.

---

[42] Forty-second annual meeting, White Sulphur Springs, W. Va., June 18–21, 1950. Resolution adopted quoted in Minutes, Third Meeting, Governors' Interstate Council on Indian Affairs, Oklahoma City, Okla., December 7–8, 1950.

Wendell Chino, Mescalero Apache, Vice President of the Governors' Interstate Indian Council, (GIIC), June 1971. Seated: Vernon L. Ashley, Sioux, past president of GIIC.

(Photo: Theodore B. Hetzel.)

Termination of Federal services became a lively topic beginning in 1955. The Council opposed any actions under P.L. 280, authorizing States to assume law and order jurisdiction over Indian country, or House Concurrent Resolution 108 (H.C.R. 108), expressing the intent of the Congress to terminate special Federal services to Indian tribes as soon as they were ready, without the consent of the Indians concerned. In 1960, the Council recommended that H.C.R. 108 should be considered as a long-range goal, not an immediate goal. The 1969 Council stated that the consent of both the Indians and the State should be obtained before any Federal termination action was taken.

At the Boise, Ida., meeting in 1963, it was pointed out that: [43]

. . . the goals of self-sufficiency can be made meaningful by

---

[43] Report of the Twenty-Second Annual Meeting Governors' Interstate Indian Council (GIIC), Rapid City, S. Dak., September 10–12, 1969, p. 10.

participation of Indians, tribal governments, Federal, State, and local comunity governments in the following objectives:

1. Full participation of Indians in American life;
2. Equal citizenship privileges and responsibilities for Indians.

States were also encouraged to organize Indian commissions to study State problems and obtain Indian points of view before making commitments on Indian policy.[44]

Four States Seek Transfer of Functions with Federal Financing

Four States—Wisconsin, Minnesota, South Dakota, and North Dakota—sought State operation of Indian programs with Federal financing in 1957. The approach was to amend the Johnson-O'-Malley Act to provide that any contracts with the four States would require reimbursement by the Federal Government for actual cost of the service, ". . . including administrative costs, of the State, political subdivision, corporation, agency or institution under such contract." [45]

The proposed definition of an Indian was broadened to include many persons not considered Indians eligible for Federal services by the Bureau. Also, the bills provided that the Federal Government pay 80 percent of the State's share of categorical aid support under the Social Security Act for Indians.

The Interior Department interpreted the intent of the bills as putting exclusive responsibility for Indians upon the Federal Government, except for minor State contributions to categorical aids. The Department opposed the establishment of the Indians ". . . as an ethnic group for which the Federal Government rather than the States is exclusively responsible" and added: [46]

> With respect to the division of financial responsibility between the Federal and State Governments for services furnished by a State to Indians who live on tax exempt land, we believe that the State has the basic constitutional responsibility and that the effect of the tax exemption on the revenue of the State or

---

[44] Palm Springs, 1960. Report of GIIC, 1969, p. 8. See Appendix C for a more in depth summary of the 1969 meeting.

[45] S. 574, H.R. 3362, H.R. 3634, 85th Cong., 1st sess., not enacted.

[46] Interior Department Report on H.R. 3362 and H.R. 3634, April 16, 1958.

local agency providing the service should be the primary factor in determining the amount of the Federal contribution.

In further clarifying its constitutional views on this matter, the Department stated: [47]

> The policy of this Department is to bring about equal and full recognition of the Indians as citizens of the States in which they reside with the rights and privileges of other citizens and with the same responsibilities and duties.

The Bureau of the Budget, in its report recommending that the bills not be enacted, stated that they would effect ". . . a drastic change in the division of State and Federal responsibilities" and that these changes ". . . would relieve the States of responsibility for providing certain service to Indians . . . even though such services are now, and would continue to be, available to other citizens of the States concerned." [48]

Nothing came of these proposals. However, bills of similar nature have been introduced regularly since 1957.[49]

If the States involved were really dedicated to the philosophy of these bills, more would be heard about them. At any rate, they provided an opportunity for the executive branch to go clearly on record favoring the goal of Indian citizens receiving the same services from the same governmental units as other citizens.

In response to the continual hammering by the States on the need for Federal financial assistance, the Bureau of Indian Affairs emphasized and reemphasized in the 1950's that:

1. Indians are citizens not only of the United States but of the States wherein they reside and fully entitled to all the privileges and prerogatives that go with that status.

2. Indians are generally included in the population base and the per capita income base used in computing various Federal grants-in-aid to the several States.[50]

The States also recognize that they can do things on behalf of the

---

[47] Ibid.

[48] Letter to Chairman, Committee on Interior and Insular Affairs, U. S. Senate, from Deputy Director, Bureau of the Budget, April 2, 1958, Bureau of Indian Affairs' files.

[49] See for example, H.R. 17624, 91st Cong., 2nd sess., introduced May 14, 1970 by Congressman E. Y. Berry of South Dakota but not enacted.

[50] For example, speech by Commissioner of Indian Affairs, Sun Valley, Ida. meeting of GIIC October 1, 1954.

Indians that the Federal Government cannot accomplish in as effective a manner, such as foster home care under certain circumstances and the work of the State health departments.[51]

Summary

In the 1950's there was recognition by the States at the policy level, as reflected by the Governors' Interstate Indian Council, of the States' responsibilities to their Indian citizens. The States admitted that they had not done all that they should for Indians; they recognized that segregation and other forms of discrimination existed. The States concerned organized with the objective of working more effectively together on mutual Indian problems including joint requests for financial assistance from the Federal Government to help meet Indian program needs.

---

[51] Mr. Jarle Leirfallom, of the Minnesota Department of Public Welfare, pointed this out in a memorandum to Governor C. Elmer Anderson of Minnesota, October 5, 1954, reporting on the Sun Valley, Ida. meeting of the GIIC.

CHAPTER FOUR

FEDERAL ACTIVITY TO TERMINATE SPECIAL RELATIONSHIPS WITH INDIANS BY RESERVATION, TRIBE, OR STATE

EXAMPLES OF EARLY ACTIVITY

A treaty with the Wyandotte Indians in 1855 read in part: [1] "The Wyandotte Indians having become sufficiently advanced in civilization, and being desirous of becoming citizens . . . are hereby declared, to be citizens of the United States." The treaty provided that those who opted for citizenship ". . . shall in all respects be subject to the laws of the United States, and to the Territory of Kansas in the same manner as other citizens of said territory."

A treaty with the Ottawas in 1862 had somewhat similar provisions.[2]

Commissioner of Indian Affairs Francis A. Walker wrote in 1874 that the choice lay between "seclusion and citizenship" for Indians. There could be no middle ground. Seclusion would not work unless it was complete. And it was "worse than useless to keep up the forms of reservations and non-intercourse" unless seclusion was complete.[3]

In 1875 Commissioner of Indian Affairs Edward P. Smith stated that the interests of all parties concerned would be benefitted if the care of Indians in New York, Wisconsin, Michigan, and Minnesota were transferred to the States.[4]

> I recommend that legislation be sought from Congress looking toward the divorcement of the United States and Indians as "citizens of a domestic sovereignty within our borders" and the transfer of the Indians and their property to the states

---

[1] Article one of Treaty of January 31, 1855 (10 Stat. 1159).

[2] 12 Stat. 1237.

[3] *The Indian Question*, Boston, 1874, p. 118.

[4] Commissioner of Indian Affairs, *Annual Report*, 1875, p. 17.

where they reside, as rapidly as both the states and the Indians
are prepared therefore.

In 1876, the Secretary of the Interior proposed legislation to
transfer responsibility for Indians to New York, North Carolina,
Michigan, Wisconsin, Minnesota, and Iowa.[5]

The "Allotment Act of 1887" was aimed at citizenship.

"We have entire faith," said the Board of Indian Commissioners
in 1899,[6] "that before very many years . . . the Indians . . . will be
better off under the general laws of our States and Territories, and
by incorporation with the great body of our American citizens
. . . ."

The so-called "forced-patent" period (1917–21) was based on
discontinuing special Federal relationships with competent Indians
and ". . . giving even closer attention to the incompetent that
they may more speedily achieve competency." [7]

In 1923, Commissioner of Indian Affairs Charles H. Burke sent a
letter to 18 governors on the desirability of "a better understanding
and cooperation between the States having Indian populations and
the Federal administration of Indian affairs," pointing out that it
was in the States' self-interest to have a well-educated, healthy and
adjusted Indian group rather than a group that was not self-sufficient. He referred to the " . . . localizing trend of Indian affairs
and the need of friendly cooperation between State and Federal
Governments preparatory to surrendering to the former the problems and progress of Indians." [8]

In 1927 hearings were held on bills that would transfer the ad-
ministration of certain appropriations for Indian affairs from the
Federal Government to the States of California, Wisconsin, and
Montana.[9]

The then Secretary of the Interior, Hubert Work, supported the

[5] Letter from Secretary of the Interior Z. Chandler to the Speaker of the House
of Representatives, January 27, 1876, quoted in J. P. Kinney, *A Continent Lost and
a Civilization Won* (Johns-Hopkins Press, Baltimore, Md. 1937), p. 179.

[6] Board of Indian Commissioners, *Annual Report*, 1899, pp. 18–19.

[7] Commissioner of Indian Affairs, *Annual Report*, 1917, p. 3.

[8] Letter from Commissioner of Indian Affairs Charles H. Burke to the Governors
of Arizona, California, Idaho, Kansas, Minnesota, Montana, Nebraska, Nevada, New
Mexico, North Carolina, North Dakota, Oklahoma, Oregon, South Dakota, Utah,
Washington, Wisconsin, and Wyoming, November 17, 1923, Bureau of Indian Affairs
(BIA) Files.

[9] *Hearings Before the Subcommittee of the Committee on Indian Affairs* (Washington, D. C.: 69th Cong., 2d sess., U. S. Senate, February 10, 1927) .

philosophy of decentralization. Commissioner of Indian Affairs Charles H. Burke suggested authorization for contracting with the State for health, education, welfare, and the like, rather than the method suggested in the bills, a concept later adopted in the John-son-O'Malley Act. John Collier, then Executive Secretary of the American Indian Defense Association, preferred a legislative state-ment of policy so there would be no discretion left with the Bureau of Indian Affairs (BIA) as to whether the States would perform the functions being discussed. The Indian Protective Association of Montana, the General Federation of Women's Clubs, local Califor-nia schools and other local groups, all favored the proposed legislation.[10]

SENATE COMMITTEE'S DESIRE TO ABOLISH THE BUREAU

"The Indian Bureau should be abolished," said the Senate Com-mittee on Indian Affairs in 1943. From 1928 to 1944, this Commit-tee made a "Survey of Conditions Among the Indians of the United States." [11]

In a partial report in 1943, the Committee made a vitriolic at-tack on Commissioner Collier's program and promulgated its view on the policy of the future.[12]

The original purpose of the Bureau, said the Committee, was to "fit the Indians into the commonwealth of citizenship" by cooper-ating with missionary groups, the States, and other divisions of the Federal Government. "It was intended as a service rather than as an administrative bureau." But this purpose was lost in the Bu-reau's complex of competing functional activities. If normal condi-tions had prevailed, the Indian would have been able to fulfill the original aims and "would have eliminated the Indian problem years ago."

Instead of the original aim "to make the Indian a citizen," the aim "appears to be to keep the Indian an Indian" and attempt to

---

[10] Ibid., pp. 11–38.

[11] Pursuant to Resolution 79, 70th Cong., 1st sess. and subsequent continuing resolutions. The Committee held hearings within every agency jurisdiction. See *Report, No. 310* (Washington, D. C.: 78th Cong., 1st sess., U. S. Senate, June 11, 1943) , p. 17.

[12] *Report, No. 310* (Washington, D. C.: 78th Cong., 1st sess. U. S. Senate, June 11, 1943) .

help him "recapture his ancient, worn-out cultures" which are but a "vague memory," and "unable to function in his present world." Non-Indians, said the Committee, would not try "to recapture our glamorous pioneer culture" even though it could be done more easily than in the Indian instance.

The Bureau was "segregating the Indian from the general citizenry" and "condemning the Indian to perpetual wardship." The Bureau's "adventitious accretions" may be reduced by "progressive elimination . . . until the whole objective is accomplished."

The final three recommendations leave no doubt of the Committee's objective: [13]

31. Beginning July 1, 1945, reduce the Central Indian Office staff to a commissioner and not more than three assistants, a chief counsel, and a clerical staff not exceeding six persons. Beginning January 1, 1946, the central office staff shall not exceed a commissioner and three clerks.

32. Beginning January 1, 1944, reduce all agency staffs to one administrative officer who shall act as liaison officer between the Government and the Indians under the agency, and the absolutely necessary clerical and custodial staff not exceeding five Federal employees in any case.

33. Beginning January 1, 1944, not more than one administrative officer and not to exceed five clerical and custodial employees may be retained at each of the eliminated boarding schools to assist in their disposition, and to act as custodians pending such disposition.

PRESSURE FOR ECONOMY AND RELATION TO INDIAN POLICY

The Congress, specifically the Senate, was also pressuring for economy. S. Res. 41, introduced by Senator William Langer, January 8, 1947, was for the purpose of determining if employment could be reduced throughout Government. [14]

At hearings held on this resolution, the recommendations of the Senate Committee on Indian Affairs [15] were reviewed and the sev-

---

[13] Ibid., p. 22 Note: As of June 30, 1971, the BIA had 14,714 full time permanent employees.

[14] *Congressional Record*, U. S. Senate, January 8, 1947, p. 168.

[15] *Report, No. 310*, op. cit.

eral Senators indicated that the Bureau had ceased to be of utility.[16] The Committee requested Acting Commissioner William Zimmerman, Jr. to list the tribes that could be separated from Federal supervision and prepare drafts of bills to accomplish the objective.[17]

Mr. Zimmerman presented the list to the Committee on February 8, 1947, with drafts of legislation to incorporate Klamath, Osage, and Menominee Tribes; plans of State control for California and North Dakota; and a bill that would permit individuals to withdraw from a tribe. These were the three alternative termination routes that Mr. Zimmerman thought possible at that time.[18]

Mr. Zimmerman pointed out that if money was saved in Group 1 (ready for immediate release from Federal supervision), it would probably be needed for Group 2 (ready in 10 years) and Group 3 (indefinite time). Even some of the draft proposals in the short run did not save much, as they provided for sharing financing with the States involved. Transfer of law and order to the States was specifically discussed. One senator asked if the States became interested in working with the Federal Government could they not help the Indians more than they were. To which Mr. Zimmerman responded,[19] ". . . in the State of California, in my judgment, if the Federal Government were to withdraw, the State could provide more services in the long run than we are now providing."

Senator Edward J. Thye was disappointed that the Bureau's suggestions would not necessarily save money—the primary objective of the Post Office and Civil Service Committee.[20] Since the Bureau would not indicate how it could save money, the Senator stated it would be " . . . necessary for Congress and each respective State to decide what they are going to tell you . . . to do."

HOUSE INVESTIGATION

In 1943 and 1944, the House had an investigation of Indian af-

---

[16] *Hearings on S. Res. 41, Officers and Employees of the Federal Government* (Washington, D. C.: 80th Cong., 1st sess., U. S. Senate, Post Office and Civil Service Committee, 1947). See, for example, p. 130 where Senator Dennis Chavez states: "I think we ought to abolish the Indian agency entirely. It is absolutely unnecessary."

[17] Ibid., pp. 253–259, January 28, 1947.

[18] Ibid., pt. 1, pp. 556–568. The list of tribes and offices and a summary of the draft legislation is included in Appendix D.

[19] Ibid., p. 576.

[20] Mr. Zimmerman had pointed out that 500 positions were involved with the Group 1 reservations and there was some discussion of savings on this. Ibid., p. 578.

fairs and its Select Committee concluded that ". . . the American Indians as a group are not ready to be 'turned loose,' "; and added ". . . the Government of the United States has not as yet discharged its obligation to the Indian to the point where the Indian Office can be abolished and the various necessary services to the Indian be discontinued." [21]

However, the Select Committee believed the goal of Indian policy was to enable the Indian ". . . to take his place in the white man's community on the white man's level and with the white man's opportunity and security status." [22] This goal was blocked by inadequate economic development, educational opportunity, and legislation, as the Committee saw it and it made recommendations in each area.

The prime emphasis was on education. "In large part, the eventual liquidation of the Indian problem and the dismantling of the Indian Bureau depends upon the degree of success achieved in the proper education of the Indian children." [23]

APPROPRIATION COMMITTEE ATTITUDES

The House of Representatives was in a budget cutting frame of mind in 1946, and reduced the Interior appropriation by 50 percent.[24] BIA was not cut as badly and most of the cut was restored by the Senate.

The important aspect of this byplay during the late 40's, however, was the attitudes of the Senate and House committees on the nature of Federal and State responsibilities for Indians. The House

---

[21] "A Resolution Creating a Select Committee of the Indian Affairs Committee to Make an Investigation to Determine Whether the Changed Status of the Indian Requires a Revision of the Laws and Regulations Affecting the American Indian," *Report, No. 2091 Pursuant to H. Res. 166* (Washington, D. C.: 78th Cong., 2nd sess., U. S. House of Representatives, December 23, 1944), p. 2. Members of the Committee were: James F. O'Connor, Montana, Chairman; Karl E. Mundt, South Dakota, Vice Chairman; John R. Murdock, Arizona; Antonio M. Fernandez, New Mexico; and Fred C. Gilchrist, Iowa.

[22] Ibid., p. 2.

[23] Ibid., p. 8.

The inadequacies of the then existing Indian education and recommendations for solution are described in Appendix E.

[24] "Interior Department Appropriation Bill," *Report, No. 1984* (Washington, D. C.: 79th Cong., 2d sess., U. S. House of Representatives, May 7, 1946). Estimates reduced from $346,765,830 to $174,652,579.

Committee said that there had been discussion for many years as "to how and when the American Indian would reach the point where he would no longer be dependent upon the Federal Government for support." The Indian Reorganization Act (IRA) had not led to Indian economic freedom; in fact, expenditures had increased. The Committee concluded that the "Congress can expect no constructive advice and assistance from the Bureau of Indian Affairs in the solution of the problem." [25]

The House Committee noted that it could spend "unlimited funds" in support of Indians. But it pointed out that the States and local communities have some obligation to the Indians and indicated that in some States, such as Oklahoma "the State is obligated to provide educational facilities for all citizens." The Committee made substantial reductions in education, relief, and administration for these reasons and urged the Bureau to engage in "a gradual reduction in activities in succeeding years." [26]

On the Senate side, there was some disagreement with the House position, Senator Cordon stating that the support of Indians "is an obligation of the United States" and "cannot equitably be transferred to a State or to communities." Senator Thomas pointed out the economic problem of applying the House position in Oklahoma.[27]

FIRST HOOVER COMMISSION

The 1948 Hoover Commission had a task force on Indian affairs which reviewed policy and organization. The underlying assumption of this task force was eventual transfer of the governmental functions performed by BIA to the States "but the financial burden should not be transferred" until the Indians were able to pay property taxes and the surplus population had been relocated. In the transitional period the Federal Government had a responsibility to catch up backlogs, as in education, bring physical facilities into good condition and facilitate Indian development. And it should

---

[25] "Committee on Appropriations," *Report, No. 279* (Washington, D. C.: 80th Cong., 1st sess., U. S. House of Representatives, April 21, 1947) , p. 15.

[26] Ibid.

[27] "Interior Department Appropriation Bill for 1948," *Hearings* (Washington, D. C.: 80th Cong., 1st sess., U. S. Senate, May 8, 1947), pt. 1, p. 500.

be determined first if the State was better able to do the job before transfers took place.[28]

The Hoover Commission cited the advocacy of its task force for "progressive measures to integrate the Indians into the rest of the population as the best solution" for their future. "In the opinion of the Commission this should be the keystone of the organization and of the activities of the federal government in the field of Indian Affairs." [29]

SUMMARY OF 1940'S

The Congress during the 1940's was dissatisfied with the pace of the Bureau in accomplishing self-sufficiency on the part of the Indians and reducing the need for the Bureau of Indian Affairs. The Senate tended to be more impatient than the House in the substantive committees, but the House more impatient in its appropriation committee. Meriam, Collier, Zimmerman, and the majority of the Hoover Commission, all envisioned increased responsibility on the part of the States and the Indian tribes. Investigations and hearings by the Senate and House between 1928 and the late 1940's [30] did not improve the humor of our legislators and ". . . there were no doubt many Congressmen who sincerely believed that the best thing ultimately for the Indian was to get him weaned away from his special status as soon as possible." [31]

The Senators made it clear in the confirmation hearings of Commissioner of Indian Affairs William A. Brophy in 1945 that they wanted a Commissioner who would be responsive to Congressional policy.[32]

---

[28] *Report of the Committee on Indian Affairs to the Commission on Organization of the Executive Branch of the Government*, October 1948 (mimeographed, never printed), pp. 98–100, 119–127.

[29] Commission on Organization of the Executive Branch of the Government, *A Report to the Congress on Social Security, Education, and Indian Affairs*, March 1949, p. 63.

See Appendix F for specific recommendations of the Hoover Commission and minority reports which are classical statements of the conflicting viewpoints on the Indian situation.

[30] "Survey of Conditions of the Indians in the United States (1928–1943) ," *Report, No. 310* (Washington, D. C.: 78th Cong., 1st sess., U. S. Senate, June 11, 1943), pp. 1–22. See also pt. 2, Supplemental Report, May 2, 1944.

[31] S. Lyman Tyler, *Indian Affairs: A Work Paper on Termination* (Provo, Utah: Brigham Young University, Institute of American Indian Studies, 1964) , p. 30.

[32] S. Lyman Tyler, op. cit., p. 29.

BOSONE RESOLUTION, 1950

Indication of the Congressional mood for a termination of special relationships with the Indians because they were Indians was portrayed in the Bosone Resolution,[33] which was approved by the House July 27, 1950, but not by the Senate. This resolution directed the Secretary of the Interior to study the respective tribes, bands, and groups of Indians under his jurisdiction to determine their qualifications to manage their own affairs without supervision and control by the Federal Government.

HOUSE REPORT NO. 2503, 1952

House Resolution 698, which passed the House on July 1, 1952, provided for an investigation of the Bureau of Indian Affairs. The Committee was to submit a report including, among other things: (1) a list of groups of Indians qualified to manage their own affairs; (2) ". . . legislative proposals designed to promote the earliest practicable termination of all Federal supervision and control over Indians . . ."; (3) ". . . a listing of functions now carried on by the Bureau of Indian Affairs which may be discontinued or transferred to other agencies of the Federal Government or to the States . . ." (4) ". . . names of States where further operation of the Bureau of Indian Affairs should be discontinued . . ." and (5) ". . . recommended legislation for removal of legal disability of Indians by reason of guardianship by the Federal Government . . ."[34]

The Committee asked the Bureau to report on the above items, and Commissioner Dillon S. Myer sent a comprehensive questionnaire to the field (August 5, 1952) in which he stated that Congressional actions indicate ". . . future appropriations will be limited largely to financing items which will facilitate withdrawal." He concluded it was necessary to help Indians ". . . become better qualified to manage their own affairs."

In his report to the Committee (December 3, 1952), the Commissioner indicated the complexity of terminal actions, and that it

---

[33] H. J. Resolution 490, 81st Cong., 2nd sess., 1950, not enacted.

[34] "Investigation of BIA, Pursuant to H. Res. 698," *Report, No. 2503* (Washington, D. C.: 82nd Cong., 2nd sess., U. S. House of Representatives, December 15, 1952) , p. 1.

was "extremely difficult to make a flat statement on which tribes
. . . are now qualified for full management of their own affairs." [35]

He listed the problems of outstanding treaty claims, surplus population on reservations, heirship land problem, need for establishing corporations to manage Indian resources, Congressional determination needed as to whether the Federal Government would
subsidize States for health and educational services, and the need for
investments to develop Indian resources.[36]

Concerning States where further operation of BIA could be discontinued, the Commissioner indicated the Bureau had been working with the Indians and the States of California, Michigan, and
Kansas. All functions were with the State of New York except for
an annual Federal payment of "$6,000 in interest and the distribu-
tion of $4,500 worth of cloth" which the New York Indians did not
seem ready to modify.[37]

Intensive programing was underway in western Oregon, western
Washington, Wisconsin, Utah, Iowa, Colorado, and Louisiana.
Other specific groups being studied to determine their readiness
for self-sufficiency were: the Quapaw and Osage areas of Oklahoma, Red Lake in Minnesota, Flathead in Montana, Klamath in
Oregon, and Fort Berthold in North Dakota. Other groups were
being subjected to more limited planning.[38]

The Commissioner's Report also included tables presenting information on the population, education, income, degree of blood,
assets, taxable value of trust land, Bureau expenditures, and the
like, by tribes and States.[39]

The House Committee stated that all Indian legislation should
be directed toward the end of the trust status ("not acceptable to
our American way of life"), and "the assumption by individual
Indians of all the duties, obligations, and privileges of free citizens"
to the end that "the Indians be assimilated into the Nation's social
and economic life." [40]

From 1950 to 1952 "more than 43 bands" and Indian groups in

[35] Ibid., p. 28.

[36] Ibid., pp. 29–30.

[37] Act of February 19, 1831 (4 Stat. 442).

[38] Report, No. 2503, op. cit., pp. 36, 37.

[39] Ibid., pp. 46–117. House Report No. 2503 included much data, previously prepared, such as the Zimmerman testimony to the Senate in 1947. Ibid., pp. 167–179.

[40] Ibid., p. 124.

western Oregon and 115 groups in California reached agreement with the Bureau of Indian Affairs "looking toward termination of Federal responsibilities and services as provided through the Bureau." [41]

The House Committee on Interior and Insular Affairs appointed a Special Subcommittee on Indian Affairs pursuant to H. Res. 89 of the 83rd Congress, March 25, 1953. This subcommittee recommended discontinuance of the operation of the BIA in California, Michigan, Nebraska, South Carolina, Texas, and Wyoming. The Committee said this could be accomplished by transfer of functions to the Indians themselves, to the States, or to other Federal agencies.

The transfer of all BIA educational, law and order, and roads activities in all States to the States was recommended.

Other BIA functions, the Committee believed, should be transferred to the Indians themselves or other appropriate Federal agencies.[42]

DEPARTMENT OF INTERIOR POLICY POSITION

Starting in 1928 with the Meriam Report, the Department moved progressively toward adoption of withdrawal of trusteeship as an objective but not through the allotment procedure. The Meriam Report stated that it was ". . . highly desirable that the states should as rapidly as possible assume responsibility for the administration of activities which they can effectively perform alike for whites and for the Indians with a single organization . . ." But the report indicated that transfer should be function by function and not necessarily occur at the same time in the various States as each situation was unique. Further, the Federal Government should carry its responsibility until the Indians and the States were ready for the change.[43]

Commissioner Collier, in a 1943 discussion of the preparation of post-war programs for the reservations, indicated that consideration should be given to what functions could be transferred to the

---

[41] Memorandum to Commissioner of Indian Affairs Louis R. Bruce on Termination from Carl J. Cornelius, Chizu Toda and Peter F. Walz, October 13, 1969, (BIA files).

[42] "Pursuant to House Resolution 89," *Report, No. 2680* (Washington, D. C.: 83rd Cong., 2d sess., U. S. House of Representatives, September 20, 1954), p. 4.

[43] Lewis Meriam and Associates, op. cit., p. 89.

tribes ". . . and how best the advisory function of the Indian Serv-ice can be strengthened and the supervisory function reduced." [44] Also such planning should consider ". . . what additional services to Indians might be assumed by State, county or municipal agen-cies, such as law and order, health, and education."

And as to the effect of each reservation plan as a whole, Collier stated: " . . . you should seek to answer the question, 'When will the group or tribe affected be in a sufficiently stable position—economic, social, political—to justify reducing federal supervision or even withdrawing it?' I say *seek* to answer, because in many cases, we can not begin to answer it; in others, we can make fairly good guesses; in some cases we can answer it and begin to implement the answer." [45]

The two long-range objectives of the Bureau of Indian Affairs, as stated by Commissioner Dillon S. Myer in 1951, were: [46]

> (1) A standard of living for Indians comparable with that en-joyed by other segments of the population, and (2) the step-by-step transfer of Bureau functions to the Indians themselves or to the appropriate agencies of local, State or Federal Gov-ernment.

In 1952, the Commissioner of Indian Affairs started off his *An-nual Report* with the following statement: [47]

> Greatly increased emphasis on the ultimate transfer of Indian Bureau function either to the Indians themselves or to appro-priate State and local agencies was reflected during the fiscal year 1952 in almost every phase of the program of the Bureau of Indian Affairs.

The Report indicated: the termination bills introduced and the conferences with the Indians and the States concerned; plans for transferring 25 additional Indian Service schools to local school dis-tricts; that the Congress had authorized the transfer of Indian health ". . . from the Bureau to appropriate State or local agencies"; [48] that funds were being sought to contract with non-Fed-

---

[44] Commissioner, "Memorandum to All Indian Service Personnel and All Indians," November 15, 1943, BIA files.

[45] Ibid.

[46] Commissioner of Indian Affairs, *Annual Report*, 1951, p. 353 of Department of Interior Annual Report for 1951.

[47] Commissioner of Indian Affairs, *Annual Report*, 1952, p. 389 of Department of Interior Annual Report for 1952.

[48] 66 Stat. 35 (April 3, 1952).

eral hospitals for Indian health services; consultations held with tribes and States concerning possible transfer of law and order responsibilities "within Indian reservations from the Federal Government to the States"; and reported on the Bureau sponsored bills for transfer of such jurisdiction in Minnesota, Wisconsin, Nebraska, California, and Washington.

In working toward the objective of Bureau withdrawal from Indian affairs, guidance was provided for the development of specific programs with " . . . primary emphasis . . . given to the principle of consultation with the Indians."

Commissioner Myer offered to work with any tribe which wished to assume "either full control or a greater degree of control over its own affairs." [49]

In early 1953, Assistant Secretary of the Interior Orme Lewis, met with the Chairmen of the House and Senate Indian Affairs Subcommittees, and subsequently with the Secretary of the Interior Douglas McKay on Indian policy. [50]

On March 13, 1953, the Assistant Secretary stated Interior's policy in a letter to the Senate and House Subcommittees, which put the Executive arm of the Government flatly on record as follows: [51]

Federal responsibility for administering the affairs of individual Indian tribes should be terminated as rapidly as the circumstances of each tribe will permit. This should be accomplished by arrangement with the proper public bodies of the political subdivisions to assume responsibility for the services customarily enjoyed by the non-Indian residents of such political subdivisions and by distribution of tribal assets to the tribes as a unit or by division of tribal assets among the individual members, whichever may appear to be the better plan in each case. In addition, responsibility for trust properties should be transferred to the Indians themselves, either as groups or individuals, as soon as feasible.

HOUSE CONCURRENT RESOLUTION 108 (HCR 108)

The high point of the termination drive came with the adoption

[49] Commissioner of Indian Affairs, *Annual Report*, 1952, pp. 390–394 of Department Report.

[50] Memorandum to Commissioner Louis R. Bruce on Termination, October 13, 1969, BIA files.

[51] Ibid.

by both the House and the Senate of House Concurrent Resolution 108 on August 1, 1953. The text follows:

Whereas it is the policy of Congress, as rapidly as possible, to make the Indians within the territorial limits of the United States subject to the same laws and entitled to the same privileges and responsibilities as are applicable to other citizens of the United States, to end their status as wards of the United States, and to grant them all of the rights and prerogatives pertaining to American citizenship; and

Whereas the Indians within the territorial limits of the United States should assume their full responsibilities as American citizens: NOW, therefore, be it

RESOLVED by the House of Representatives (the Senate concurring), That it is declared to be the sense of Congress that, at the earliest possible time, all of the Indian tribes and the individual members thereof located within the States of California, Florida, New York, and Texas, and all of the following-named Indian tribes and individual members thereof, should be freed from Federal supervision and control and from the disabilities and limitations specially applicable to Indians: The Flathead Tribe of Montana, the Klamath Tribe of Oregon, the Menominee Tribe of Wisconsin, the Potawatomi Tribe of Kansas and Nebraska, and those members of the Chippewa Tribe who are on the Turtle Mountain Reservation, North Dakota. It is further declared to be the sense of Congress that, upon the release of such tribes and individual members thereof from such disabilities and limitations, all offices of the Bureau of Indian Affairs in the States of California, Florida, New York, and Texas, and all other offices of the Bureau of Indian Affairs whose primary purpose was to serve any Indian tribe or individual Indian freed from Federal supervision should be abolished. It is further declared to be the sense of Congress that the Secretary of the Interior should examine all existing legislation dealing with such Indians and treaties between the Government of the United States and each such tribe, and report to Congress at the earliest practicable date, but not later than January 1, 1954, his recommendations for such legislation as, in his judgment, may be necessary to accomplish the purposes of this resolution.

This resolution was in harmony with Interior's policy and set the stage for aggressive action on all fronts. The objective was to transfer the functions of BIA to the States. Not only was proposed legislation to be submitted by Interior on the four States and specific Indian tribes mentioned in the resolution by January 1, 1954, but the accompanying report [52] set forth five areas of action that included all of the major suggestions for getting BIA out of business since the early 1940's.

Action taken during the first and second sessions of the 83rd Congress following the passage of HCR 108 included the enactment of Public Laws 277, 280, and 281 which repealed the Indian liquor law, conferred State civil and criminal jurisdiction over certain Indians and authorizing similar extension to the remainder, and repealed certain statutes having to do with personal property and the sale of firearms.[53]

TERMINATION ACTIONS

Legislative recommendations were submitted by the Department to the Congress at the beginning of the 1954 Congressional session for the groups defined in HCR 108, and the Indians of western Oregon.[54]

Ten termination acts were passed from 1954 to 1958: Alabama and Coushatta Tribes of Texas; California Rancherias and Reservations; Klamath Tribe of Oregon; Menomine Tribe of Wisconsin; Ottawa Tribe of Oklahoma; Paiute Indians of Utah; Peoria Tribe of Oklahoma; Uintah and Ouray Ute Mixed Bloods of Utah; Western Oregon (60 bands); and Wyandotte Tribe of Oklahoma.

In 1959, termination legislation was passed for the Catawba Indians of South Carolina and in 1962 for the Ponca Tribe of Native Americans of Nebraska.[55]

---

[52] Report, No. 841, (Washington, D. C.: 83rd Cong., 1st sess., U.S. House of Representatives, July 15, 1953), pp. 1–4.

[53] House, Report, No. 2680, op. cit., September 20, 1954, p. vi.

[54] Commissioner of Indian Affairs, Annual Report, 1954, p. 228. The Western Oregon group was submitted because the Indians involved on several occasions had expressed their desire for early severance from Federal trusteeship.

[55] See Appendix B, Table III, for table giving dates, membership, land acreage, and current status for all tribes having terminal legislation.

CHAPTER FIVE

REAPPRAISAL OF PHILOSOPHY IN THE 1960's

INDIAN REACTION TO TERMINATION

The termination policy expressed in House Concurrent Resolution 108 (HCR 108), legislation enacted such as P.L. 280 transferring law and order to certain States and authorizing other States to unilaterally assume civil and criminal jurisdiction over Indians, the vigorous withdrawal programing at the Indian agencies in consultation with the tribes concerned, and proposed termination legislation " . . . sent a wave of apprehension" through Indian country. In some tribes factions developed—those that favored and those that opposed termination. The Governors' Interstate Indian Council (GIIC) had favored termination, but ". . . grew more cautious in 1954 and set up minimum conditions that should be met by the Federal Government prior to termination," which included agreement by the Indians, the State concerned, and the Federal Government before any action on termination.[1]

Not all tribes listed by the Bureau of Indian Affairs (BIA) from 1947 on as ready for termination were interested in this action. Some of these tribes were specifically mentioned in House Concurrent Resolution 108—Flathead, Turtle Mountain, and the Potawatomi Indians of Kansas and Nebraska, for example. No termination legislation has been enacted for any of them. Nor has termination legislation been enacted for any of the Indians in Florida or New York, two of the four States mentioned in HCR 108. The statute for the Alabama and Coushatta Indians of Texas was not really termination of special services, but a transfer of the responsibility for such services from the Federal to the State Government.

Those tribes that opposed termination and made their desires

---

[1] Memo to Commissioner of Indian Affairs Louis R. Bruce on Termination from Carl J. Cornelius, Chizu Toda, and Peter F. Walz, October 13, 1969, Bureau of Indian Affairs, (BIA) files; minutes of various Governors' Interstate Indian Council (GIIC) meetings.

known successfully blocked attempted termination legislation. There was no official tribal opposition to the passage of those proposals that were enacted. The Indians, the States concerned, and the Bureau worked closely together on the proposed legislation for the Menominee and Klamath reservations. The leadership of both tribes and of both States concerned were favorable to termination at that time.[2]

During the period from 1953 to 1960 the Bureau strongly pushed programs leading to self-sufficiency: universal education of all Indian children; emphasis on education in public schools when possible; and economic improvement both through improved management of his own resources by the Indian and increased ability of the Indian to take advantage of off-reservation resources. Tribes were encouraged to take on increased responsibilities for management of their own affairs. In 1956, Commissioner Glenn L. Emmons issued a directive to the field on consultation with the tribes in the development of tribal programs: [3]

> I emphasize that the important thing is for each group to have as a goal, with or without legislation, the development of the group to the point where, from a realistic point of view, special services or assistance because of Indian status will no longer be necessary.

However, the opposition to the policy of rapid termination was so strong that it affected the willingness of many tribes to embark on new programs that might make them more self-sufficient. Commissioner Emmons' directive received little implementation. Tribes were afraid that a successful new program would lead to termination. [4] Thus there was a significant psychological block to Indian participation. Without such participation, fundamental progress was impossible.

READJUSTMENT OF FEDERAL APPROACH

Secretary Seaton's Statement

In 1958, Secretary of the Interior Fred A. Seaton believed it necessary to reassure the Indian people. He interpreted House Concur-

---

[2] See Appendix H 3 and 4 for discussion of Klamath and Menominee.
[3] Memorandum to Field Officials, April 12, 1956.
[4] Memo to Commissioner Louis R. Bruce on Termination, op. cit.

rent Resolution 108 as stating " . . . an objective, not an immediate goal" and stated that a tribe would not only have to *understand* and *concur* in a plan for severing its relationship with the Federal Government, but also would have to have an adequate educational level before he would recommend termination.[5]

Secretary Udall's Task Force

Early in his administration Secretary Stewart L. Udall appointed a task force to review the Indian program.[6] One of its main conclusions was that the emphasis on termination had impaired Indian morale and produced a "hostile or apathetic response" to Federal Indian programs. It would be wiser to put emphasis on social, economic and political development ". . . to the point where special services to this group of Americans are no longer justified. Then termination can be achieved with maximum benefit for all concerned." The task force did not list "termination *per se*" as one of the Bureau's main objectives, as it had been during the 50's. As stated by the task force " . . . if development, rather than termination, is emphasized during the transitional period, Indian cooperation—an essential ingredient of a successful program—can be expected." [7]

Policy Development in the 1960's

Both Indian Commissioners Philleo Nash (1961–66) and Robert Bennett (1966–69) pushed the objective of Indian development—economic, social, and governmental—and Indian involvement in such development. They did not talk termination. The Senate Committee on the Interior tried to force Bennett to take a stand favoring termination during his confirmation hearings, but Bennett successfully sidestepped the issue.[8]

---

[5] Fred A. Seaton, Radio Broadcast, September 13, 1958, Window Rock, Ariz.

[6] *Task Force on Indian Affairs*, Report to the Secretary of the Interior, July 10, 1961. Members of the task force were: W. W. Keeler, Chairman; Philleo Nash, James E. Officer, and William Zimmerman, Jr.

[7] Ibid., p. 6.

[8] "The Nomination of Robert LaFollette Bennett of Alaska to be Commissioner of Indian Affairs," *Hearings Before the Committee on Interior and Insular Affairs* (Washington, D. C.: 89th Cong., 2d sess., U. S. Senate, April 1, 1966).

In an unusual procedure, the Senate Committee filed a written report on Commissioner Bennett's nomination. (*Executive Report No. 1* (Washington, D.C.: 89th Cong., 2d sess., U.S. Senate, April 8, 1966).) It cited House Report 2680 of the 83rd Congress and the list of tribes ready for termination and berated the Bureau for not taking action and not responding to the Committee's requests for legislation. The Committee pointed out that the Colville Tribe wanted termination yet the Committee had received minimal cooperation from the Bureau. The Committee expected Mr. Bennett to be more responsive. The Senate Committee, obviously, was pro termination.

Expansion of Federal Services

The objectives of Nash and Bennett were facilitated by the social legislation enacted during the Kennedy and Johnson years. This legislation resulted in expanded services to Indians as well as to non-Indians such as: the Elementary and Secondary Education Act; the Education Professions Development Act; the Vocational Education Act; the Higher Education Act; the Economic Opportunity Act; and increased funds for the above programs as well as for housing assistance, manpower training and economic development. As a result, many Federal agencies developed programs providing additional opportunities for tribes and individual Indians.[9]

Omnibus Bill

Secretary Udall, too, pushed for Indian economic development and desired some landmark Indian economic development legislation.[10] He visualized a multimillion dollar recreational development at Pyramid Lake, Nev., for example, which is owned by the

---

[9] Federal funding for Indian reservation programs for fiscal year 1970 totaled approximately $600 million of which $309 million, about 50 percent, was through the Bureau of Indian Affairs. The breakdown by department was: Agriculture, $22 million; Commerce, $22 million; Defense, $2 million; Office of Economic Opportunity, $33.5 million; HEW, $170 million; HUD, $22.5 million; Interior, $314.5 million; Labor, $6.5 million; Small Business Administration, $4.5 million; and Veterans Administration, $500 thousand. The implications of this increase in Federal activity is discussed further in Chapter VII.

[10] At a Santa Fe meeting with Bureau of Indian Affairs (BIA) officials, followed by a meeting with tribal representatives, Secretary Udall pointed to the need to remove the "shackles" of Indian dependence and announced that "the BIA, in consultation with Indians and others, will develop 'a big piece of legislation' to accomplish that end." *Albuquerque Journal*, April 16, 1966.

Pyramid Lake Tribe (Paiute) and admirably located to serve the West Coast population complex.[11]

In response to Udall's urging, the Bureau prepared a preliminary draft of a possible Economic Development Bill for discussion purposes, primarily to determine what points seemed to make sense to the various specialists in the Bureau and the Department and in order to develop a framework for review and suggestions by the Indian community. A copy of the "July 4 draft," (it was dated July 4, 1966) as it was dubbed, leaked to the National Congress of American Indians (NCAI) and it was reproduced by NCAI and distributed to all tribes and was immediately attacked as having been prepared without Indian consultation and that it threatened the loss of tribal land because of a suggested authorization for tribes to mortgage such land to obtain capital for economic development.

Commissioner of Indian Affairs Robert L. Bennett held regional meetings to obtain Indian desires and attitudes concerning this and other proposed legislation. Most of the Indian desires were already authorized by law (e.g., more and better education, community social development, employment assistance, water development, community physical development, better law and order, etc.) but funding was inadequate. New legislation was not required. In one area there was agreement that new legislation was needed—the desirability of increasing the authorization and funding of the revolving loan fund. There was not too much opposition to loan guarantee and insurance provisions.[12]

The proposed Economic Development Bill was modified substantially as the result of Indian input, but it still contained the authority for a tribe to mortgage its tribal land. It also contained the tribal proposal of a large revolving loan fund which the tribes

---

[11] The Bureau of Outdoor Recreation stated the recreational potential of Pyramid Lake as "a recreation source of national significance" due to its "leviathan proportions" and "wealth of aesthetic . . . phenomena." . . . "A properly developed Pyramid Lake will help meet the water-based recreation needs of a combined day-use and weekend/vacation use . . . zone population of 13,814,243 in the year 2000. Visitation to Pyramid Lake in that year should total 2,375,000."

Preliminary Study, not for public release, dated November 1968, pp. 14–15.

[12] David E. Walker, Jr. *An Examination of American Indian Reaction to Proposals of the Commissioner of Indian Affairs for General Legislation, 1967,* Northwest Anthropological Research Notes, Fall 1967. See also Alan L. Sorkin, *American Indians and Federal Aid* (The Brookings Institution, Washington, D. C., 1971) for a discussion of the contents of the proposal, p. 97 ff.

wanted so that mortgaging of their land would not be required. The Department theory was to put everything in one bill to enhance the passage of less popular items. Thus it was dubbed the "Omnibus Bill." Also, it was hoped that it would stand out historically as "landmark legislation" such as the Indian Reorganization Act (IRA) of 1934. If items were acted on piecemeal, they would lack dramatic impact.

At the conclusion of the field hearings, Commissioner Bennett invited tribal leaders to Washington, gave them the use of the Bureau auditorium and let them hammer out what they wanted. The main theme was that many of the provisions of the bill were not their idea and they were suspicious. They definitely opposed mortgaging of Indian land. They went on record favoring a $500 million revolving loan fund.[13]

They sent a letter to the President incorporating their reactions.[14]

The Administration Bill was forwarded to the Congress on May 16, 1967, and hearings were held.[15]

No legislation was enacted. A clear message for those who will see —the Indians have to initiate and propose before they will support new policy or new legislation. Policy action cannot be "time-tabled" by outside groups such as the Government with any expectation of Indian agreement and support. Indians must be involved. The ideas must be their ideas.

Involvement

During the 60's Indian involvement was stressed. Two schools were contracted for Indian operation—Blackwater on the Pima Reservation and Rough Rock on the Navajo.

---

[13] The Bureau's authorized fund at the time totaled approximately $25 million.

[14] Letter to the President from the Indian Conference on Policy and Legislation, Washington, D. C., February 2, 1967, signed by Norman Hollow, Chairman; Earl Old Person, cochairman; and Roger S. Jourdain, cochairman. The conference "rigorously opposed" certain provisions, agreed others had possibilities, pled for more time to study, and stressed the need for "repudiation of the ideas" behind HCR 108 and a "consent" amendment to P.L. 280. BIA files 4513–1966–013– Part 5.

[15] "Indian Resources Development Act of 1967," *Hearings Before the Subcommittee on Indian Affairs on H. R. 10560* (Washington, D. C.: 90th Cong., 1st sess., U. S. House of Representatives, July 13 and 14, 1967). The companion bill in the Senate was S. 1816. The Senate held hearings July 11, 1967 and May 15, 31, and June 1, 1968. No hearings were published.

Commissioner Bennett did not hold traditional hearings on the Omnibus Bill. He set the date and time and asked the Indians present to elect a chairman, appoint subcommittees, and come up with a report. He, as Commissioner, presented the possibilities for legislation at the beginning of the session. The Indians ran the meeting.

The Bureau of Indian Affairs developed a program that provided for contracting by the Indians of any community so that they could operate their school if they wanted to take over the responsibility from BIA. By Indians contracting to assume services, the Commissioner estimated the possible reduction of 4,000 Federal positions over a period of years. This was a Bureau-initiated idea and has been approached cautiously by the Indian Community.

Commissioner Bennett also believed that the numerous Federal and State programs and services for Indians should be coordinated by Indian tribal leadership on the reservation—rather than attempt to do it for the Indians through the BIA superintendent or some other official.

Nor would Commissioner Bennett fall for paternalism. When a tribe complained bitterly about a problem and asked the Commissioner what he was going to do about it, he would likely respond in the following vein: "What do you think ought to be done? It's primarily your problem, not the Bureau's. We'll help if we can but we need to know how you think the problem should be resolved." This often came as a shock, and sometimes the tribe worked out its problem when it thought it through. When the Indians came up with a specific solution they, in effect, took the leadership with the Bureau helping.

Indian Advocacy

Commissioner Bennett also regarded the BIA as an advocate of the Indian cause, not as the representative of the dominant segment of society in dealing with the Indians. Bureau policy and recommendations, therefore, were "pro-Indian," reflecting Indian desire rather than what others might consider a more balanced view which took into consideration other factors such as the interests of the taxpayers who were funding the programs or non-Indian water users competing for the same water supply.

The Kennedy Committee hearings and report also took an

Indian advocacy role and stimulated national interest in the Indian situation.[16]

REVERSAL OF SOME STATE ATTITUDES

Two samples will be cited of State changes in viewpoint.

California

In the 1950's the California Indians, the Governor, and the legislature endorsed termination of Federal activity. The Congress passed the Rancheria Act[17] which provided the mechanism for termination of various California Indian groups. Many of the functional activities—such as, education, welfare, law and order—were performed by the State and its instrumentalities for its Indian citizens in the same manner as for its other citizens. In large measure, the State had assumed most governmental responsibilities for California Indians by the end of the decade.

In the 60's the State reversed itself, supported by many Indian residents, and pressed hard for education assistance in the form of reinstatement of Johnson-O'Malley funds and authority for their children to attend Federal boarding schools. The State has also sought Indian Health Service aid for sanitation and domestic water systems, and the Indians have requested the Bureau of Indian Affairs for repair and installation of irrigation works. The State now believes the Indians of California should have the same Federal housing assistance as Indians in the other States. In short, the State and many of its Indian citizens appear to want the Federal presence on Indian matters, either in the form of funds or federally supplied services.

Nebraska

Nebraska assumed civil and criminal jurisdiction over Indian reservations in the State in 1953.

---

[16] *Hearings on Indian Education, Special Subcommittee on Indian Education* (Washington, D. C.: 90th Cong., 1st and 2d sess., U. S. Senate, Committee on Labor and Public Welfare, December 14 and 15, 1967, Washington, D. C. and January 4, 1968, San Francisco, Calif.) , pt. 1.

"A Resolution Authorizing an Investigation into the Problems of Education for American Indians," *Report, No. 91–501, Indian Education: A National Tragedy—A National Challenge* (Washington, D. C.: 91st Cong., 1st sess., U. S. Senate, Special Subcommittee on Indian Education, Pursuant to S. Res. 80, November 3, 1969) .

[17] 72 Stat. 619, as amended.

In 1968, Nebraska's desire to retrocede law and order responsibility on the Omaha and Winnebago reservations was discussed with the Bureau of Indian Affairs and on April 16, 1969, the Nebraska legislature enacted a resolution retroceding to the United States jurisdiction assumed under P.L. 280 in 1953, except for motor vehicle operation on roads and highways. Reasons given in the resolution were: steadily increased costs of law enforcement; insufficient land tax base; and the State assistance to county had increased each biennium.[18]

The Thurston County Board of Supervisors, which has jurisdiction over both tribes, first endorsed the request for retrocession [19] and then urged the Federal Government to refuse retrocession.[20] The reasons for the Board's reversal were:

. . . Further study of the effects of retrocession leads the said County Board of Thurston County, Neb., to believe that a multitude of problems would arise if jurisdiction over Indians and Indian Territory were retroceded to the Federal Government; and

. . . Said retrocession would not be in the best interests of the entire population of Thurston County, Neb. . . .[21]

The two tribes took opposite positions—the Omahas favoring retrocession [22] and the Winnebagos opposing such action.[23]

The Attorney General for Nebraska urged that jurisdictional questions be thought through before final action was taken.[24]

On October 16, 1970, the Secretary of the Interior accepted retrocession for the Omaha portion of Thurston County only.[25]

Governors' Interstate Indian Council

In his address to the 1970 Governors' Interstate Indian Council meeting, Council Chairman John Rainer stated that HCR 108 was

---

[18] Legislative Resolution No. 37, April 16, 1969.
[19] Resolution, July 15, 1969.
[20] Resolution, April 9, 1970.
[21] Ibid.
[22] Tribal Resolution No. 69–33, January 29, 1969.
[23] Tribal Resolution No. 69–19, April 7, 1969.
[24] Letter to Commissioner Louis R. Bruce from Clarence A. H. Meyer, Attorney General, State of Nebraska, March 25, 1970.
[25] 35 *Federal Register* 16598 (1970). On February 1, 1971, the Nebraska legislature passed Legislative Resolution 16, which purports to rescind the offer of retrocession, which Interior states is of no validity.

a threat to Indians, and, if it had been implemented, the States would have had to assume full responsibility for Indians. The GIIC provides a vehicle for States to cooperate on forward-looking programs for building Indian communities, not terminating them, he continued. "The basic role of the state, in exercising its responsibilities to the Indians," he said "should be one of full cooperation with Indian groups in giving as much assistance as possible to build up their political, economic, judicial, artistic, social and cultural resources." [26]

No one took issue with the antitermination stand at the meeting. The tone of the session was one of working out the best procedures between tribes, the States, and the Federal Government, for improving the Indian condition.

SOME COMPARISONS OF THE JOHNSON AND NIXON PRESIDENTIAL MESSAGES

The whole history of Indian policy served as a backdrop for the Johnson and Nixon Presidential messages. However, the negative impact of HRC 108 and the original language of P.L. 280, the expansion of Federal services through the legislation of the 60's, Indian reaction to the Omnibus Bill, the obvious need for Indian involvement, the strong Indian advocacy positions adopted by the Bureau and the Kennedy Committee, the reversal of some State attitudes, and special Presidential task force reviews of the Indian situation were of particular importance.[27]

Much of the basic philosophy in both messages is the same—rejection of the termination policy, the necessity for Indian involvement, working with Indians, the necessity of developing Indian leadership, expansion of credit, improved schools and Indian participation in operating the schools, and the elevation of Indian responsibilities to the higher reaches of the Federal Government (e.g., National Council on Indian Opportunity). The emphasis is on transfer of control and responsibility from the Federal Government to *Indian communities* rather than to State or local government.

However, President Nixon's message launched consideration of

---

[26] GIIC meeting, Tulsa, Okla., June 11, 1970.

[27] A more detailed summary of these two important messages and reference to the Presidential task forces is in Appendix G.

several important innovations which built upon the common underlying philosophy. The most important of these were in the form of requests for legislation: repeal of House Concurrent Resolution 108 and an affirmative declaration by the Congress of the Federal Indian responsibility; empowering tribes with final decision authority on whether to take over administration of Indian service programs of Interior or Health, Education, and Welfare; the establishment of an Indian Trust Counsel Authority as an Indian advocate on trust matters such as land and water to avoid conflict of interest within Interior and Justice; and the creation of the position of Assistant Secretary for Indian and Territorial Affairs in Interior.

Not requiring immediate legislation was official Presidential endorsement of Federal Indian action in the urban area, and support for seven pilot urban centers.

If these legislative requests are enacted they will indeed constitute an "historic step forward in Indian policy."

EMERGENCE OF THE PHILOSOPHY OF PLURALISM

The philosophy of pluralism was most succinctly stated by President Nixon, both in his preelection statement and his message to the Congress.[28]

We must recognize that American society can allow many different cultures to flourish in harmony and we must provide an opportunity for those Indians wishing to do so to lead a useful and prosperous life in an Indian environment.

The Johnson message contained the same assumption, as did many of Commissioner Bennett's statements.

The statement to the GIIC by John Rainer also emphasized the strengthening of Indian communities but in addition stressed cooperative effort between the Indian communities and the *States* as well as with the Federal Government.

In the following chapters some of the aspects of the present and future relations between the Indians, the States, and the Federal Government will be reviewed. This review will include attitudes and actions related to the concept of maintaining the integrity of the Indian individuals and communities within the larger culture as long as that is the Indians' choice.

---

[28] Preelection statement, September 27, 1968.

CHAPTER SIX

RELATIONS BETWEEN INDIAN CITIZENS AND STATES TODAY

The States are inevitably involved with their Indian citizens as they are with all of their other citizens. However, in those States in which some Indians have a special relationship to the Federal Government, the States' interface with some of their Indian citizens may be different in many respects than that of other State citizens. Police and court functions or the educational system of the State may not be applicable to Indian citizens in certain reservation areas, for example. However, as indicated in Chapter III, many State and local governmental functions are provided to Indian communities even though the Indians have special Federal arrangements for other services and their land is in trust and not subject to real estate taxes.

Certain governmental functions for Indian communities would be difficult to provide through the Federal Government. Examples are foster home care or specialized institutional care for dependent or handicapped children. Also, specialized State or private institutions frequently have the only service available for the mentally ill or the aged and infirm requiring institutional care. Judicial authority is necessary to place children in foster homes without the consent of parents, or for placement in State institutions. The Federal Government does not have such authority, nor does the Federal Government operate children's institutions. It is necessary to utilize tribal court authority in areas within the jurisdiction of a tribal court, and State or local court authority in other areas. Tribes and the Bureau of Indian Affairs (BIA) have jail facilities only for short-time custody. The State correctional institutions are the only feasible source of service for the majority of Indians sentenced for long terms. Federal prisons are available only for those who are convicted of Federal offenses.

Territorially, Federal Indian reservations are within State

74

Spokane tribal officials meet with the Governor of the State of Washington and State officials on Spokane tribal issues. Left to right: (back row) William Jeffries, Assistant to Governor for Indian Affairs; (front row) Al McCoy, Tribal Councilman; Robbie Flett, Tribal Councilman; Anne Flett, Tribal Secretary; Glenn Galbraith, Executive Secretary of Tribe; and Governor Dan Evans. Alex Sherwood, Chairman, not shown.

(Photo furnished by William Jeffries.)

boundaries. They are also included in county boundaries. As has been developed in earlier chapters, one of the main historical trends has been to devolve special Federal services to the appropriate local and State jurisdictions. The current apportionment of responsibilities among the three levels is described in this chapter.

HOW MANY INDIANS AND WHERE ARE THEY?

Table I, Appendix B, "Indian Population, Land, Education, Law and Order, and Other Services" presents many of the basic statistics pertinent to understanding the relationship between the Indians, the States, and the Federal Government.

The table indicates that in 1970 there were 827,000 (827,091) Indians and Alaska Natives in the United States. The five States with 50 thousand or more of these were:

TABLE 1—STATES WITH 50,000 OR MORE INDIANS

State	Population		
	Indian	Total	Percent Indian
Oklahoma _____	97,731	2,559,253	3.8
Arizona _____	95,812	1,772,483	5.4
California _____	91,018	19,953,134	0.5
New Mexico _____	72,788	1,016,000	7.2
Alaska _____	51,528	302,173	17.0
Total _____	408,877	25,603,042	1.6

These States (10 percent of the States) account for almost one half of the Indian population.

States with 10,000 or more Indians (excluding the above five States) were:

TABLE 2—STATES WITH 10,000 OR MORE INDIANS

State	Indian Population
North Carolina _____	43,487
Washington _____	33,386
South Dakota _____	32,365
New York _____	28,330
Montana _____	27,130
Minnesota _____	23,128
Wisconsin _____	18,924
Texas _____	18,132
Michigan _____	16,854
North Dakota _____	14,369
Oregon _____	13,510
Illinois _____	11,413
Utah _____	11,273
Total _____	292,301

Eighteen States (36 percent of the States) 10,000 or over have 701,178 Indians (85 percent of total).

If the States are ranked by those with the greatest percent of Indians to the total State population there is overlap with the above lists, but there are some differences. Following are the States in which Indian (or native) population is 1 percent or more of the total State population:

TABLE 3—STATES WITH INDIAN POPULATION ONE PERCENT OR MORE OF TOTAL

State	Percent of Total Population Indian or Native
Alaska	17.05
New Mexico	7.16
Arizona	5.40
South Dakota	4.86
Montana	3.91
Oklahoma	3.82
North Dakota	2.33
Nevada	1.62
Wyoming	1.50
Utah	1.06

California, with the third highest Indian population in absolute numbers, has less than 1 percent (.46) classified as Indian. Others of the 18 States with 10,000 or more Indians in which the Indians are less than 1 percent of the State population are: North Carolina (.86), Washington (.98), New York (.16), Minnesota (.60), Wisconsin (.43), Texas (.16), Michigan (.19), Oregon (.65), and Illinois (.10). Wyoming (1.50) and Nevada (1.62), on the other hand, each have less than 10,000 Indians but the Indian portion is more than 1 percent of their total populations.

BIA has estimated that there are 477,458 (57.7 percent) Indians eligible for Federal services in the service area of the Bureau of Indian Affairs (BIA) —on or near a reservation or other Indian land held in trust by the Federal Government.[1]

Indians have moved in large numbers to metropolitan areas such as New York, Chicago, San Francisco, and Los Angeles. The 1970 census indicated that there are approximately 310,000 Indians in

[1] Table I, Appendix B. The 1970 BIA figure of 477,458 includes Arizona, New Mexico, and Alaska figures in excess of the 1970 Census figures for the total Indians in these three States; if the service population number for these three States was reduced to the Census total, there would be a net reduction of 28,604 for a revised total of 448,854 in the BIA service area. This leaves approximately 378,237 (45.7 percent) Indians in urban areas and non-BIA rural areas who receive any benefits or services primarily from the State or local governments. Note: The March, 1971 figure is reported to be 488,083 by the Bureau of Indian Affairs (BIA).

such metropolitan centers. Another 50,000 are in smaller urbanized areas of 2,500 and up—not including the metropolitan areas. The remaining 467,000 are in rural areas.

RELATIONSHIP OF GOVERNMENT TRUST RESPONSIBILITY FOR INDIAN LAND TO SPECIAL SERVICES FOR INDIANS

Indian land which is held in trust by the Federal or a State Government is controlled by the respective Government as to sale, lease, or other use. Such trust land is a basic factor in determining the relationship of the Indian to his various governments. Tribal governments—with chairmen, councils, courts, police, and various tribal services—exist only where there is a reservation consisting of trust land.[2]

There are 25 States with Federal trust land. Thus it will be noted in Table I that in the 14 States where the tribal government is involved in law and order, there is a trust land base. It will be noted, too, that the existence of trust land does not automatically involve the tribe as a governmental entity in law and order. In many instances the State has assumed jurisdiction over some Indians or Indian communities. In 35 States, law and order is primarily a State function for Indians the same as for their other citizens.

No State without Indian land held in Federal trust has BIA schools. However, in only two instances, North Dakota and Mississippi, do the Federal schools have a majority of the Indian children. In all other States either all or a majority of the Indian children are in public or private schools.

Federal field installations of BIA and the Indian Health Service (IHS) are concentrated in those States where Indian land is held in Federal trust. New York is an exception, but even there Indian

---

[2] In some States Indian land under Federal trust is a sizeable portion of the total land area. For example, land ownership in Arizona is as follows:

Sector	Percent
Indian	27.03
Federal	44.91
State	13.12
Private	14.94

From an article by Senator Barry Goldwater, "Arizona's Indians: Americans Before Columbus," *Arizona Progress* inserted in *Congressional Record,* July 12, 1971, E 7525.

Lumbee Indians in front of Old Main at Pembroke, N. C. State University campus, originally a Lumbee Indian school. From left to right: Brenda Brooks, Nick and Janie Locklear, Lewis R. Burton, Lumbee poet and historian, and Earl Hughes Oxendine, Lumbee educator.

(Photo: *New York Times.*)

land cannot be alienated without Federal approval. As exceptions, the BIA has field offices in Ohio, Texas, and Illinois related to employment assistance and industrial development—both programs, however, are related strictly to reservation Indians.

States with special organizations for Indians (Indian Commissions or equivalent) have trust land, either Federal or State. However, not all States with trust land have special organizations. The size of the Indian population, though important in many instances, is not the governing criterion.[3]

Trust land, then, is the basic criterion for special Federal and State activity for Indians. The reason for this is threefold: first, the

---

[3] For example, until 1971 there was no State organization or special services for the large number of Lumbees in North Carolina (no trust land). The largest special State organizations for Indians are for small groups in Maine and Texas (State trust land). The Federal Government provides some services for a few small groups, too, e.g., 268 Chittimachas in Louisiana.

existence of trust land in many instances stems from treaties or other agreements between the Indians concerned and the State or Federal Governments (or the colonial governments preceding them); second, the existence of land held in trust imposes a responsibility on the trustee to carry out his trust responsibilities; and, third, where the tribe or the Federal Government performs governmental functions normally provided by State and local government, special adjustments are required by both the State and Federal Governments. For the most part State Indian trust land, like Federal trust land, is not subject to a local or State real estate tax.

INTERFACE OF INDIAN, STATE, AND FEDERAL GOVERNMENTS IN EDUCATION AND LAW AND ORDER

The basic structure of our Federal system provides for State and local government with certain functional responsibilities, such as education and police and court systems. The Federal level concentrates on international relations, defense, and national programs such as those for commerce, agriculture, labor, natural resources, the federal legal and judicial system, education, and welfare. Where functions seem to be duplicated above, such as education, the operation and management of the function is generally with the State and local jurisdictions with grant-in-aid assistance from the Federal level plus statistical and research services on a national basis. Insofar as grant-in-aid programs involve conditions or criteria, they also may have considerable impact on policy and operation at the State and local levels. But the official with whom the citizen comes in contact is a local or State official as a general rule.

However, a Navajo Indian living in the State of Arizona may attend a tribal, State, or Federal school. No other segment of the population has this option. An Oglala Sioux on the Pine Ridge Reservation in South Dakota is not subject to the State police or the State courts—but to tribal police and courts under the general supervision of the Federal Government. For certain offenses, the jurisdiction is automatically with a Federal court. When he leaves the reservation he is subject to local and State police and local and State courts. Thus, some law and order functions traditionally local and State in nature, are performed by tribal or Federal employees on reservations in 15 States where the Indian residents are eligible for special Federal services. However, there is no standard pattern and the relationships are in constant flux. These two areas, education and law and order, will be examined to indicate the variation in patterns of responsibility.

Education

In education, for example, a vast majority of Indian children in school on Federal reservations used to be educated either by mission schools or Federal schools. However, the mission and other private schools now have about 6 percent and Federal schools about 26 percent of the total Indian children in school in States with federally recognized Indians. The remaining 68 percent are in public schools.[4]

Of course, all Indian children not members of tribes recognized by the BIA are educated in either public or private schools. The Federal policy has been to transfer BIA schools to local and State jurisdiction when all parties concerned were in agreement.

A financial problem faces a public school with an appreciable number of Indian children living on non-taxable land, if the school district obtains part of its revenue from a real estate tax. Relief in such instances should come from the Department of Health, Education, and Welfare (HEW) (P.L. 874 funds). However, under the provisions of the Johnson-O'Malley Act [5] BIA can reimburse States and school districts to make up for this tax loss if it determined that P.L. 874 (64 Stat. 1100) and other Federal, State and local resources cannot compensate a school district for this loss. Johnson-O'Malley funds are primarily used to provide compensatory education for disadvantaged Indian children. In fiscal year 1970, over $16 million in such funds were disbursed to the States.[6]

Of the estimated 129,785 (127,596 ages 6–18 and 2,189 over 18) Indian children in public schools in those States in which BIA operates schools and/or provides Johnson-O'Malley funds, only 72,081 Indian public school students received Johnson-O'Malley funding in 1970. The States and localities provided the same funds

---

[4] See Table I, Appendix B. Although there has been a steady rise in the percentage in public schools, movement has been slow during the last four decades. 52 percent were in public schools in 1930. See Alan L. Sorkin, *American Indians and Federal Aid*, (Washington, D. C.: The Brookings Institution, 1971), p. 22.

[5] See Chapter II for description of this act.

[6] See Table IV, Appendix B, for State distribution.

Senior high school English classroom, Sisseton Public Schools, with both Indian and non-Indian students.

(Photo: U.S. Department of the Interior, Bureau of Indian Affairs.)

for the other Indian children in public schools (57,203) as for non-Indian children.[7]

For the education function, direct service to the Indian citizen by the Federal Government has been changing to service by the State, with Federal financial support as appropriate.

HEW grant-in-aid funds are available for all students, including Indians, and many educational facilities and programs with a substantial number of Indian participants are benefiting from these programs.[8]

When served by a public school, Indians and others in the school district may vote for the school board and participate in parent and

---

[7] *Johnson-O'Malley Student Statistical Summary Report,* 1970, BIA. The States included in the above totals are: Nebraska, North Dakota, South Dakota, Colorado, Kansas, Montana, Wyoming, Alaska Iowa, Minnesota, Wisconsin, Oklahoma, Mississippi, New Mexico, Arizona, Nevada, Utah, Idaho, Washington, and Florida. All Indian children in other States are fully funded by State or private schools, with such Federal aids as are available for all school systems meeting the criteria. See Table IV, Appendix B.

[8] For example, Elementary and Secondary Education Act, P.L. 815 (facilities) 64 Stat. 967, and P.L. 874 (program) 64 Stat. 1100.

Tuba City Public School Board members, left to right: Hadley A. Thomas, Superintendent, Creek Tribe; George J. Outie, Hopi Tribe; Phillip Miller, non-Indian; Ray Amick, non-Indian; Ernest Manuelito, Navajo Tribe; Paul Blatchford, Navajo Tribe; Mrs. Evelyn Elliott, district secretary, non-Indian.

(Photo: U.S. Department of the Interior, Bureau of Indian Affairs.)

civic activities related to school policy. The Indian influence is determined by their relative numbers and degree of participation. BIA statistics indicate that in 1971 there were 232 public school districts with Indian membership on the school boards totaling 631 Indian board members. Some of these boards have an Indian majority, such as those at Tuba City (Navajo) and Whiteriver (White Mountain Apache). Public schools operate under State law and State departments of education which frequently specify minimum course requirements, minimum standards for and approval of proposed school facilities, minimum teacher qualifications and other personnel criteria, and frequently operate functions that logically are State-wide such as the teacher retirement system. State funds for public schools are distributed to local school systems on a per capita basis, sometimes in accordance with a special formula. The local school system thus may have income from the State, the locality (generally from a property tax), and from the Federal

Government because of funds channeled through the State.

A new option for Indian communities is now available—local operation of a school under a contract with BIA. Five schools are operated in this manner: Rough Rock and Blackwater schools in Arizona, the Ramah Navajo school in New Mexico, the Stefan school in South Dakota (200 students, high school level), and a school for the Miccosukee in Florida. These five schools had a total enrollment of approximately 761 pupils in 1971. Under this option the State and local public school system, if any, is bypassed. Funding is entirely Federal or a combination of Federal and private.[9]

Minimum curriculum standards and requirements are spelled out in the contracts and generally equal or exceed State curriculum requirements. Flexibility is provided for Indian input relating to Indian cultural or other programs which are in addition to the minimum requirements. As in the case of federally operated schools, State funds distributed to public schools would not be received by a school under BIA contract.

Another option is that of tribal corporations being responsible for the use of Johnson-O'Malley funds in a given State. As of July 1971, BIA had contracts with the United Tribes of North Dakota, the Nebraska Inter-Tribal Corporation, and the United Sioux Tribal Corporation of South Dakota. In these circumstances, the tribal corporation negotiates a contract with the State for the use of these funds in the education of Indian children in public schools.

Another phenomenon is a spcial provision for Indian education by the State. Maine actually operated three Indian day schools with tribal enrollment of over 200 children in 1970.[10] Indian elementary students also attend public schools off the reservation and all high school students attend off-reservation schools. The tuition for each student is paid by the State.[11]

New York has been actively engaged in the education of Indian children since 1846, at which time State operated Indian schools were inaugurated on several reservations. The State no longer oper-

---

[9] Rough Rock, for example, receives the average BIA amount per capita for each pupil and, in addition, has received funds from the Office of Economic Opportunity and the Donner Foundation to more than double this amount.

[10] One on the Penobscot Reservation and two on the Passamaquoddy Reservation. Letter to author from Meredith A. Ring, Supervisor of Indian Education, State of Maine.

[11] Maine Statutes, Title 20, Sec. 1452–1454.

ates Indian schools, but contracts with three boards of education for the operation of the three remaining State-owned reservation schools. The State contracts with seven other districts for the education of Indian reservation children through grade 12. All tuition and transportation charges are paid by the State.

In post secondary training the Indian student has a distinct advantage over his non-Indian neighbor as New York State is currently subsidizing him up to $1,100 each year.[12]

Up until 1971, Colorado provided tuition-free education for qualified Indians at Fort Lewis College, Durango, and continues to provide tuition-free education to Colorado Indian residents.[13] This college has an intercultural program which is of assistance to many Indian students. In a free, six-week, summer pre-college course the college gives assistance in registration procedure, study habits, and an introduction to campus living. Extra help sessions are provided for individuals in academically weak areas and tips are given on social behavior. Personal guidance and counseling are available. Some students taking the pre-college course stay at Ft. Lewis and others go on to other colleges. It is reported that dropout rates have been greatly reduced.[14]

The Virginia State Department of Education, which formerly operated special schools for the Pamunkey and the Mattaponi Indians, is responsible for the payment of tuition, cafeteria meals, and provision of free textbooks for Indian children who reside on the Pamunkey and Mattaponi Indian reservations in King William County. These children now attend the county schools.[15] No special provisions are made for the children of other Indian groups such as the Chickahominys, the largest in Virginia.[16]

In Wisconsin, the State supervisors of Indian education and superintendent of public instruction have tried to develop understanding among all professional people of the special problems Indian students face, as well as to maintain close consultation with

---

[12] *Annual Report of New York State Interdepartmental Committee on Indian Affairs, 1968–1969.* Letter from John R. Hathorn indicates current subsidy of $1,100.

[13] Sec. 124–14–12, Colorado Revised Statutes, 1963.

[14] Response of Lyle C. Kyle, Director, Legislative Counsel of the Colorado General Assembly, to Governors' Interstate Indian Council (GIIC) questionnaire of April 1970.

[15] J. G. Blount, Jr., Assistant Superintendent, Administration, Virginia State Board of Education, letter to author dated August 11, 1970.

[16] *Indians of the Eastern Seaboard* (Washington, D. C.: U. S. Department of the Interior, Bureau of Indian Affairs, 1968).

principals of schools with a large Indian enrollment, teachers of Indian students, the students themselves, their parents, and tribal leaders. Wisconsin has two monetary programs for aiding Indian young people. The college scholarships program, funded by the State and BIA, makes it possible for any Indian student in the upper two-thirds of his class to attend a Wisconsin university. The State vocational grant program provides a support of $20 per week to Indian students attending vocational schools.[17]

Many State programs such as the visiting coordinator program in Oklahoma [18] are funded under the Federal Johnson-O'Malley program but the examples that preceded are illustrations of special efforts that use State funds in whole or in part for the benefit of Indians.

Law and Order

One of the amenities desired by people living together in communities is freedom from violence and adherence to rules of behavior that the community decides contribute to the common good. Historically, Indians had their own governing systems, then, when placed on reservations, the Army or the BIA frequently established the rules and enforced them. Two separate law and order systems

---

[17] *Handbook on Wisconsin Indians* (Madison, Wisc.: Governor's Commission on Human Rights, 1966) , p. 52.

[18] The visiting coordinator program is the most popular Oklahoma Indian school program among Indian parents and Oklahoma public school people. Ten coordinators work in different areas of the State. Their duties are:

1) visiting schools and conferring with school personnel in order to learn the problems confronting the Indian students and attempting to locate and enroll all school-aged Indian children in an area; attempting to alleviate problems which might keep children out of school, or cause them to leave.

2) visiting Indian homes and explaining the importance of regular school attendance; explaining various school policies and regulations, school lunches, and other school matters; encouraging parents to attend school sponsored meetings.

3) counseling with Indian students and dropouts to encourage them to further their education; helping students make decisions concerning higher education or vocational training.

4) cooperating with the local branches of government, the State Department of Institutions, Social and Rehabilitation Services, Employment Office, the Federal Bureau of Indian Affairs, and with local organizations, such as civic groups and churches; attending related meetings such as those of the tribal council.

5) arranging for medical care, transportation, free lunches, etc., for students unable to provide these for themselves.

Twenty-Second Annual Report of Indian Education in Oklahoma, State Department of Education, Oklahoma City 1969, pp. 3 and 4.

developed, one on reservations and one in non-Indian areas surrounding the reservation.

With the Allotment Act and the breakup of many reservations, non-Indians secured land within the old reservation boundaries. The increasing acculturation to non-Indian ways and the need for earning a living led many Indians to find employment off the reservation. Thus, along with the movement that led to the Indian citizenship act of 1924, came mobility and increased intermixing, both on and off the reservation. Today approximately 43 percent of known Indians live in urban and metropolitan areas away from the reservation. They are subject to State and local law and order.

These developments put a strain on the dual law and order system. Many tribes have their own law and order codes, their own courts and judges, and their own police, sometimes operated in cooperation with a BIA special officer. When an Indian commits an offense within the traditional reservation boundary he is subject to the tribe's or BIA's jurisdiction. However, if he commits an offense outside of the reservation, he is subject to State or local jurisdiction.[19]

The converse is not true, however. If a non-Indian commits an offense on an Indian reservation he is not subject to the jurisdiction of the tribal police or courts.

Many awkward situations develop. Attempts to ameliorate the situation have taken three courses. First, under P.L. 280 [20] States and tribes can agree on State jurisdiction for all citizens and territory in the State. Second, neighboring jurisdictions may cross-deputize, so that, for example, a Navajo policeman may arrest a non-Indian under State authority. And, third, the improvement of tribal judicial procedures and development of civil rights of individuals more in line with non-Indian custom may eventually result in parity, that is, authority of tribal courts to try non-Indians for offenses committed on the reservation.

This area of relationships between the tribe and Indian individuals with non-Indian communities and individuals around them is in constant flux.

As the result of the above trends, there are a variety of arrangements in States with Federal reservations. Eleven such States have

---

[19] Except for designated major crimes which automatically come under the Federal courts.

[20] See Chapter III for discussion of this act.

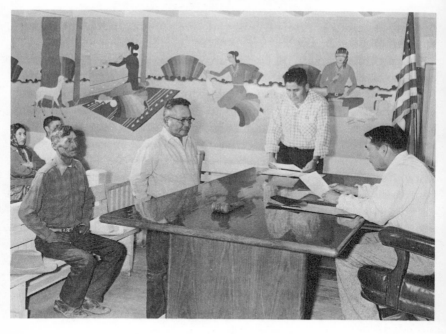

Navajo Tribal Court trial in process.
(Photo: U.S. Department of the Interior, Bureau of Indian Affairs.)

law and order jurisdictions over all citizens, including Indians and other natives, whether such citizens are on or off the reservation: Alaska, California, Florida, Iowa, Kansas, Louisiana, Missouri, Nebraska, New York, Oklahoma, and Wisconsin. Eleven other States have Federal jurisdiction on at least some reservation areas and either or both tribal and State jurisdiction over some actions or areas: Idaho, Michigan, Minnesota, Montana, Nevada, North Carolina, New Mexico, Oregon, South Dakota, Utah, and Washington. Four States have Federal and tribal jurisdiction only on Federal Indian reservations. They are: Arizona, Mississippi, North Dakota, and Wyoming.[21]

All 24 States without Federal reservations or Indian land held in trust exercise civil and criminal jurisdiction over all of their citizens including Indians.

---

[21] See Table I, Appendix B.

STATES' APPROACH TO THEIR INDIAN CITIZENS

Twenty States have established special organizational arrangements for some aspects of their relationships with Indian citizens. Four States have some special services but no special organizational arrangements. The remaining 26 States have no special provision for their Indian citizens.

The breakdown is as follows:

TABLE 4—INDIANS SERVED BY STATE, FEDERAL AGENCIES

States	Total Indian Population	BIA Service Population	State Service Population
26 with no special organization or services	186,079	63,038	123,041
4 with services	34,886	8,626	26,260
20 with special organizational arrangements	606,126	377,290	228,836
Totals	827,091	448,954 [1]	378,137

[1] The difference between 448,954 and 477,458 shown in Table I, Appendix B, is the lower Census figures for the States of Alaska, Arizona, and New Mexico than the number of Indians BIA says it is serving in those States. The 448,954 includes only the 1970 Census total in the States mentioned.

In the 26 States [22] with no special organization or services, the total Indian population is 186,079. Only 63,038 of them are recognized as being eligible for service by the Federal Government in the States of Alaska, Iowa, Louisiana, Mississippi, North Carolina, and Oregon. If Alaska, with its 51,528 Natives is excluded, of the 134,551 Indians in the remaining 25 States only 11,510 are recognized and eligible to receive special services from the Federal Government. The remaining 123,041 receive whatever service they get from the States and localities, or Federal services available to all citizens.[23]

The four States of Colorado, Connecticut, Virginia, and Wisconsin which have some special programs or services, but no special organizational entity for Indians, have a total Indian population of 34,886 Indians of which 75 percent receive the same services as other citizens and only 25 percent are eligible to receive some services from the Federal Government.[24]

[22] See Table I, Appendix B, for breakdown by State.
[23] See Appendix H 3 for more details on these States.
[24] See Appendix, H 4, for more details on these States.

The remaining 20 States with special organizational arrangements for serving Indians have 73 percent (606,126) of Indians in the United States.[25]

These 20 States are shown on Table I, Appendix B, under the heading "Special State Organization" with a separate column for each of the following subheadings: "State Indian Commission or Equivalent," "State Director or Coordinator" and "Director's Staff." One or more of the three subcolumns will be checked for each of the 20 States.

Too much detail would be required to describe each State situation for these 20 States.[26]

The discussion that follows will summarize: State philosophy concerning Indian citizens; characteristics of State commissions or other organizations; functions of coordinators or directors of Indian affairs; activities of commissions and coordinators; and importance of State departments and institutions to Indian citizens.

States' Philosophy Concerning Their Indian Citizens

Views concerning the relationships of Indians to the Federal and State governments have shifted as circumstances have changed. The Constitution declared that Indians not taxed would not be counted as "free persons" in determining State representation in the Congress. The term "Indians not taxed" was also used by various Federal and State laws to exclude Indians from voting. Some State constitutions and statutes held non-taxed tribal Indians were not citizens, for example, the constitutions of Idaho, New Mexico, and Washington. Arizona denied Indians the right to vote on the basis that they were under guardianship.[27]

---

[25] States with 5,000 or more Indians or Natives not included in the above 20 States are: Alaska (51,528) ; Colorado (8,836) ; Illinois (11,413) ; Louisiana (5,366) ; Missouri (5,405) ; North Carolina (43,487) ; Ohio (6,654) ; Pennsylvania (5,533) ; and Wisconsin (18,924) . Alaska, Colorado, Louisiana, North Carolina, and Wisconsin are discussed in Appendix H 3 and H 4.

States with federally recognized Indians not having special State Indian organizational arrangements are: Colorado, Wisconsin, Alaska, Iowa, Louisiana, Mississippi, North Carolina, and Oregon.

[26] The State statutes, description of State organization, and State activities alone take up approximately 90 pages in the *State Directory: State Organizations and Activities for Indian Citizens* (Draft for Review and Correction) Theodore W. Taylor, December 1970.

[27] *Federal Indian Law* (Washington, D. C.: United States Department of the Interior, Office of the Solicitor, 1958), pp. 526–532 discusses Indian suffrage.

Porter v. Hall, 271 p. 411 (Ariz. 1928) see "Legal Status of Indian Suffrage in the U. S." 19 Calif. L. Rev. 507 (1930) .

Historically there were practical problems with Indians voting in State elections. Indians living on a Federal reservation were frequently not subject to State or local laws while on the reservation. If they voted for State and county officials they participated in making laws or levying taxes not applicable to them but applicable to others. This situation is still true and it raises bothersome questions of equity from the non-Indian point of view.

Over the years various Indians became citizens by treaty or special statute such as the Allotment Act. In 1924, all Indians not previously considered citizens became such.[28] Remaining State barriers to Indian voting began to fall. For example, in 1948 the Arizona Supreme Court declared that the disenfranchisement of Indians in Arizona was unconstitutional overruling the earlier case of *Porter v. Hall*.[29] New Mexico followed Arizona's decision in 1962.[30]

Maine amended its constitution in 1954 to remove "Indians not taxed" from those excepted from voting. Some Maine Indians publicly opposed the removal of the constitutional exception and the granting of the right to vote because they saw it "as a step towards the termination of the special Indian-State relationship." [30A]

All Indian citizens in all States now have the right to vote in local, State and Federal elections on the same basis as other citizens. Today the importance of the State to its Indian citizens and the reciprocal—the importance of Indian citizens to the State—is specifically recognized in many States by State statutes, establishment of State Indian commissions, and the fact that State officials work closely with Indian leaders. This occurs in States with large numbers of Indians such as Arizona, New Mexico, and Oklahoma, as well as in States with relatively few Indians such as Florida, Texas, and Maine. Thus many State attitudes have changed for the better in recent years.

Arizona's Commission on Indian Affairs Chairman Bill Alcaida, of the Colorado River Reservation, recognized the interrelationship when he said: "The problems confronting Arizona Indians in attaining a place of social, economic, and political equality with other citizens within the state and nation are complex and will take both time and patience to solve." He continued that he hoped

---

[28] 43 Stat. 253.

[29] *Harrison v. Laveen*, 196 P. 2d 456 (Ariz. 1948).

[30] *Montoya v. Bolack*, 372 P. 2d 398 (N.M. 1962).

[30A] Letter to Thomas Tureen from Edward C. Hinckley, former Commissioner of Indian Affairs for Maine, March 24, 1972.

the information in the Commission's report to the Governor would "prove to be encouraging and helpful as you evaluate the progress being made by the Commission in its program of cooperation with state and federal agencies, tribal councils and others, including our legislators, to bring about circumstances that will definitely include the cooperation of the Indian citizens of Arizona as an important part of the state's future." [31]

The statute in Oklahoma provides that "It shall be the purpose of the Oklahoma Indian Affairs Commission to work toward promoting unity, purpose, and understanding among the Indian people of the State, Indian leaders of the State, the various Indian agencies both Federal and State, and the Executive and Legislative branches of the State Government." [32]

Further examples of State philosophy will be found in Appendix H1.

Characteristics of State Commissions or Other Organizations

Analysis of Table I, Appendix B, indicates that the States with federally recognized Indians, even when they have an Indian Commission and an executive director or coordinator, have minimum staff support for these activities—the maximum being four persons including the director. The two States with a substantial staff are two of those States that have assumed complete State responsibility for all of their Indian citizens: Texas with 25 persons and Maine with ten persons, not including the staff of the Maine State Department of Indian Education and ten and a half teachers. Thus, it is obvious that except for Maine and Texas, the State's focal point for Indian affairs, when they have one at all, is poorly staffed and financed. [33]

Eleven of the 20 States considered in this category established their Indian commissions or other State Indian program by statute. The Governor, through executive order or otherwise, set up the organization in six States. [34]

The Governor is on the commission in only four States, and is

---

[31] Chairman of Arizona's Commission on Indian Affairs letter to the Governor, transmitting the 1968–69 Annual Report of the Commission.

[32] Oklahoma Indian Affairs Commission, *Biennial Report,* May 8, 1967—June 30, 1969, p. 1.

[33] See Appendix H 2 for further details on funding.

[34] Washington is not included in above breakdowns as no information was received. California has no formal organization, but had one until 1969. Maine does not have a commission but has a State Department of Indian Affairs.

ex-officio or honorary except in the case of North Dakota, where he is chairman. Five States have State executive department representation on the commissions; in two States it is ex-officio. Only two States have members of the legislature on the commission.

Fifteen States have Indian members on the commission and the Indians are the majority in ten State commissions. In four of these States all members are Indian, and in two, Texas and New York, all members are non-Indian.[35]

North Dakota and Minnesota have interesting variations. In addition to the Governor, representatives of State executive departments, and the tribal chairmen or their designees from the four State reservations, North Dakota provides that a representative of the county commissioners' organization who lives in one of the counties bordering the reservation be on the commission.

Minnesota is one of the States where the Governor and the commissioners of education, public welfare, conservation, and business development, are ex-officio members of the Indian commission. Red Lake, Consolidated Chippewa, and the Sioux group each appoint one Indian member to the commission and have the authority to remove them. The House and Senate each appoint three members. Only three members at large are appointed by the Governor. Thus, in Minnesota the Governor does not appoint the voting majority as ex-officio members do not vote.

Of the 16 States having commissions, ten are chaired by Indians, six by non-Indians.[36]

In all cases where there is a State appointed commission or board, it reports to the Governor. Even in Utah, where the statutes state that the Board of Indian Affairs is in the Department of Social Services, the Governor appoints the members with the advice and consent of the Senate and the Board's reports are submitted to the Governor and the Legislature, as well as to the Department of Social Services.

---

[35] Seventeen States are reported above. The other three are California (no organization now), Montana (no commission as such), and Washington (no information available).

[36] Washington, California, Maine, and Montana have no commissions or equivalent in the State organization. Montana, however, has an Intertribal Policy Board which is all Indian and composed of two representatives from each reservation and two delegates representing landless Indians. The State Coordinator of Indian Affairs attends all meetings and, upon formal incorporation of the Board in 1969, was the initial registered agent and incorporator. There is a very close liaison between this board and State officials.

Functions of Coordinators or Directors of Indian Affairs

The executive director or coordinator of Indian affairs generally is the director of the staff for the commissions, and in seven of the States is appointed by the commission. In five States the executive director or coordinator is appointed by the Governor but in most cases the statute specifies that he is to carry out the staff work under the policy direction of the commission. In Montana, the coordinator works closely with the Intertribal Policy Board made up of two representatives from each reservation. He is appointed by the Governor from a list of five nominees agreed upon by the tribal councils in Montana. In Nevada, the executive director is appointed by the Governor upon the recommendation of the commission.

In New York the Director of Indian Affairs is chairman of the Interdepartmental Committee on Indian Affairs, made up of representatives of the State departments of: Commerce, Conservation, Education, Health, Transportation, Social Services, Mental Hygiene, and State Police.

In South Dakota the Governor appoints ". . . a coordinator to assist in the administration of the duties, responsibilities, and activities of the Commission of Indian Affairs." The coordinator serves at the pleasure of the Governor, has such powers and duties as assigned by the Governor, and is paid a salary determined by the Governor. However, the Governor is an honorary member of the commission and can influence coordination between the coordinator and commission. The coordinator legally reports to the Governor, but, in fact, works closely with the commission.

In Maine, the Commissioner of Indian Affairs is appointed by the Governor and he is the policy and administrative head of the only State department of Indian affairs in the United States.

The Texas Commission of Indian Affairs is appointed by the Governor with the advice and consent of the Senate. The Commission in turn appoints the Superintendents of the two Texas Indian communities.

Activities of Commissions and Coordinators

Gathering Information, Reports and Recommendations

All commissions and coordinators (or directors) have duties of assembling information about: (1) the Indian condition in the State; and (2) State, Federal, and other programs available to Indians. This information is gathered through such activities as studies, task forces, questionnaires, visits to tribes (and to State and Federal agencies), hearings, and meetings.

On the basis of information collected, State commissioners are responsible for reporting the situation as found and making recommendations, generally to the governor and the State legislature. These reports are annual, biennial, or special, depending on the situation. These commissions thus have an opportunity to exercise influence on State Indian policy and implementation. New York's interdepartmental committee on Indian affairs has recommended changes in Indian law and other statutes—both to the State legislature and the Federal Congress. Recently the legislature changed the qualifications for school board members to make Indians eligible for election to the board at St. Regis, and New York took the lead in obtaining Federal statutes assigning the State authority over Indians for civil and criminal law.

Some find it difficult to gather pertinent information and Utah has recommended a manual on Federal programs and effective information on how to make use of such programs. It was suggested these programs could be under such general headings as: housing, health, education, community development, and roads.[37]

Liaison Activities

One of the functions of commissions and their staffs is to maintain liaison between tribal councils, local governments, State departments, State legislature, and Federal activities both in the executive and legislative branches.[38] Arizona prints reports of State and Federal activities for Indians side by side for all fields of activity such as education and health. When there seems to be lack of communication or coordination of effort is needed, the Executive Director of the Arizona Commission of Indian Affairs tries to resolve the situation through conferences and joint meetings of

---

[37] Frank Allen, Consultant, response to GIIC questionnaire, April 1970. This suggestion poses a real challenge. See, for example, the *Listing of Operating Federal Assistance Programs Compiled During the Roth Study,* prepared by the staff of Representative William V. Roth, Jr. (Washington, D. C.: U. S. Government Printing Office, 1969). The Office of Minority Business Enterprise, Office of Economic Opportunity, and the Office of Management and Budget have also worked on this problem.

[38] See, for example, "Arizona Commission of Indian Affairs: Rules and Regulations," mimeograph, undated.

tribal, local, State, and Federal officials concerned, when appropriate.[39]

The Florida Commission on Indian Affairs discovered that one of the main concerns of the Florida Indians was the lack of effective law enforcement on Indian reservations. The commission secured a promise from the State for additional law enforcement funds for Indian communities. This commission also obtained legislative enactment of long-term lease authority for Indians on State Indian reservation land, making it easier for Indians to finance capital improvements.[40]

In Maine the Penobscot and Passamaquoddy Indians vote for Representatives and Senators to the State Legislature as do Indians in the other States.

In addition, Maine has a unique provision for two Representatives, one each elected by the Penobscot and Passamaquoddy Tribes, who attend the sessions of the State Legislature, but cannot vote or speak on the floor. However, they act as much needed lobbyists presenting the needs and desires of the Indians.

Wyoming indicated the importance they attach to liaison by stating that their greatest accomplishment " . . . has been the greatly increased communication and understanding between tribal leaders, individual Indian citizens and the non-Indian . . ." especially in towns bordering the Wind River Reservation. As one result there is a better understanding of police and court jurisdiction on and off the reservation. Another is that a number of tribal members are now employed by a computer parts manufacturer in Riverton.[41]

Facilitation of communication and followup action by the State Government is the objective of the Indian advisory council and annual Indian conference in Idaho. Each tribe nominates two representatives and the Governor invites them to two meetings, the spring meeting coinciding with the Annual Indian Conference. At the conference discussions are on any topic desired by the participants, followed by visits by Indians with various State executive department heads. In 1970, the program included an address by the Governor and panels on education, legal problems, employment and training, State welfare and foster homes, health, communica-

---

[39] Response to GIIC questionnaire of April 1970.

[40] Charles L. Knight, Chairman, Florida Commission on Indian Affairs, in response to GIIC questionnaire of April 1970.

[41] Response to GIIC questionnaire of April 1970.

tion (between State, Indian tribes, and Federal Government), industrial development, water and treaty rights, education and training of prisoners of the Idaho State Penitentiary, and law and order. Both the Commissioner of Indian Affairs and the Executive Director of the National Council on Indian Opportunity from Washington, D.C., participated in the conference.[42]

In 1967–68 the studies made by and recommendations of the Nevada Indian Affairs Commission emphasized coordination of effort between parties concerned and effective action to meet problems. Studies covered activities of Indians, BIA, and State agencies concerned with Indians and concluded with recommendations.[43]

For example, under Indian education it was reported that only 97 Nevada Indians attended the Stewart Indian School (BIA) and that the vast majority of the Indian students attended public schools throughout the State "where they face unique problems in a predominantly non-Indian environment." Neither the BIA staff nor the State Department of Education did much counseling with this public school group of approximately 2,300 Indian students. The report recommended "That a study be conducted of the Federal Relations and Programs Branch of the State Department of Education with the objective of determining ways of more effectively budgeting funds and scheduling staff's time so as to provide more on-the-job counseling in public schools."

Under social services the report pointed out that general assistance, social services, child welfare and foster care were contracted to the State by BIA and recommended that the rest of the social services activities be contracted also.

Many other programs could be cited.

In its summary the report stated: "It is hoped the Governor, 1969 State Legislative body, the Nevada Congressional Delegation, and others will review this report and sense its urgent call for necessary changes." [44]

As another example of a procedure for interchange of informa-

---

[42] Richard D. Hughes, Administrative Assistant to the Governor of Idaho, response to GIIC questionnaire.

[43] Subjects included education, social services, employment assistance, housing, roads, credit, realty, reservation programs, land operations, law and order, tribal operations, intertribal council, community action agencies, Neighborhood Youth Corps, youth recreation and cultural enrichment program, work incentive program, emergency food and medical services, community developers, alcoholism program, and senior citizens program.

[44] Report of the Nevada Indian Affairs Commission, 1967–68.

tion and coordination of action, the Executive Director of the Nevada Indian Affairs Commission attends the staff meetings of BIA's Nevada Indian Agency.[45]

Concrete results of teamwork are seen in the establishment of plants in rural Oklahoma to provide payroll for the disadvantaged, including Indians. Private business, State and Federal agencies, and Indian tribes have worked together to achieve this result.[46]

Work with Tribes and Services to Tribes

Commissions run the gamut of activities from providing assistance in long-range economic planning, such as in Florida, to the provision of fairly complete assistance and services for Indian groups, such as in Texas. Several examples of service to tribes are mentioned in earlier portions of this section, such as obtaining law and order funds from the State in Florida and helping in establishing new plants in Oklahoma. Following are other examples:

In Texas, the three man commission appoints the superintendents of the two Indian communities, finances a considerable staff out of State funds,[47] and is working with the tribes in the development of tourism and accompanying activities to provide jobs for individual Indians and income for the tribe. The objective is to develop each community to the point where it can financially support its own programs of health, education, housing, and economic welfare.

A tourist complex has been built on the Alabama-Coushatta reservation in Texas centering on native Indian activities. In 1968, 113,414 tourists visited this complex and they spent $195,370. This complex is being enlarged through additional capital investment and the Alabama-Coushatta Tribe expects it to help provide a sound economic base for the reservation. Other programs on the reservation were: Head Start, Neighborhood Youth Corps, adult education, and youth programs. A Federal mutual help housing

---

[45] Ross Morres, Executive Director, telephone conversation with author, October 15, 1970.

[46] Discussions with Messrs. George Hubley and Prentiss Mooney, BIA; Marvin Franklin, Phillips Petroleum; also see Dewey F. Bartlett, former Governor of Oklahoma, *The Okie-Type Company: An Innovation* (undated).

Oktronics, Inc., located in Okemah, produces electrical equipment and employs 19 Indians, 5 Negroes, and 26 Whites, Cherokee Nation Industries, Inc., wholly-owned and managed by the Cherokee Nation, employs 51 people, mostly Indian.

[47] There are 17 paid State employees at Alabama-Coushatta and eight paid State employees at Tigua.

New Mexico Commission on Indian Affairs meeting March 4, 1970. Standing, John C. Rainer, executive director, left to right, sitting: Jardy L. Jones, mayor of Chama; James T. Nahkai, Jr., Navajo; Preston Keevama, San Juan Pueblo; Joe Watson, Jr., Navajo, chairman; Dolores Chandler, secretary; William C. Schaab, attorney.

(Photo: U.S. Department of the Interior, Bureau of Indian Affairs.)

project will provide 40 new three bedroom brick homes to replace and supplement present substandard housing.[48]

The responsibilities of the Utah Board of Indian Affairs are unique. Thirty-seven and one-half percent of the net oil and gas royalties from Navajo land in Utah is paid to the State of Utah to be expended by the State for the health, education, and general welfare of the Navajo Indians residing in San Juan County.[49] The Board supervises expenditures from this fund, and works with an Indian advisory committee on the priority of activities requiring funds. Its March 23, 1970 report indicates that funds were allocated for education, health, housing, and roads.

The Board and the Director of the State Division of Indian Affairs are also working with the Utah Paiute groups to carry out provisions of Public Law 90–584 of October 17, 1968. This was an

---

[48] Assistant Superintendent Roland Pancho, response to GIIC questionnaire, April 1970.

[49] P.L. 403, March 1, 1933 (47 Stat. 1418). This income was approximately $675,000 from April 1, 1968, to March 31, 1970. BIA Finance Office.

act to provide for disposition of over $7 million appropriated by the Congress to pay an Indian Claims Commission judgment in favor of the Southern Paiute Nation of Indians for payment on land taken about 1860. The appropriation amounts to approximately $7,200 for each eligible Indian. Five of the Southern Paiute groups are in Utah [50] and the act provided that the funds were to be used in accordance with a plan agreed upon between the governing bodies of the Paiute groups in Utah and the Utah Board of Indian Affairs.[51]

The State Board and the Paiute Indian groups have agreed on setting up six-man advisory groups for each Paiute community to work up a distribution plan for the funds for that community. These groups are made up of three Indians and three non-Indians from neighboring jurisdictions. The objective is to obtain more inter-involvement of the Indian and non-Indian groups as well as to provide expert advice to the Indians by knowledgeable members of the non-Indian community such as bankers and used car salesmen.

This is an interesting approach providing primarily for State-Indian responsibility in the decision process. In contrast, for Paiute groups in Arizona and Nevada, the statute provides for disposition of the funds in such manner as decided upon by the Indian group and approved by the Secretary—leaving out State participation.

Legislation has been passed in Nevada providing that: (1) Indians are to receive surplus property in the same priority as counties, cities, and fire departments; (2) Indians are not required to have permits to gather pine nuts; (3) Indian land is to be exempt from the possessory tax; (4) Indians are to be exempt from paying for fishing and hunting licenses; and (5) Indian use of peyote is exempted from narcotic provisions.[52]

---

[50] Cedar City Paiutes, Indian Peaks, Kanosh, Koosharem, and Shivwitz. All but the Cedar City group have been terminated.

[51] The act also provided that a meeting between the Board of Indian Affairs and the various Paiute groups would be called in accordance with rules promulgated by the Secretary of the Interior, and that the plan agreed upon required the approval of the Secretary. The Secretary was not to be responsible for the administration of the funds. The regulations promulgated by the Bureau for the Secretary provide for BIA representation at meetings between the Paiute and the Board of Indian Affairs until a plan is approved. Thereafter, a BIA representative would not be present unless requested by a Paiute group. A BIA representative would attend all meetings of the Cedar City group (not terminated) unless otherwise decided by the BIA Area Director. 35 *Federal Register* 16186 Thursday, October 15, 1970.

[52] Frank Durham, Chairman, Nevada Indian Affairs Commission, in response to GIIC questionnaire, April 1970.

The New Mexico Commission on Indian Affairs helped organize the Indian Community Action Program funded by the Office of Economic Opportunity. This took "months of consultation among Indian leaders, officials of the University and the federal government." [53]

The New Mexico Commission worked closely with the New Mexico Employment Security Commission in starting an Indian Human Resources Development program, employing 21 Indians as interviewers. The Commission also: worked with the State Department of Labor in establishing a Concentrated Employment Program for northern New Mexico; worked with BIA in planning for the Roswell Employment Training Center; encouraged tourism; assisted U. S. attorneys in locating and interviewing Indian witnesses concerning Indian water rights; worked with Indian leaders, school boards, and the State Director of Education to obtain educational programs that fit Indian needs; visited Indian students in college to try to cut attrition rate; worked with tribes to help them conform to the Civil Rights Act of 1968; and, with the help of a Field Foundation grant, and in cooperation with the University of New Mexico School of Law, hired an attorney to assist tribal governments in drawing up or revising their constitutions and law and order codes.[54] The Executive Director assisted in programs of voter education and registration of Indians so they could use their right to vote and thus actively participate in county, State and national elections.[55]

The four reservations in North Dakota—Standing Rock (partly in South Dakota), Ft. Berthold, Devils Lake, and Turtle Mountain—have joined together as the United Tribes of North Dakota. The North Dakota Indian Affairs Commission has aided them in this move to strengthen tribal actions and influence. The United Tribes of North Dakota Development Corporation was incorporated in January 1968 to enable the United Tribes to receive Federal funds and carry out planning and development. The chairmen of the four North Dakota tribes form the board of directors, and the Executive Secretary of the State Indian Affairs Commission is the non-voting secretary of the Corporation.

On June 24, 1969, a prime contract was executed between the Corporation and BIA giving the Corporation full responsibility for

---

[53] New Mexico Commission on Indian Affairs, *Annual Report*, 1968.
[54] Ibid.
[55] John Rainer, Report to GIIC, 1970.

establishing and operating a family training center for Indians at Bismarck, N. Dak. First year operating funds in the amount of $1,080,000 were provided by the Federal Government. The Corporation subcontracted with Bendix for on-site operation. Mr. Theodore Jamerson, a Standing Rock Sioux, was employed as the first "Coordinator" for the training center to supervise the operation of the subcontract with Bendix. Needless to say, a tremendous amount of groundwork and promotion was required to launch a project of this magnitude. Officials of the four tribes, the Executive Director of the State Indian Affairs Commission, BIA (area and central offices), other Federal agencies and authorities such as representatives of the Labor Department, the National Council on Indian Opportunity, and members of the Congress were involved.

The Corporation has also established a planning staff, with which the Executive Director of the Commission cooperated, and economic development plans were completed for each reservation during 1969. A Statewide Economic Advisory Council was created by the Corporation with State business and other leaders as members. A Center for Economic Development was sanctioned by the Corporation at North Dakota State University, funded by OEO and the university. This center had 18 different projects under study during 1969.

The North Dakota Indian Affairs Commission, through its Executive Director, also worked with: the State Indian Education Committee on use of Johnson-O'Malley funds for the education of Indian children in the public schools; the State Indian Committee on Higher Education; a two-day workshop for tribal council members; legislation on Indian scholarships; the Commission budget; clarification of foundation payments for Indians in public schools; establishing authority for school boards to enter into cooperative agreements with BIA schools; legislation to express State policy regarding tribal councils and to express State support for the family training center. The Executive Director of the Commission also worked with the North Dakota Council of Churches and the United Tribes in identifying and initiating worthwhile projects.[56]

---

[56] Austin G. Engle, Jr., Executive Director, North Dakota Indian Affairs Commission, response to GIIC questionnaire, April 1970.

Importance of State Departments and Institutions to Indian Citizens

The most important State services to Indians are through the various divisions of the State Government. The foregoing analysis of State commissions or other special activities has indicated that they function primarily as informational channels and help with liaison and coordination of Indian, local, State, and Federal programs. They also make recommendations which, if carried out, have to be implemented by legislative or executive action by one or more of the governments involved. It is clear that the State departments of education and law and order perform services for many Indian citizens. Florida's government has provided 104,800 acres of State trust lands to the Seminoles and Miccosukees, plus 143,620 acres of land for use under a revokable license. The State also dedicated three parcels of land on the Tamiami Trail to the Miccosukees. The Miccosukee restaurant, service station, and store are on two of these parcels.

In Texas the State plans to provide over $300,000 in capital funding for the Tiguas in 1972–73 and help them obtain over $1 million additional capital funding from Federal agencies. Maine, New York, Virginia, and Wisconsin have special provisions for the schooling of Indian children.

Several States, such as Oklahoma, have cooperated in developing payroll through industry. Wisconsin has passed special appropriations and rendered special services to the Menominees.[57]

The State employment services, largely funded by the Federal Government, are widely used by Indian citizens, including those on Federal Indian reservations. Categorical welfare aid, also funded in large part by the Federal Government, is administered by the States for all of their citizens, including Indians.

The States contribute to agricultural extension programs for Indians and many State judicial and institutional services are the only ones available to its Indian citizens.

However, the record indicates that the States are pinched for funds and that many needed services are non-existent or inadequate. Such services as counseling for Indian children in the schools, police protection in Indian country where there is State law and order, roads and road maintenance, housing, and the like,

---

[57] See Appendix H 4 for some of the Menominee details.

are all too frequently inadequate. Historically, many States have recognized responsibilities but have not performed them. The main excuse is lack of funds. They sometimes rationalize that Indians are a Federal responsibility.

Use of the taxing power and the priorities on the use of funds are within the States' discretion. Indians have not had a high priority in many instances. California is an example of this. Although California has 91,000 Indians, they constitute less than one half of 1 percent of the population. It is a question of priority as to whether the State will fund effective Indian programs from its own resources. As Acting Commissioner William Zimmerman, Jr. pointed out in the 1940's, California could provide an adequate program for Indians if it chose to do so.[58]

SUMMARY

Five States have half the national Indian population. The next 13 States in terms of numbers of Indian citizens have 35 percent of the Indian population. The last 15 percent of the Indians is scattered through the remaining 32 States.

Trust land is the primary basis for both State and Federal activity especially for Indians. Sixty-eight percent of the Indian children in States with Indians eligible for special Federal services are in public schools. Thirty-five States have law and order jurisdiction over all of their citizens, including their Indian citizens. Eleven States have a mixture of Federal, State or tribal law and order jurisdiction over reservation Indians, and but four States have Federal and tribal jurisdiction only over such Indians.

Twenty-four States have special services for Indians, and 20 of these have Indian commissions or other special organizational arrangements.

The States have adopted a positive attitude toward their Indian citizens as indicated by statutes and executive orders in 17 States— the emphasis being on the importance of Indian participation in the social, economic, and political life of the State. However, with a few notable exceptions, State programs for Indians are poorly funded and poorly staffed. The commissions in many instances are window dressing. However, whatever the motive in the establish-

---

[58] *Hearings on Sen. Res. 41, Post Office and Civil Service* (Washington, D. C.: 80th Cong., 1st sess., U. S. Senate, 1947), pt. 1, p. 576 ". . . in the State of California, in my judgment, if the Federal Government were to withdraw, the State could provide more services in the long run than we are now providing."

Adrian Fisher, chairman, Colorado River Tribal Council, with Governor Jack Williams (Arizona) at dedication of tribal museum and library, 1970.
(Photo: U.S. Department of the Interior, Bureau of Indian Affairs.)

ment of such commissions and coordinators, they provide a foot in the door. Indians, as well as forward-looking State officials, will use them to their advantage.

States have also learned that Indians must be involved in decisions affecting them and in many instances are trying to facilitate necessary Indian participation not only through Indian commissions, but by appointment of Indians to State executive agencies, and by establishing procedures for consultation with Indians on matters affecting Indian welfare.

The increasing activity of Indians in public school affairs is indicative. Not only are Indians on school boards, but they have been elected to State legislatures and to the United States Congress,[59] and many appointments to responsible executive positions both in

---

[59] Some States where Indians have been elected to the State legislature are: New Mexico, Arizona, Montana, Idaho, Alaska, and Oklahoma. Ben Reifel (Sioux) of South Dakota just retired from the U. S. House of Representatives. See Marion E. Gridley, *Indians of Today* (4th ed.; Chicago: Indian Council Fire, Inc., 1971). See also *Indian Record*, Bureau of Indian Affairs, January 1967.

the government and in private industry. The Chairman of the Board of Phillips Petroleum, for example, is Chief of the Cherokee Tribe in Oklahoma. There are still many Indians, however, who have not mastered the interface with the white culture surrounding them and some do not want to. Some of these live on a bare subsistence basis on their trust land or in urban slums.

Some States are attacking this problem, in cooperation with Indian leadership and Federal agencies, by endeavoring to develop an economic base where the Indians live in the rural areas—as illustrated by the Alabama and Coushatta in Texas and the Cherokees in Oklahoma. Texas' urban group, the Tiguas, are also involved in the development of a program aimed at making them economically self-sufficient.

Today, as never before, there is a public awareness of the disadvantaged, the problems of poverty, and support for basic civil rights. The possibilities for State participation in improving the condition of our Indian minority against this backdrop are discussed in Chapter IX.

CHAPTER SEVEN

CHANGING NATIONAL POLICIES

The United States is in a revolutionary period: non-whites are demanding a share of the power; our most respected institutions and public authority are under attack; new values and lifestyles are springing up; and technological change alters our way of life with ever-increasing velocity.[1]

Minorities, as well as the majority, are caught in the vortex of this change. Much of the social legislation of the Johnson Presidency reflected aspects of our changing times: civil rights, aid to education in various forms, the war on poverty, housing, manpower training, and economic development to name a few. National programs for the citizenry as a whole have affected Indian-State-Federal relationships in the past. Their impact in the future may even be more dramatic.[2]

EXAMPLE OF IMPACT IN THE 1960's

With the expansion of Federal help to housing, a program was developed between the Departments of Housing and Urban Development (HUD), Health, Education, and Welfare (HEW), and

---

[1] Fletcher Knebel, "Enlightened Self-Interest in Time of Change." *The Sunday Star,* Washington, D. C., January 10, 1971. The impact of this change, especially technological, is discussed by Alvin Toffler, in *Future Shock,* (New York: Random House, July 1970). Vine Deloria, Jr. describes the importance of ethnic groups in considering public policy. He made this point in his address to Smithsonian Institution International Symposium, November 18, 1970, in his article, "The Imperative: Not to Do Good but to Do Right," *The Sunday Star,* Washington, D. C., July 4, 1971, and on NBC TV program "Speaking Freely," July 18, 1971. 8:30–9:30 a.m.

[2] Richard Schifter points out that these programs have lessened the relative influence of the BIA in Indian communities in "Trends in Federal Indian Administration," *South Dakota Law Review,* Winter 1970. James Sundquist points out that these programs have changed the nature of our Federal system in James L. Sundquist with collaboration of David W. Davis, *Making Federalism Work* (Washington, D. C.: The Brookings Institution, 1969), especially pp. 1–13.

Navojo hogan, Crownpoint, N.M., 1964. Typical home and surroundings of many Bureau of Indian Affairs boarding school children.

(Photo: U.S. Department of the Interior, Bureau of Indian Affairs.)

Bureau of Indian Affairs (BIA) to eliminate substandard Indian housing. In 1966 there were 19,000 units of standard housing; in 1970 there were 30,560 such units. The agencies and tribes concerned are aiming for 8,000 units a year until substandard housing is eliminated—and came close to the annual goal in fiscal year 1971. Prior to the 1960's the BIA had not had a housing program as such. The major funds for this program are from HUD which is in business for the total population, not just Indians.

The Office of Economic Opportunity (OEO) funded Community Action Programs on Indian reservations as well as elsewhere. Grants are made to Indian tribes by OEO. The Indian tribe receiving the grant developed and administered the program. This gave Indians experience and confidence, and, along with community development minded superintendents who had done much along the same line for many years, provided much of the impetus of the present drive for self-determination.[3]

The various statutes providing for aids to education have helped

---

[3] OEO funds to Indian tribes totaled $27 million in fiscal year 1971.

Modern housing funded by the Department of Housing and Urban Development at Camp Verde Indian Reservation, Arizona.

(Photo: U.S. Department of the Interior, Bureau of Indian Affairs.)

both public and Federal schools in supplying compensatory education to Indian children.

The Economic Development Administration (EDA) has funded many Indian commercial and industrial endeavors, and recently the cumulative total from the mid-60's to 1971 reached $100 million.[4]

The examples could continue and details be provided, but the point being made is that social programs for all the people are catching up with many special programs that used to be just for Indians, and, in many instances, surpassing what was formerly available to Indians. If such national programs continue to expand, they may provide most of the services to Indians historically provided by BIA and Indian Health Service (IHS).

---

[4] EDA funds for Indians in fiscal year 1971 totaled $21,813,000. Information from EDA Indian Desk.

PROGRAM CONSIDERATIONS FOR THE 1970's

Population Location Policy

Increasing attention has been directed to the concentration of population along the eastern seaboard, Florida, Chicago, and the west coast—with the starvation of rural area vitality and increasing problems of the big megolopolises. There is some thought that this movement to the city may not be the most healthy thing for individuals or for the country—economically or socially.[5]

The BIA program has contributed to migration from the country to the city through its employment assistance and vocational training program. Indians apply for relocation and training in the urban areas for the same reasons others go there—the city has most of the jobs. Many Indians would rather stay on the reservation if they could have the same or nearly equivalent economic opportunity. Evidently this is true for non-Indians as well.

If national policy should be developed and adopted to provide incentives for dispersion of economic activity to small towns and rural areas, such a policy would not only affect Appalachia, but many Indian reservations anxious for more payroll and a desire on the part of their residents to live and work in their homelands.

---

[5] Senator Henry M. Jackson sponsors a bill to put medical doctors in rural areas with a shortage of medical service, *Anchorage Alaska News*, January 24, 1970. President's First Annual Report on Government Services to Rural America, *Congressional Record*, House, March 1, 1971, p. 933.

An excellent discussion of the history of action directed toward the revival of rural and non-metropolitan areas, as well as suggestions for future action, is found in: James L. Sundquist with the collaboration of David W. Davis, *Making Federalism Work* (Washington, D. C.: The Brookings Institution, 1969), p. 130 ff.

James L. Sundquist, *Where Shall They Live* (Washington, D. C.: The Brookings Institution, 1970), Reprint 172. Sundquist points out that we had an early population policy of western development supported by subsidies to railroads, turnpikes, river navigation, opening of public lands to settlement, and controlling Indians on reservations. We now have no clear sense of national purpose on population distribution. If all social and economic costs of migration, loss in values in the country, increase in transportation, welfare, and other costs in the city were included in a cost/benefits analysis it would "no doubt show that, as a general rule, it is far more economical from the standpoint of the *whole* society to create new economic opportunities where people are rather than allow existing communities to die while building other whole communities from the ground up in the name of 'economic efficiency'."

Population Size

The population explosion and its effect on crowding, resources, pollution, and other aspects of our life is becoming a matter of national and international concern. Open discussion of contraceptive practices and abortion is relatively recent, as is Government funding for family planning assistance, both in this country and abroad.

Indian communities, on or near Federal trust land, have one of the highest rates of population increase in the country, averaging about 2.5 percent per year during the last decade.[6]

Poverty, limited economic opportunities, and rapid population increase spell trouble—the community has to run fast to stay even. Too many people for the resources of the reservation are a critical problem for many tribes. This is one of the reasons for the employment assistance and relocation program and its past support by the tribes and the Congress.

In 1965, Secretary of the Interior Stewart L. Udall, inaugurated a policy of providing birth control and family planning information through pertinent bureaus of the Interior Department. Use of such information by Indians and others was to be on a voluntary basis.[7] HEW adopted a similar policy in 1966.[8] BIA and the Indian Health Service (IHS) have cooperated in this program on Indian reservations through BIA social workers and IHS nurses and physicians.

Recently there seems to be a dip in the rate of population increase on Indian reservations, but it is too early to tell whether it is a trend.

If there is increasing national acceptance on limiting the number of children, it could have an impact on Indian as well as other communities. Increased levels of education, competition in the non-Indian world, and higher Indian incomes could affect family size if Indians react the same as other groups.

Income Strategy Approach to Welfare

Revision of the national and State systems of helping those temporarily in need could have major impact on the Indian condition. Moynihan states that the most powerful determinant of behavior

---

[6] Information from Chief Statistician, Bureau of Indian Affairs, July 16, 1971.
[7] Memorandum to Bureaus, June 17, 1965.
[8] Memorandum to Heads of Operating Agencies, January 24, 1966.

and well being is the level and security of an individual's income. He, and others, including President Nixon and the Chairman of the House Ways and Means Committee, believe the Government should adopt an income strategy and insure a minimum income.[9]

Should such a program become law, 80–90 percent of BIA's general assistance caseload probably would qualify. Depending on the wording of the statute, this would change the Federal agency from BIA to a new Federal activity serving all eligibles regardless of race for the base payment provided in the law.[10]

Revenue Sharing

The States receive considerable revenue sharing at the present time. Should the amount of funds available to State and/or tribes through revenue sharing (either "general" or "special") be substantially increased this would have to be taken into consideration.[11]

Job Creation

Public works programs have been used to invigorate the economy, frequently with lasting public benefits in preservation of human pride and stamina, training for the world of work, as well as in providing public facilities and preservation of resources of value to the Nation. Such programs as the Works Progress Admin-

---

[9] Daniel P. Moynihan, "One Step We Must Take," *Saturday Review*, May 23, 1970, p. 20.

Elliot L. Richardson, "H.R. 1: A Far Reaching Proposal for Welfare Reform," *The Washington Post*, June 21, 1971.

An illuminating discussion on the options available for welfare and family assistance, including current family assistance planning proposals and how they might be integrated into other welfare programs, is found in Charles L. Schultze, Fried, Rivlin, and Teeters, *Setting National Priorities, The 1972 Budget* (Washington, D. C.: The Brookings Institution, 1971), pp. 172 ff.

[10] If the present figure of $2,400 for a family of four is used, States or BIA would have to supplement this amount in many instances if BIA recipients were not to suffer a lowering of the amounts they are now receiving (based on State standards for Aid for Dependent Children).

[11] The President's proposals were very modest and would result in very little impact on Indian reservations. However, the amounts involved could be substantially increased. If so, and programs other than BIA met or exceeded present BIA services in any function, it is reasonable to expect that the Indians would receive such services from the same source as anybody else. It should be noted, however, that although Indians have been included in Census figures to determine grants to States, it frequently appeared to them that they did not receive their share of services from the States.

istration (WPA), Public Works Administration (PWA), and Civilian Conservation Corps (CCC) in the high unemployment era of the 1930's were prominent aspects of public policy—a policy of maintaining income through constructive work. Many Indians trace the development of work habits and ability to compete in the non-Indian world to the CCC program on Indian reservations.[12]

Subsequent policy in this tradition can be found in the Area Redevelopment Act (ARA) of 1961[13] and later the Public Works Acceleration Act in 1962,[14] the Economic Opportunity Act of 1964,[15] the Public Works and Economic Development Act of 1965, and various provisions for housing assistance and other programs.

The "Emergency Employment Act of 1971"[16] authorizes $750 million for fiscal year 1972 and $1 billion for fiscal year 1973 to provide unemployed and underemployed persons with "transitional employment in jobs providing needed public services during times of high unemployment, and, wherever feasible, related training and manpower services to enable such persons to move into employment and training not supported by this Act." In September, 1971, the Department of Labor announced that $8.4 million of these funds would be allotted to Indian tribes.[17] No estimate of the number of jobs this would provide Indians was made by the Labor Department. If it cost $10,000 a job for wages, overhead, equipment, etc., there would be 840 jobs; if $5,000 a job, 1,680 jobs would result. BIA's March 1971 figures indicate 60,000 Indians unemployed and 29,000 in temporary employment for a total of 57 percent of the Indian labor force.[18] Not all will accept the types of employment stemming from this legislation, but if half of them, say 45,000, are interested it is obvious that the funds available are but a small beginning.

Richard Schifter had in mind a major job creation program for

---

[12] Discussion with Richard Schifter, Counsel, Association on American Indian Affairs, July 21, 1971. Alan Sorkin also reports that Indians looked favorably on WPA in the 1930's. Alan Sorkin, *American Indians and Federal Aid*. (Washington, D. C.: The Brookings Institution, 1971), p. 102.

[13] 75 Stat. 47.

[14] 76 Stat. 920.

[15] 78 Stat. 508.

[16] 85 Stat. 154.

[17] Press Release, Sept. 28, 1971.

[18] *Indian Population, Labor Force, Unemployment, and Underemployment; by Area: March 1971,* Statistics Division, Bureau of Indian Affairs.

Indian reservations as a model to demonstrate its possible application to the total economy in the following comment:

> It is the opinion of this writer that federal programs could indeed be developed and executed which would within a decade have the effect of raising the standard of living of Indian people to that of surrounding communities.

> Because the Indian reservation population is, when compared to the general population of the United States, exceedingly small (less than 0.2 percent), the funds necessary to do this job could be obtained without making a significant impact on total federal expenditures.[19]

It might take $225 to $450 million (on the basis of assumptions indicated above) to provide 45,000 additional jobs on Indian reservations. A program of this nature would have a significant impact: welfare loads would decrease, housing would improve, diets and health would improve, more of the available labor force would acquire work habits, Indian-operated retail and commercial enterprises could be established and have a chance to prosper, tribes might consider tapping some of this income through tribally operated commercial enterprises or through a tribal tax to support needed tribal programs, and the like.

*   *   *   *

Action in one or more of the above policy areas could have major impact on present Indian programs and possibly eliminate the need for some of the present ethnically-oriented Government activities.

---

[19] Richard Schifter, "Trends in Federal Indian Administration." *South Dakota Law Review,* Winter 1970, p. 18.

Actually, the 1970 Census indicates that Indians comprise .41 percent of the total population (see Table I, Appendix B).

A job creation program can also be attacked through the private sector with Government subsidy. Whenever unemployment rises, interest in some form of job creation increases. See Charles L. Schultze, *Setting National Priorities,* op. cit., p. 191 ff. for a brief history and discussion of current status.

CHAPTER EIGHT

FEDERAL OBLIGATIONS TO INDIANS

The exploitation of the Indians under the Articles of Confederation led to the constitutional provision of Federal control over commerce with the Indians. Treating Indian groups as foreign nations logically put negotiations in the hands of the central government under its treaty-making authority. However, even the central government proved powerless against the settlers, hunters, and gold seekers in their violation of territory reserved to the Indians. Indian wars ensued and the central government's war-making power was a prime factor in Indian relations during much of the 19th Century.

Treaties generally provided for a reservation area, education of Indian children, education of adults in the arts of farming and related frontier skills.

In 1971, what are the current requirements for special attention to Indians on the part of the Federal Government? Treaty making and war making are no longer required. Sixty-eight percent of Indian education in the 22 States with federally recognized Indians is in the hands of the States; law and order and other services are frequently provided by the States. However, there are several areas that are peculiarly of a Federal responsibility in nature and should continue to be a Federal responsibility until resolved. They stem from treaties, agreements, and court decisions.

RESERVATION BOUNDARIES

There is hardly a reservation that does not have a boundary question in need of resolution. Vital economic interests are involved—both Indian and non-Indian. The erroneous survey of the Crow-Northern Cheyenne boundary and the Yakima boundary are two examples. On May 20, 1972, President Nixon returned 20 thousand acres of timberland to the Yakima Tribe. These lands had been erroneously included in the National Forest boundary in 1907. Money and personnel are necessary for cadastral surveys, boundary determinations, negotiation, and court action where required. The Federal Government has been negligent in its trust responsibility on boundary questions.

WATER RIGHTS

Water is necessary for life, and on many reservations preservation of Indian water rights is the most critical issue.[1] Arrayed against the Indians are non-Indian water users (frequently Irrigation Districts), the Bureau of Reclamation whose clients are the non-Indian water users, and often the State Governments which respond to the pressure of the powerful irrigation interests and large urban areas needing an expanded water supply.

Further complicating the scene is the western State legal philosophy of use of scarce water by appropriation (largely on the basis of use) as against the traditional doctrine of riparian rights and the Winters Doctrine which the Indians rely upon for protection.[2]

The governmental authority with the best chance of assisting the Indians in this issue is the present Bureau of Indian Affairs (BIA) with the assistance of the Department of Justice, as long as BIA acts as the Indians' advocate. The proposed new Trust Counsel Authority could strengthen Indian advocacy in the Federal and State Governments and in the courts and help resolve Indian water rights.[3]

The March 24, 1971 Supreme Court decision on the Eagle River case (Colorado) held that Indian water rights are subject to adju-

[1] William H. Veeder, "Federal Encroachment on Indian Water Rights and the Impairment of Reservation Development," in *Toward Economic Development for Native American Communities*, a compendium of papers submitted to the Subcommittee on Economy in Government (Washington, D. C.: 91st Cong., 1st sess., Joint Economic Committee, 1969), p. 460.

[2] See Veeder, op. cit., p. 469, Winters vs. U.S. 143 Fed. 740,741 (CA 9, 1906); Winters vs. U.S. 148 Fed. 684 (CA 9, 1906).

[3] "To provide for the creation of an Indian Trust Counsel Authority," transmitted by Executive Communication, April 28, 1971. Purpose is to provide independent legal counsel and representation for the preservation and protection of the natural resource rights of the Indians. Provisions are incorporated in the following bills: H.R. 2380, H.R. 7689, S. 2035, and H.R. 9358, 92nd Cong. 1st sess., introduced only.

On October 4, 1971, Secretary of the Interior, Rogers C. B. Morton, stated: "To insure effective advocacy of Indian water rights, I am establishing an Indian Water Rights Office. It will serve as an interim body until enactment . . . of an Indian Trust Counsel Authority." Press conference, Interior Dept., October 4, 1971. The office will report to the Commissioner of Indian Affairs.

Eagle Creek, on the Mescalero Apache Reservation in New Mexico, is one of the unspoiled spots that attracts campers, picnickers, and fishermen to the exploration of Indian reservations.

(Photo: U.S. Department of the Interior, Bureau of Indian Affairs.)

dication in State courts under certain circumstances, but if there is conflict between Federal rights (including Indian rights) and State court action, the Supreme Court can take the case for review.[4]

Although the tribes continue to possess the priorities they have always had, non-Indians may institute water suits that will require court defense by the tribes.[5]

This case also points to the desirability of Indians strengthening their relations with the States and the general citizenry so that there will be an understanding of the Indian water rights and greater State interest in preserving them. In States where the Indians have a significant percentage of the voting power or other assets in demand by non-Indians, careful use of this power on a coordinated basis by the State Indian residents may have significant results.

The Federal Government should stay on this problem until it is resolved.

HEIRSHIP LAND

There are 10.7 million acres of individually owned Indian land in trust with the Federal Government. Original allotments of the land were in the name of one individual. However, upon the death of the original owners, and the death of subsequent heirs, the ownership of this land has become so fractionated that many owners cannot effectively use the land. The result is that much of it is not used or is leased by the BIA on behalf of the owners and the income divided in accordance with percentage of ownership. It is hard to do anything with land in multiple ownership because of difficulty in contacting all owners and obtaining their agreement to a proposed sale, lease, or other use. Fractional shares of individual ownership in a piece of land may be such grotesque figures as 837/4,515,840. Payments to many owners from lease income or sale

---

[4] United States vs. District Court in and for the County of Eagle, et. al. (No. 87) and United States vs. District Court in and for Water Division No. 5, et al., (No. 812) Supreme Court of the United States, decided March 24, 1971.

[5] Tribal attorneys, William H. Veeder of BIA, Senators Alan Cranston and John V. Tunney, and Congressman Jerry L. Pettis were very concerned with the handling of this case by Justice. It is an illustration of the need of constant vigilance and a strong Indian advocate on the Federal scene.

See "Conflicts of Interest in Proceedings Before the Supreme Court of the United States" by William H. Veeder, filed with the Supreme Court on March 23, 1971, and a part of the record.

may be 10 cents or less. The administrative costs to the Government are great.

Solutions have been proposed from time to time.

One of the main proposals was Senator Frank Church's bill in 1961.[6] In 1963 this bill [7] was passed by the senate but not acted upon by the House.

Provisions of this bill were: Where there were up to ten owners, any one or more owning a 50 percent or larger interest may request the Secretary of the Interior to sell or partition the land. In tracts with 11 or more owners, the requirement is reduced to one or more owning at least 25 percent of the land. There were provisions to protect the tribe in the event the land constituted a key tract. Where land was in part owned by individuals with unrestricted interests the above provisions would apply only upon agreement of the non-trust owners. If non-trust owners do not agree, the Secretary, upon percentage request indicated above, can consent to a judicial partition for purchase at appraised value or to meet the high bid. The tribe also had the right to meet the high bid. Trust interests in minerals was also authorized to make loans for the purchase of such lands. Authorization was provided for land consolidation sales or exchanges between tribes and individuals.[8] Indian testimony on the various proposals has made clear that any solution must include the following:

(1) retention of land title, to the maximum extent, in Indian ownership; and

(2) recognition of the equity of Indian owners.

In addition to the above, the executive and the Congress have indicated that the solution must: (1) not place large demands on the Federal Treasury for its accomplishment; and (2) provide a means for substantially eliminating the problem.

---

[6] S. 1392, 87th Cong., 1st sess.

[7] S. 1049, 88th Cong., 1st sess.

[8] The Department's proposed "Indian Resources Development Act" in 1967 had an heirship section based largely on the Church formula. The heirship section was again submitted to the Congress by the Interior Department as a separate bill in 1969.

Former Commissioner Bennett worked on a bill incorporating four different formulas, making it optional for tribes to choose the one suiting them. It never got out of the Bureau of the Budget.

There have been many proposals and bills and not all can be mentioned here. For a summary of the history and issues involved see Stephen A. Langone, "The Heirship Land Problem and Its Effect Upon the Indian, the Tribe, and Effective Utilization . . . In A Compendium of Papers," Joint Economic Committee, op. cit., p. 519.

Federal involvement in this problem is inescapable. Indian land owners are losing income because of poor land utilization, and the taxpayers are footing the bill for a heavy administrative expense. Action is needed. The Federal Government should take the initiative in cooperation with the Indians concerned and apply the necessary resources to achieve a solution.

PAYMENTS IN LIEU OF TAXES

As long as Indian land is under Federal trust and cannot be taxed by the State, Federal funds should continue for school and other local services performed by local or State Government for Indians living on trust land, when such services are normally funded by a local real estate tax.

Indian areas need to become more productive so that tribal income can support necessary tribal programs and the State taxes (other than real estate) yield appropriate revenues for necessary services. Until this is accomplished special grants to either the Indians or the States in which they reside may be necessary for continued progress toward self-sufficiency.

SETTLEMENT OF INDIAN CLAIMS

The Indian Claims Commission Act, 1946 [8A] provided for the review of Indian tribal claims against the United States, including actions affected by fraud, duress, unconscionable consideration and mutual or unilateral mistakes. Review and adjudication of these claims is a responsibility of the Federal Government.[9]

EFFECTIVE TRIBAL GOVERNMENT

The Federal Government has authorized tribal government by law. Therefore, it should continue to do four things until the tribes decide they no longer need Federal assistance:

[8A] 60 Stat. 1049.

[9] As of October 1, 1971, the Indian Claims Commission had made final awards of $395 million, of which $388 million had been appropriated by the Congress. An additional $50 million in claims has been awarded by the Commission but is in various stages of appeal action. The above represents the amounts awarded for 198 dockets. 246 other dockets are pending at the Commission (decision on award not yet made). One hundred-sixty-six dockets have been dismissed by the Commission.

Meeting of the Chief, Vice President, and Treasurer of Minto, Alaska Tribal Council.
(Photo: U.S. Department of the Interior, Bureau of Indian Affairs.)

(1) Provide technical advice on: constitutional provisions; proposed amendments to governing documents; election, enrollment, legislative disputes and procedures; and other problems which daily confront local governments.

(2) Arrange for sufficient financial support for basic governmental positions and other expenses until the tribes have sufficient resources to provide for themselves.

The BIA has supplemented tribal income for improved tribal management for 25 tribes in fiscal year 1972 (total cost $200,000). Increased funds are being requested of the Executive and the Congress for the next two fiscal years.

(3) Help provide appropriate training for tribal officials in both policy formulation and administrative procedures, so that they can be effective in working toward the tribes' goals. Training programs have been initiated by BIA, both directly and through contract.

(4) Help develop tribal corporate mechanisms for nongovernmental functions, such as land enterprise, cattle herds, or other business or commercial activity.

Without an effective government, self-determination may be an empty phrase for an Indian group.

Meeting of the Constitutional amendment committee, Chippewa Cree Tribe of Rocky Boy's Reservation, November 17, 1971. Left to right around table: Patrick Chief Stick, Sr., Jacob Ahtone, Bureau of Indian Affairs, Billings Area Tribal Operations Officer, William Saddler, William Morsette, William Corcoran and Edward Eagleman.

(Photo: U.S. Department of the Interior, Bureau of Indian Affairs.)

SELF-SUFFICIENCY

The goal of self-sufficiency—the ability of the Indian people to stand on their own feet—seems to be accepted by many Indians and Government policy makers. "Most everyone will claim the same goals for Indians—economic self-sufficiency, the fulfillment of promises made by the Federal Government, and a standard of living comparable to that of other American communities."[10]

In historical context, it seems appropriate that the Federal Government continue to work with Indians, Indian organizations, and the states until it is mutually agreeable that this goal has been

---

[10] Louis R. Bruce, Commissioner of Indian Affairs, George Washington University Symposium, March 17, 1971.

achieved. The current and last administrations adopted an Indian policy of full partnership, consultation, and self-determination which is supportive of this objective and emphasizes this responsibility.[11]

Reservation life has much security to offer Indians who are not at home in the non-Indian world.

They will not starve; there is the custom of sharing and they know the welfare system.

They like to be with relatives and friends and live according to familiar customs.

There is no tax on their land or their house.

They may have a lease income from their land.

If needed, subsidized housing is being made available.

They have free schools—subsidized largely by non-Indian tax-payers if the State relies heavily on a real estate tax for school construction and operation.

They have free medical and hospital service—a real security in this time of frightening escalation in hospital and medical costs.

Tribal assets (the reservation land, trees, minerals, or tribal economic activities) and the possibility of income from an Indian claim presented to the Indian Claims Commission, both may be more secure in the Indian's mind if he remains a reservation resident.

The tradition of a subsistence economy, plus the above factors, makes it not only possible for an Indian to exist with relatively little effort and considerable security on the reservation, but often it may be a more desirable option than trying to adjust to the non-Indian society and economy with its differing sets of values and standards.

---

[11] Meriam stated this goal in the 1920's: "The fundamental requirement is that the task of the Indian Service be recognized as primarily educational, in the broadest sense of the word, and that it be made an efficient educational agency, devoting its main energies to the social and economic advancement of the Indians, so that they may be absorbed into the prevailing civilization or be fitted to live in the presence of that civilization at least in accordance with a minimal standard of health and decency." Meriam: op. cit., p. 21.

Likewise the object of the Fund for the Republic Study ". . . was to promote a better understanding of the special status of these people as United States citizens and of what should be done by and for them to facilitate their entry into the mainstream of American life." Commission on the Rights, Liberties, and Responsibilities of the American Indian: *A Program for Indian Citizens* (Fund for the Republic, January 1961), Preface iii. See Selected Bibliography, Brophy for members of the Commission.

Navajo Indian looks óver lumber at Navajo Forest Products, Inc., where he works. Navajo Forest Products is a Navajo-owned sawmill that processes Navajo tribally-owned timber.

(Photo: U.S. Department of the Interior, Bureau of Indian Affairs.)

The city, where most jobs are, lures some. But payment of rent, taxes, health care, strange surroundings, strange customs, prejudice, and loneliness—may be the negative side of the city picture for many. It is a wonder that as many do accept the challenge of the relative insecurity of the non-Indian environment. It is manifestly a much more difficult adjustment for a reservation Indian than for some one raised in the city environment.

The objective of self-sufficiency must be attained either in the reservation setting or away from it. The Federal Government has set its hand to the task and should see it through in cooperation with the Indians and the States.[12]

---

[12] In reviewing a draft of the above statement on self-sufficiency, former Commis-

PERPETUAL OBLIGATION?

The claim of some Indians, especially "professional" Indians, that the taking of their land and other historical happenings created a debt on the part of non-Indians to Indian descendants in perpetuity is obviously not in consonance with self-sufficiency. A literal interpretation of some treaty language could lead to this conclusion. Perpetual recognition of the Indian and his contribution to our heritage, and perpetual right to retain his culture or such portions as he chooses—these will continue. Most tribes indicate a desire to build up individual and tribal competence, increase economic resources and payroll, and look to the day when they can support themselves and their governmental institutions.[13]

Many times public sympathy is whipped up by citing the social indices of the Indian condition indicating poor housing, high unemployment, low literacy, low average age at death, high school dropout rates as compared with the white population. In the national guilt over the historical treatment of Indians, the country

---

sioner Robert L. Bennett indicated his belief "that the goal of self-sufficiency is stated more or less as the ethical justification for expenditure of funds realizing that as a basic matter, this will be a continuing goal because economic standards continue to rise faster than Indian communities can achieve economic parity. Stated in another way, Indians will always be in poverty because the income standard of the poverty level will always rise faster than Indian people are able to achieve these levels of income." Letter to author dated November 5, 1971.

The above has proven all too true for many reservation and unsuccessful urban Indians. But the author does not believe it need necessarily remain so if sufficient resources are available to meet their needs, unless the Indians involved prefer it that way.

[13] Theodore W. Taylor, "Indian Organization Questionnaire, Compilation of Responses," July 1971. This is not a new attitude:

Treat all men alike. Give them all the same law. Give them all an even chance to live and grow.

All men were made by the same Great Spirit Chief. They are all brothers.

The Mother Earth is the Mother of all people, and people should have equal rights upon it.

We only ask an even chance to live as other men live. We ask to be recognized as men.

Let me be a free man . . . Free to work, free to trade, free to choose my teachers, free to follow the religion of my fathers, free to think and talk and act for myself—and I will obey every law or submit to the penalty.

Chief Joseph of the Nez Perce Indians 1879

OEO Poster 6164–1 March 1971

continually flagellates itself with statistics, the poor job society has done to help the Indians, and the evils of paternalism.[14]

In contrast to the horror statistics are the evidences of improvement in Indian health, education, and housing, very seldom mentioned by the headline hunters and the budgeteers.[15]

The Health of Indians and Alaska Natives has been substantially improved. Infant death rates are down 51 percent from 1955; tuberculosis death rates are down 75 percent; gastroenteric death rates are down 53 percent, and death rates from influenza and pneumonia are down 36 percent.

Indian post high school education is increasing in geometric progression. In 1934, for example, 71 Indian students were in post high school education, only 15 completed the year, and none graduated. In 1944 133, were in post high school education, 30 completed the year, none graduated from a four year school.

Since 1949, when the "grant" program for post high education was instituted, there has been a rapid change.

HIGHER EDUCATION GRANTS

Year	Grants	Completing one Year	Graduating
1949	178 (and loans)	68	1
1959	400	340	52
1969	3,189	2,647	225
1971	6,500	5,525	330 BA & BS, 15 Advanced degrees
1972	10,000 (est)	8,500	450–500 (est)

Note: Some vocational and other non-college included in above grant totals

The Bureau of Indian Affairs (BIA) estimates that only half of the Indian students in higher education are receiving BIA grants. Some do not meet "need", "blood quantum", or other criteria.

---

[14] See for example: "The Forgotten American." President Johnson's Indian Message to the Congress, March 6, 1968; President Nixon's Indian Message to the Congress, July 8, 1970.

Indian Education: A National Tragedy—A National Challenge, Report No. 91–501, Special Subcommittee on Indian Education (Washington, D.C.: 91st Cong., 1st sess., U. S. Senate, Committee on Labor and Public Welfare, 1969).

For a more balanced and rational view, see *The Education of Indian Children and Youth,* University of Chicago, December 1970.

[15] Statement by Director of Indian Health, copy of Opening Statement prepared for presentation to the respective Appropriation Committees of the U. S. Senate and the House of Representatives, April 1971, p. 8.

Some are funded by tribal and State Governments. Others are unaware of or uninterested in the program.

It is interesting to note that the estimated number of Indian high school graduates in 1971 was 8,933 from the following: public school 6,000; BIA schools 2,353; mission and private schools 580. Three years ago 78 percent of Indian college students were choosing "educational" fields as a major. In 1971 only 48 percent chose educational fields and other professions are gaining recruits such as law, health, and science. In the 1971–72 school year there are 104 Indians in the Indian Law program, and 150 applicants had to be turned down due to lack of funds.[16]

For the details of substantial improvement in Indian housing see Chapter VII.

Returning to the question of the obligation of non-Indians, the white invasion was certainly not Indian initiated. But no one else alive today was responsible for it either. The two cultures—European and Indian—were (and still are in many instances) very dissimilar.

Despite many well-meaning efforts from the days of Jefferson to the present, many Indians have refused to be helped to stand on their own feet in the environment in which they found themselves because to them this was not a desirable goal. Thus, Indians bear some of the responsibility for their current condition. If Indians prefer a bare subsistence living for some of the reasons cited earlier and in the discussion on attitudes, there is not much the Government or anyone else can do about it. Certainly, the Indian environment at the time of Columbus is impossible to resurrect. Indians, the Government and the general public need to face reality. Adjustments are required. Such adjustments have to be willed by the individuals concerned if they are to occur. As Alan Fry, Superintendent of a Canadian Reserve puts it, sometimes Indians are "the hardest god-damned people on earth to help." [17]

Concerning Fry's statement, former Commissioner Bennett commented that one of the reasons for this is that people are always wanting to help Indian people achieve the goals of the "helper" and not of the "Indians." And this is very true. The author believes that when the goals of the Indian are not the same as those of

---

[16] Education information from Division of Student Services, BIA, December 7, 1971.

[17] Alan Fry, *How a People Die* (Garden City, N. Y., Doubleday, 1970), p. 58. Note: Of particular pertinence to this point is the discussion on pp. 64–69.

the majority society around him, the majority society should not try to change those goals except insofar as they interfere with the rights of others. Conformance with health laws, minimal education requirements, and not requiring an economic subsidy of a different nature or magnitude from others, are aspects of this consideration. Both the States and the Federal Government recognize the validity of a pluralistic society. But, in both cases, the underlying assumption is that various cultural groups will accommodate themselves sufficiently to their environment so that they are economically self-sufficient as in the examples of the Amish and the Hutterites. Both the States and the Federal Government are desirous of helping Indians achieve this objective.

Ray Paddock (Eskimo)[18] commented "that the only way the Indian is going to be self-sufficient is to beat the white man at his own game—good leadership, good government, good management, and respected political influence. This will be painful to some groups who want to retain the old ways, but these groups will never be competitive unless they take that step . . . ."

As everyone is aware, many Indians have successfully made adjustment and learned that they can make their way in the non-Indian world and still retain valuable portions of their culture and their Indianness, if they so desire.[19]

'I'm not familiar with tribal organizations and customs,' Thomas Jimboy, a Haskell (Indian school) graduate and a Lawrence (Kan.) resident said. 'My family didn't function within a tribe. But nevertheless I take pride in Indian tradition and don't want to see it lost.' Most of the Indians attending the reorganizational meetings in Lawrence insist being an Indian is more than having a sense of customs and traditions, and that participation in business and industry off the reservation cannot damage the Indian identity.

'These kids can retain their culture and still make it in the white man's world,' Wesley Benito, education director of the Apache tribe at Whiteriver, Ariz. said. 'They don't want to be assimilated by the white man's society, but they want to

---

[18] On the staff of the Indian Desk, Economic Development Administration, U. S. Department of Commerce, in a memo to Ray Tanner of the same office, dated November 11, 1971.

[19] Robert W. Butler, "Haskell Molds Indian Identity," Kansas City, Mo., *Times*, February 18, 1971.

compete in it. We want to be better than the white man. We've been playing a tax-eating role for too long.'

Former Commissioner of Indian Affairs Robert L. Bennett said, '. . . Indians think their way of life is better and this accounts for their reluctance to become too quickly involved in the mainstream of society.'

James Wilson, an Indian and former Director of the Office of Economic Opportunity Indian desk in Washington stated: [20]

Many of the concerns of the traditional Indians about the changing values of the young Indians were relieved when these young Indians found that they could be productive members of this society, and still be Indian in every sense of the word. This was a real breakthrough for a lot of us.

Margaret Mead has suggested that some Indian tribes like the Aztecs and the Incas were greedy, too. "I don't believe in stereotypes like 'the white man' and 'the American Indian.' I believe in people." Dr. Mead has said also that she didn't "care whose ancestors took land away from whose ancestors. I don't intend to adopt the sins of my ancestors or their virtues. What we're concerned about is what is going on now." [21]

One fact stands clear—progress from the non-Indian viewpoint will not occur until the Indian wills it.[22]

The best intentioned, enlightened and ably administered policy and program will not have much result without Indian involvement and Indian desire to achieve the goal. The Indians, then, as

---

[20] Stan Steiner, *The New Indian* (New York: Dell Publishing Co., 1968), p. 94.

[21] Margaret Mead, A Symposium on the American Indian, March 17–20, 1971, The George Washington University Center, as quoted in *The Evening Star*, Washington, D.C., Friday, March 19, 1971, p. C–9.

See also, John C. Ewers, "When Red and White Men Met," reprinted from *The Western Historical Quarterly*, April 1971: ". . . intertribal warfare among neighboring tribes, even those who spoke dialects of the same basic language, was both common and prolonged." p. 134. "At times Indians butchered their fallen foes . . . Firsthand accounts of intertribal actions repeatedly referred to mutilation of the dead or dying—the taking of arms as well as scalps as trophies, even in the dismembering of the privates. . . ." p. 142.

Concerning finding a scapegoat for the sad plight of the Indians in the far west, see pp. 146–148 in which is found: "Frankly, I believe there is enough blame for the sorry state of the Indians in the American West today so that we can all have a share of it—including the Indians who are most vocal in passing the buck for their plight to the white man."

[22] William A. Brophy, and Sophie D. Aberle, *The Indian, America's Unfinished Business*, Report of the Commission on the Rights, Liberties, and Responsibilities of the American Indians (Norman, Okla.: University of Oklahoma Press, 1966), p. 5.

individuals and as groups, share a portion of the responsibility for their current posture.[23] It may not be a culpable responsibility. In many instances Indians may be culture or environment bound. But, with a firm desire and with help, which is available, Indians have demonstrated that they can adjust and become self-sufficient.

There is no obligation to subsidize any group in perpetuity. In the writer's judgment, based on a western culture orientation, this would be a death warrant to the integrity and dignity of any such group. The purposelessness and degradation of the human potential one finds in some reservation situations tend to confirm that, without a worthy objective posing a continuing challenge to the best in an individual, people disintegrate. This seems to be just as true of Indians as anybody else.

---

[23] "We often blame the white man for our lack of progress but we must also shoulder a large part of the blame," Black Elk, *The Rough Rock News,* November 17, 1971, from speech delivered to the National Indian Education Conference, November 4–6 1971, Albuquerque, N. M.

CHAPTER NINE

VIABILITY OF STATES: DISTRIBUTION OF INDIAN SERVICES

The States recognize that Indians are State citizens. They have gone on record as desiring to help those Indians, who have not already done so, achieve the objective of self-sufficiency. Even for federally recognized Indians they perform a sizable portion of various service functions, such as education and law and order, for State Indian residents.

Where do the Indians and the States go from here?

The future role of the States with regard to their Indian citizens will be determined by the following considerations: Indian attitudes and goals, changing national policies, the nature of Federal obligations to Indians, the initiatives taken and the vitality of the States, the effectiveness of tribal governments, Indian power, and Indian culture and its adaptive ability. An additional factor will be the adoption of one or more of the policy options discussed in this chapter.

THE STATES—ARE THEY VIABLE?

Whether the State and local governments can be dynamic parts of the Federal system is important in considering their relationships to the Indian people and tribal governments. Public administration and political science literature is replete with the shortcomings of State executive, legislative, and judicial standards and performance.[1]

---

[1] *The Advisory Commission on Intergovernmental Relations* (Washington, D. C.: Advisory Commission on Intergovernmental Relations, October 1969), presents recommendations to strengthen States and make them effective partners in the Federal system, pp. 29 and 32. See also the *Eleventh Annual Report* (Washington, D. C.: Advisory Committee on Intergovernmental Relations, January 31, 1970) for a discussion on the States and federalism in the 60's and for the 70's. The *Twelfth Annual Report,* January 31, 1971, brings the progress up-to-date. Recommendations for intergovernmental research are found in *Public Administration Review*, May/ June 1970, p. 272.

One of the problems is State revenue. But it is not the only problem—political spoils, lack of accountability resulting from the long ballot, poorly staffed legislative committees, incompetent officials, overlapping jurisdictions, and accepted discriminatory practices against minority groups are still all too prevalent in some State and local governments.

Effective and fair State and local government is a must for Indian acceptance. This type of State and local government is not evident to many Indians and some react to memories of recent discriminatory history even when State attitudes and services have substantially changed.[2]

The State revenue picture is still bleak, but policy proposals such as income maintenance, Federal takeover of welfare, revenue sharing, increased use of the income tax by States and localities may improve State and local revenue sources.

Sundquist and Davis suggest a "differential approach" (e. g. working through some States and bypassing others on the same programs based on the competence of the States concerned) in involving the States as vital participants in the Federal system. They view the Federal system as a single, and not a dual system. They also point out that the States have functions and authorities that need to be effectively integrated into the system to help in resolving community problems.[3] The Bureau of Indian Affairs (BIA) has certainly found this to be true in education, domestic relations, foster care, law and order in many cases, institutional care, and welfare.

If the States will modernize and become effective participants in the Federal system—and citizens, including Indian citizens, develop confidence in them—they can truly become the main operating arm for many activities of Government.

Many of the present direct services to Indians by the Federal Government are normally provided other citizens by local or State Government. If local and State services were better and more responsive than present direct Federal services, the Indians would likely opt for them in their own self interest.

---

[2] James J. Kilpatrick comments that over the last 10 or 15 years States have sought to "cast off the fetters of horse-and-buggy constitutions" with discouraging results in some instances. In 1970 at least 40 States voted on constitutional questions. *The Evening Star*, Washington, D. C., Oct. 29, 1970 (A–13).

[3] James L. Sundquist, with collaboration of David W. Davis, *Making Federalism Work* (Washington, D. C.: The Brookings Institution, 1969), p. 270 ff.

As Merriam puts it:[4]

> The basic premise of the American Federal system is that a strong national government should unify and coordinate the national purposes and endeavors, supplemented by vigorous, autonomous State and local units exercising primary governmental functions in their respective spheres.

As indicated in earlier chapters, the States began taking increased initiative in Indian affairs in the 1950's and 60's. Many States have adopted forward looking policy positions with regard to their Indian citizens and are seeking to work with them and the Federal Government in the resolution of problems. States have changed along with the Federal Government from the philosophy of complete homogenization to a position that Indian groups have the right to retain their identity. They believe this can be done while at the same time the Indians work out an accommodation with the non-Indian culture so that the latter can be self-sufficient and be a vital part of State and national life.

Indians can help in the revitalization of State Governments by working with them to make State services more responsive to Indian needs, through the development of adequate policies and programs and through joint efforts to improve funding to make such policies and programs come to life. They can work with the States to obtain necessary financial help from the Federal Government and they can work with the States in developing healthier reservation economies which will not only help individual Indian and tribal income but improve State revenue prospects as well. Many States and their local sub-divisions are receptive to this type of Indian initiative. Indian leadership, too, is recognizing the interdependence of Indian and non-Indian communities in viable economic development plans and in the execution of those plans.

The author agrees with Sundquist that effective government "demands that the States be brought effectively into the Federal-State-local chain of relationships." [5]

---

[4] Robert E. Merriam, *Federalism Today* (Washington, D. C.: Jump-McKillop Memorial Lectures, Graduate School Press, U. S. Department of Agriculture, 1969), p. 6.

[5] James L. Sundquist, op. cit., p. 267.

In 1949, the Hoover Commission pointed out that one of the prime problems in Federal administration was the "failure to make the most of potential cooperation from State and local government and private organizations." From The Commission on Organization of the Executive Branch of the Government, *General Management*

On April 11, 1969, President Nixon appointed an Advisory Council on Executive Organization. One of the Council's assignments was to consider ". . . the organizational relationships of the Federal Government to States and cities in carrying out the many domestic programs in which the Federal Government is involved. x x x The Council will work closely with the Office of Intergovernmental Relations established by the President under the supervision of the Vice President to serve as a liaison between State and local governments and the President." [6]

POLICY OPTIONS ON DISTRIBUTION OF FUNCTIONS BETWEEN STATE AND FEDERAL GOVERNMENTS

As the history of Indian policy demonstrates, various policy courses are available to the Nation and its Indian citizens. Several of the options that might be adopted in whole or in part at this stage in our history should be evaluated by Indians and others concerned with Indian affairs. Indians, it will be noted, are not unanimous. Some groups are pressing for conflicting policies.

Expand Federal Services to All Indians

There is a vocal group pressing for extension of special Federal services to all Indians, not just those on Federal reservations and presently eligible for special Federal services because of their Indianness. Representatives of urban Indians take the leadership in this movement, assisted by other groups such as State Indian commissions and governments who would like to have Federal funds for their nonrecognized Indians, and Congressmen from States with non-Federal Indians. Interest in Indians seems to be at an all-time high, and these groups would like to cash in on such interest. For example, in February, 1972, the Passamaquoddy Tribe asked the Bureau of Indian Affairs and the Department of the Interior to recommend to the Department of Justice that a suit be instituted against the State of Maine challenging the State's assumption of authority over the tribe. The Interior Department stated that no

---

of the Executive Branch (Washington, D. C.: Report to the Congress, February 1949), pp. 42–43.

[6] *Weekly Compilation of Presidential Documents,* Week Ending Friday, April 11, 1969, p. 530.

treaty exists between the United States and the tribe and that the States of Massachusetts and Maine have acted as trustees for tribal property for over 200 years. The Department refused to request litigation and suggested that the tribe seek remedy in the appropriate State Court or the Indian Claims Commission or Court of Claims of the United States.[6A]

The leadership of the Federal Indian groups, on the other hand, is adamantly opposed to the BIA and the Indian Health Service (IHS) extending their services to urban and other nonreservation Indians. They have criticized the BIA for being influenced by the urban groups and see any steps toward expanding coverage to others as diminishing services to themselves.[7]

This policy cleavage has resulted in the birth of a new national Indian organization of tribal leaders. Up to the present the National Congress of American Indians (NCAI) has been the primary national Indian organization. But when NCAI seemed to embrace the urban and non-Federal groups under its banner, the federally recognized groups decided to form a new organization, the National Tribal Chairmen's Association (NTCA). This organization may generate considerable pressure on State and Federal executives, and in lobbying with State legislatures and the Federal Congress.[8]

The purposes outlined in the constitution and bylaws of NTCA are to improve consultation between the U. S. Government and federally recognized Indians; assist in directing Federal programs and funds for federally recognized Indians; to approve local and national Indian policies before they are implemented by the Federal, State and local governments; to demand that Indians receive their fair share of all federally funded programs; to insure continuance of the Federal trust relationship; to demand that every Federal agency recognize Indians for whom the Federal Government has trust responsibility; to employ treaty rights and privileges for promotion and protection of the human and natural resources of Indian reservations or groups; to cultivate relationships among Indian reservations; to demand that consultation become a fact; to

---

[6A] Letter from Acting Solicitor, Interior, to Assistant Attorney General, June 20, 1972.

[7] See, for example, Dave Earley, "Feds Too Concerned Over Urban Indians," *Gazette*, Billings, Mont., February 21, 1971.

[8] Constitution and Bylaws adopted July 12, 13, 14, 1971, Albuquerque, N. M., signed by chairmen of 52 tribes.

support and complement the National Congress of American Indians; and for any other purposes deemed proper and necessary. The emphasis is on federally recognized reservation Indians and their relations to local, State, and Federal Governments. There is no mention of urban Indians.

The urban Indians have been recognized by both Presidents Johnson and Nixon. President Johnson asked the National Council on Indian Opportunity to look into the urban Indian situation and make recommendations, and President Nixon has asked the Office of Economic Opportunity (OEO) to take the lead in pilot projects for urban Indians.

The OEO, the Departments of Health, Education, and Welfare (HEW), Housing and Urban Development (HUD), and Labor have joined to create a Model Urban Indian Center Program "to provide badly needed services to Indians living in cities." [9]

Services of these centers include employment assistance, information and referral, youth activities, recreation, family counseling, economic development, housing development, health and education, and cultural heritage programs. If these centers meet some of the needs of urban Indians it will reduce the pressure for extension of Bureau of Indian Affairs (BIA) services to the urban areas.

The establishment of the Model Urban Indian Center program is a definite break with past Federal policy of limiting special Federal services to Indians to those who were eligible under treaty or other agreement and were connected with land held in trust by the Federal Government.

BIA had contracted with several urban Indian groups in recent years to perform some of the functions of the Bureau Employment Assistance offices in cities, and had encouraged urban Indian organizations to improve their situation. This, plus speeches and comments indicating possible increased activities by BIA in the urban area, led to the reservation Indian reaction and a positive statement

---

[9] *NCIO News*, Vol. 1, No. 5, May 1971, Washington, D. C. Federal grants totaling some $880,000 will be used to upgrade Indian centers in Los Angeles, Minneapolis, Gallup, and Fairbanks, and to establish a central research, technical assistance, and a coordinating office in New York City. Office of Economic Opportunity (OEO) Director Frank Carlucci said the project represented a "major step in the implementation of President Nixon's 1970 Indian message," which directed OEO to take the lead in providing special assistance to the growing urban Indian population.

of policy by the Assistant Secretary of the Department of the Interior limiting BIA programs to trust land related Indians.[10]

The President stated the BIA mission as involving the reservation Indians and not those that had left the reservation in his July 9, 1970 message to the Congress. The Chairwoman of the House Appropriations Subcommittee on Interior and Related Agencies, however, muddied the water somewhat when she stated: [11]

> The Committee believes that the Bureau of Indian Affairs should reassess its relationship to off-reservation Indians who now constitute 40 percent of the country's Indian population. While the Bureau's primary responsibility is to assist Indians living on reservations, the Bureau can and should do more to assist Indians to adjust to city living. Where practicable, referral and employment assistance services of the Bureau's areas and field offices should be made available to any urban Indian requesting such services. Bureau personnel should assist urban Indian organizations in the development of new programs to meet the needs of urban Indians.

Special Federal services to urban Indians on the basis of their ethnic background poses three problems. First, the additional funds required (42 percent of U. S. Indians are not eligible for BIA services) which is of concern to the federally recognized Indians, leading to the formation of the National Tribal Chairmen's Association. If additional funds are not obtained for any special services to urban Indians, the Federal reservation groups suspected they would receive less service. If additional funds are to be obtained, considerable sums could be involved and this is of concern to Federal budget balancers.

Second, the problem of determining Indian eligibility is difficult in the urban scene.

The basic question arises: Who is an Indian? This is a subject of considerable controversy among Indians, especially in discussions of who should receive special governmental services because of their Indianness.

Federal reservation-oriented tribes have authority to determine their own members. However, the Federal Government decides

---

[10] Memorandum to Commissioner of Indian Affairs from Assistant Secretary of the Interior Harrison Loesch, January 16, 1970.

[11] Julia Butler Hansen, House Floor, in presenting BIA budget, *Congressional Record*, June 29, 1971, H. 6021.

who is eligible to receive money from Indian claims awards and Indian trust funds.[12] Federal provision of free education is limited to Indians of one-fourth or more Indian blood by Federal statutes. Tribal membership, in some instances, may include persons with very little Indian blood.

Eligibility for Federal services for federally recognized reservation Indians is relatively easy to determine from tribal membership rolls, per capita payment rolls, and other blood quantum records.

The identity of nonreservation and urban Indians is a problem of entirely different magnitude. If they are enrolled members of a federally recognized tribe, but living away from the reservation, the answer is relatively simple. But for those who cannot prove membership in a Federal tribe, the problem is difficult, if not insoluble, in many instances. If they can trace their ancestry back to a federally recognized Indian tribe, they may confirm their identity. But many persons with Indian blood cannot do this, especially on the eastern seaboard, because their ancestors were never federally recognized or on a Federal roll. Others, who have lived in an urban area for one or more generations, may have lost track of their ancestral line, at least not know how much Indian blood they have, and may not know the name of the most recent Indian ancestor who had a tribal affiliation. Thus, many nonreservation rural and urban Indians would have difficulty proving they were Indians if called upon to do so.[13]

The difficulties in this question of "Who is an Indian?" make extremely hazardous the extension of special services (Federal, State, or city) to Indians as an ethnic group who are not members of a recognized Federal or State tribe. It will be informative to review the experience of the OEO led urban pilot program inaugurated in 1971. If it is to work at all, the administering officials will almost have to take the individual's word. Since there are probably millions of people with some Indian blood who normally no longer

---

[12] Current members may wish to restrict claims payments to current membership or to reservation residents whereas the Claims Commission may prescribe payment to all heirs of members at time of transaction for which payment is being made.

[13] This analysis is on blood quantum and membership in a recognized tribe. It has no relation to the cultural definition of an Indian. Culturally some full-bloods or near full-bloods are members of the non-Indian culture; whereas some individuals with no or little Indian blood may be completely Indian in a cultural sense; e.g., *Little Big Man*. Any criteria for eligibility is likely to be somewhat arbitrary, of necessity.

consider themselves Indian, this possibly could open up pandora's box especially in a recession period in our economy.[14]

It may be appropriate to reevaluate our concept of ethnic identification. Why should not 51 percent or more blood quantum determine the ethnic origin of an individual if such classification is considered necessary? Is white blood so inferior that one-fourth or one-eighth negro, chicano, oriental or Indian blood is controlling as to the ethnic definition of the individual involved?

Who is an Indian? [15]

Because of the problem of identity, assistance based on economic or cultural needs irrespective of ethnic origin would be easier to apply in non-reservation and urban areas. As we have seen, even in reservation areas, as programs applicable to the total population catch up with BIA Indian programs, BIA drops out of the picture or reduces its services. Categorical aids under social security, employment services, certain training programs and education are examples of this phenomena.

The third aspect concerns the concept of State and local responsibility for their citizens. As we have seen, the Indian policy position of the Federal Government since the 1950's has been that States are responsible for all of their citizens, including Indian citizens. The States also recognized some responsibilities and initiated the Governors' Interstate Indian Council. There was and is some logic to special Federal programs on Indian reservations with non-taxable land, stemming from treaties or other commitments to the Indians concerned. But what is the rationale in the nonreservation scene? The only argument the author has encountered is that the black community has taken over programs for the disadvantaged in the urban areas and the Indian is not getting his fair share. If this is so, there may be better ways of correcting the problem than establishing direct Federal programs for Indians as an ethnic group in an urban situation.

---

[14] Nancy Ostreich Lurie estimates there are approximately 10,000,000 people in this country with some Indian blood in "The Enduring Indian", *Natural History Magazine*, November 1966.

[15] Discussions on definition of an Indian:

League of Women Voters, *Indians of Minnesota* (St. Paul, Minn.: North Central Publishing Co., 1971), pp. 17–24.

Handbook on Wisconsin Indians (Madison, Wisc.: Governor's Commission on Human Rights, 1966), pp. 10–11.

Federal Indian Law (Washington, D. C.: U. S. Department of the Interior, Office of the Solicitor, 1958), pp. 4–12.

Continue and Increase Present State and Local Responsibilities

The general historical trend has been to transfer Federal responsibility for funding and services special to Indians to the States and their localities. As developed in earlier chapters, there are many interrelationships between tribal governments and individual Indians and local and State governments. The federally recognized Indians realize the importance of this relationship but also want to retain Federal money and service. All other Indians, of course, are completely under the jurisdiction of the States or localities at the present time.

This option may become financially possible if general support programs become available to the States and Indians through other than BIA and Indian Health Service programs for all disadvantaged individuals, including Indians, at as high or higher level than now funded or services provided through the BIA and Indian Health Service (IHS), e.g., the implementation of one or more of the possible activities described under Federal programs earlier. If Indian economies improve and they contribute greater returns to State revenue, this might also affect the long run picture.

Transfer of full responsibility to the State is supported by those who take the view that Indian citizens are the responsibility of the States as are their other citizens. As we have seen, both the Congress, the Federal Executive, and many States supported or went along with this view in the 1940's and 1950's. The Allotment Act had this option as an objective. There is no active push for transfer to States without Federal assistance at present.

States would certainly resist this option if increased State expenditures from their own tax structure would be involved, which would generally be the case under present circumstances. Many States could not afford to take over present Federal Indian programs without Federal financial assistance.

Indians receiving Federal services would also strenuously resist as they would be concerned about adequate State resources to perform the responsibilities, as well as concerned about State attitudes and objectives, in some instances. They also want to retain the status of direct Federal relationships.

Continue and Increase Present State Responsibilities and Support by Transfer of Federal Funding

This option involves continuing present State responsibilities for Federal Indians and adding operational and service responsibility now performed by Federal agencies, such as BIA, IHS, HUD, OEO, HEW and the Economic Development Administration (EDA). This is the same as the preceding option, except that present Federal funding would go along with the responsibility and continue for as long as needed by the State.

As we have seen, some States have advocated this approach for certain programs. The Hoover Commission stated: [16]

> The Commission recommends that, pending achievement of the goal of complete integration, the administration of social programs for the Indians should be progressively transferred to State governments.
>
> The States should receive appropriate recompense from Federal funds until Indian taxes can help carry the load. The transfer to the States should be accompanied by diminishing activities by the Bureau of Indian Affairs.

This procedure would give greater assurance to the Federal Indians than option 2 that program quality and volume of services could be continued as the States would have the necessary funds. Transfer of responsibility could be accomplished more rapidly without unfavorable impact on quality of services than in option 2.

One of the concerns of Indians is that they feel they are at a political disadvantage in pressuring for services whenever they are in competition with other state groups due to the small number of Indians. They know that funds received by BIA have been devoted to Indian programs. Federally recognized Indians ask why they should be required to compete with others in their States for their share of funds when they feel it would be of serious disadvantage to them.

Most tribes would probably resist this process if a direct wholesale approach was made to transfer the present special BIA and IHS services to States along with the funds. They prefer the present arrangement. The present process of transferring a school, for

---

[16] The Commission on Organization of the Executive Branch of the Government (Hoover Commission), *Indian Affairs* (Washington, D. C.: The Commission, March 1948), p. 65.

example, from BIA to the State school system now occurs whenever the Indian community and the State (or local school system) agree on the move. Funds to assist Indian children in public schools are available from HEW and BIA. So this option is in effect as illustrated by the example of education, but operates on a concensus and piecemeal basis.

The urban Indians could be helped by the Federal Government using this option. Funds would be provided the State to help finance Indian centers in cities, or finance general centers with an Indian desk. This would be a preferable form of Federal assistance as compared with direct Federal involvement in view of the complications discussed in option 1.

Continue Present Federal Support but Transfer Operations Directly to Indians

This option would not disturb present State responsibilities and services, presumably, but instead of adding present Federal responsibilities to the States they would be transferred directly to an organized Indian group under statutory authority, contractual arrangement, or grant of funds. An example would be the transfer of BIA operation of an Indian school to tribal or Indian community operation under a contract.

Of the three methods cited above, contracting and takeover under statutory authority have been used. Takeover of many BIA functions by the Zuni Tribe in January 1971 was under an old statute.[17]

However, the only viable procedure at the present time is by contracting, as the other alternative of "grants" has not been authorized for the Bureau.[18]

Both BIA and IHS are aggressively offering to contract functions

---

[17] 4 Stat. 737, Act of June 30, 1834. Transfer of authority was January 10, 1971. (This 1834 statute [4 Stat. 735] provided for the organization of the Department of Indian Affairs).

However, the Congress has requested that the Bureau obtain current legislation authorizing Indian takeover of BIA functions. Such legislation was proposed in President Nixon's Indian message and suggested legislation was submitted to the Congress on April 1, 1971, by the Secretary of the Interior: Executive proposal 32, "To provide for the assumption of the control and operation by Indian tribes and communities of certain programs and services provided for them by the Federal Government and for other purposes."

[18] The Bureau can make grants to certain individuals, such as employment assistance trainees and college students, but not to a tribal group or other organization.

to Indian tribes or multi-tribal organizations. The Indians are slowly experimenting with this process. The option can be executed rapidly when the Indians are ready and desire to take over a function.[19]

When tribes opt for the contract route, the States are not involved except insofar as increased tribal responsibility may result in the State negotiating with a tribal official rather than a BIA official, for example, on a contract for financial support of Indian children in public schools.[20]

This option not only maintains the direct Federal-Indian relationship, but it may strengthen the Indian's hand in negotiations with the State power structure.

Under current policy the use of this option could increase at a rapid rate if the Indians desire that this be so.

Adopt Basic Policy of Using Options Most Pertinent for Given Situation

Instead of adopting a single policy or method as a panacea in an attempt to resolve the so-called "Indian Problem" (such as allotment, termination, contracting, Indian takeover, extension of Federal services to all Indians, etc.) this option recognizes that different situations exist and that varying practices which seem most appropriate for bettering the Indian condition of particular communities or reservations need to be applied.

The present "self-determination" and "consultation" policies, as well as the growing sophistication and power manipulating ability of Indian tribes and pan-Indian organizations, means that Indian involvement will have a major influence in decisions on future governmental actions affecting their welfare. Indians are wary of panaceas and instant solutions. Their leadership will take appropriate and often differing roads depending on the circumstances of each Indian group.

---

[19] Over 800 contracts between BIA and the tribes were in effect on October 4, 1971, varying from the management and operation of educational and social welfare programs to the rental of dump trucks. *Interior News Release,* Oct. 4, 1971.

[20] The Bureau has contracted with the following tribes and tribal organizations for the negotiation of Johnson O'Malley funding for Indians in State public schools: United Tribes of North Dakota Development Corp. (for North Dakota) ; United Sioux Tribes of South Dakota Development Corp. (for South Dakota) ; and the Omaha Tribe of Nebraska (for Nebraska).
BIA Education Office, as of July 1971.

Changes in Federal and State functions with regard to Indians will result when desired by the Indians and when such changes are consistent with general State and national policies.

This "evolutionary process" of dealing with the circumstances of each tribal group does not fit into a neat and specific policy package. It is somewhat amorphous. It is harder to sell to those that are putting up the money, such as the Congress and the State legislatures. However, in the author's judgment, it is the sound approach.

CHAPTER TEN

THE INDIAN POTENTIAL

Indian attitudes and goals, the nature and effectiveness of tribal government, Indian influence and power, Indian culture and adaptive ability—along with education, economic condition, and relationships with the other governments and society in general—will play a vital role in the unfolding of Indian potential.

INDIAN ATTITUDES AND GOALS

The philosophy of pluralism expressed by President Nixon and many of the States, the responsiveness of all branches of the Federal and State Governments to Indian desires, and the increased sensitiveness of the population at large to the problems and aspirations of ethnic minorities provide a receptive and supportive environment for serious consideration of the goals of Indian people.

Like others, the Indians do not speak with one voice. Many reservation Indians are alarmed at some of the philosophies and tactics of militant urban Indians, yet the militants receive a good percentage of Indian newspaper coverage. Indians in one community may have a different set of problems and different resources with which to meet them than Indians in another community. There is also a difference in attitude toward adjusting to the non-Indian world among Indian communities, and sometimes sharp cleavages on this matter within such communities.

Discussion of differences in attitudes in adjusting to the non-Indian world, planning for each community, and general attitude of Indian leaders of federally recognized Indian groups follow.

Traditional vs. Adaptive Attitudes

Earlier chapters traced some of the problems of adjustment between Indian and non-Indian culture. The overflowing hordes of non-Indians, their materialistic economic system, and their exploitive attitude toward nature (land, buffalo, trees, deer) made it im-

145

possible for the historic Indian social and economic system to continue. Without necessary adaptation to the non-Indian world, the Indian either has to be subsidized or perish.

The Indian, as Margaret Mead has pointed out, has tenaciously clung to many customs and traditional views [1] which do not encompass the folk ways required in an industrial or postindustrial society. Many have described the drama and pathos, failure and victory, involved in the collision of the Indian and European cultures.[2]

Even college educated Indians sometimes have doubts about non-Indian ways.[3]

The history of Indian education includes the problem of antagonism toward the schools from parents and grandparents.

The importance of working with the home was mentioned in Visiting Coordinator Program in Oklahoma, Chap. VI, education discussion in footnote. Home opposition to non-Indian education was one of the reasons advanced for boarding schools. The culture conflict was the underlying reason for the problem. Many accounts neglect this difficult aspect of the Indian education challenge. It is recognized by some students of the subject.[4]

---

[1] Margaret Mead at "A Symposium on the American Indian," The George Washington University, March 17–20, 1971, as reported in *The Evening Star*, Washington, D. C., March 19, 1971, p. C9.

[2] Dan Cushman, *Stay Away Joe* (4th ed., Great Falls, Mont.: Stay Away Joe Publishers, 1968) .

Harry James, *Red Man, White Man* (San Antonio, Tex.: Naylor Co., 1957).

Hal Glen Borland, *When the Legends Die* (Philadelphia and New York: J. B. Lippincott Co., 1963) .

Thomas Berger, *Little Big Man,* (New York: The Dial Press, 1964) .

Alan Fry, *How a People Die* (Garden City, N. Y.: Doubleday, 1970).

John C. Ewers, "When Red and White Men Met," reprinted from *The Western Historical Quarterly*, April 1971.

[3] "They look at the mainstream, and what do they see: ice cream bars and heart trouble and neurosis and deodorants and getting up at 6 o'clock in the morning to mow your lawn in the suburbs. They see that in the mainstream the urban and suburban men are trapped; once you get a job it's climb, climb, climb. If you get heart trouble, it's the price you pay.

"It's a strange thing. When you get far enough away from the reservation, you can see it's the urban man who has no identity. So he gets money. Or power. To feel secure, to protect himself. But he hasn't any roots, any land, any soul."

Vine Deloria, Jr., in Stan Steiner, *The New Indians* (New York: Dell Publishing Co., 1968) , p. 86. See also p. 93 for Mel Thom's critique of the American system.

[4] Francis McKinley, Stephen Bayne, and Glen Nimnicht, *Who Should Control Indian Education?* (Berkeley, Calif.: Far West Laboratory for Educational Research and Development, 1970) , pp. 13–14, points to some of these factors.

Many Indian communities have been polarized on the degree to which non-Indian ways are to be accepted—the traditionalist groups opposing change and the adaptive groups pushing for change. Traditionalists in Taos, Santo Domingo, and Hopi, for example, up until recently have opposed electricity and water piped into the home. Others in the same communities wanted these amenities. Some Indian groups do not want a written constitution, others do. Some want every decision of the tribe to be made by a general council made up of all adult members; others believe this cumbersome and prefer an elected representative council or a combination of the two processes.

Community Goals

It has long been recognized that plans and goals for Indians should be developed community-by-community to fit their own circumstances. Many attempts have been made to do this for Federal reservation Indians, especially from the time of John Collier (1930's) to the present.

In addition to the resistance of many Indians to adaptive change forced by the destruction of their traditional way of life, there have been two main difficulties in developing and following through on meaningful reservation (Indian community) goals. The first is that there was minimal Indian involvement in such plans and goals. As a result of the Allotment Act period—stamp out everything Indian —tribal governments were emaciated or non-existent as viable organisms prior to the Indian Reorganization Act (IRA). They had to be nurtured and developed, which takes time. Therefore the reservation superintendent and his staff in large measure prepared the early plans.

O. E. Rolvaag, *Peder Victorious* (New York: Harper and Brothers, 1929) points to the anguish of a Norwegian mother as her son absorbs English and non-Norwegian ways in an American public school and rejects much of the traditional culture. See particularly pp. 194–197.

In a study on San Carlos, Edward A. Parmee, *Formal Education and Culture Change* (Tucson, Ariz.: University of Arizona Press, 1968), the tendency to try to negate home influences is described, p. 109. An excellent summary of the differences between Indian culture and the dominant culture is presented in Madison L. Coombs, *The Educational Disadvantages of the Indian American Student* (Las Cruces, N. M.: Educational Resources Information Center (ERIC), Clearinghouse on Rural Education and Small Schools (CRESS), New Mexico State University, July 1970), p. 48 and ff.

The second difficulty was the lack of any recognizable relation-ship between such plans as were developed and the appropriation process. The plans and goals were on a geographical basis for an Indian community or a reservation. However, the appropriations were on a functional basis—such as total amounts for education, re-source development, and roads for all Federal Indians. If the Exec-utive or the Congress favored certain functional activities they were well funded. Others might be starved to death. After the appropria-tion the pie was divided by the Bureau of Indian Affairs (BIA) among the field jurisdictions. The funds and personnel available to the reservation communities often bore little relationship to com-munity plans or priorities. Enthusiasm for such planning waned on the part of both Bureau of Indian Affairs (BIA) field personnel and the tribal leaders after repeated experiences of this nature.

The Indian Reorganization Act required tribal participation in the budget process. The logistics and timing of the budget cycle make such participation difficult. Thus, this requirement has been largely ignored. However, the recent use of automatic data process-ing has facilitated analysis, timely reports and feed back, and im-proved the effectiveness of tribal participation in the budget proc-ess. Reservation program plans are now being developed with tribal participation and an effort is being made to provide the tribes information on the modifications of their plans as they go through the review channels to the Congress.

Tribal governments have been greatly strengthened since 1934 and are therefore much more viable instruments for expressing Indian needs and goals than formerly. Many, however, lack finan-cial resources to support necessary governmental activities. Most even find it difficult to pay salaries for tribal officials. Only a few have the funds to support even a minimum administrative staff that would provide basic service to political policy officials and provide some continuity.

Tribal officials recognize this and are endeavoring to develop revenues to support adequate government services. Until such time as this happens they want continued and increased Federal and State support.[5] For example, Peter MacDonald, chairman of the

[5] "Indian Organization Questionnaire," April 2, 1971.

Results of "Indian Organization Questionnaire" mailed to 245 tribal leaders (federally recognized) and 17 pan-Indian groups by the author April 2, 1971. Twenty-three percent responded. Results used here were summarized and sent to respondents. No one has suggested modification of the summary.

Meeting Navajo Tribal Council.
(Photo: U.S. Department of the Interior, Bureau of Indian Affairs.)

tribal council for the Navajo Nation, is reported by the October 3, 1971 *New York Times* as being "concerned that the Navajos must develop an economy that will sustain their present population as well as the population that can be expected in the next several generations."

To achieve development, tribal leaders have a strong desire for continued direct relationships with the Federal Government where that now exists, and some tribal officers desire expanded relationships in specific areas such as law and order. They want continued Federal and State funding and they want such funds increased. However, such funding is considered a transitional support for as long as they consider it necessary to meet their goals.[6]

Indian attitudes toward the States and their localities are somewhat ambivalent. The concensus seems to be that tribes and their members are inevitably involved with State and local institutions, even those tribes and their members with maximum direct Federal

---

[6] A Minnesota Indian commenting on Office of Economic Opportunity and Bureau of Indian Affairs programs said: ". . . it must be noted that each and all of these programs are the product of Federal funding and can only continue to function as long as this funding is renewed. Essentially, what we have is induced, subsidized progress and employment. What we need is free enterprise based on merit, competition, and profit. Our proposed EDA tourist complex is a first step in that direction." James Hull, Community Action Program, Grand Portage Reservation, in League of Women Voters, *Indians of Minnesota* (St. Paul, Minn.: North Central Publishing Co., 1971) p. 120.

involvement. A few do not like the relationship, some do not trust the States, but many of these, as well as the majority of the others, indicated a positive (though watchful in some instances) attitude toward trying to work with all pertinent governments and other sources of help for bettering the Indian condition.[7]

Indian goals must take into account related non-Indian communities and their goals, and vice-versa. For example, 93 percent of the respondents recognized that cooperation from the non-Indian community is needed for economic development. Neighboring towns, county governments and State departments, as well as private consultants, were regarded as important because of geographical relationships and involvement in the general economy and because of need for expertise now lacking in many Indian communities.

Education of Indian children is to a considerable extent (68 percent) under State law in local public schools in those States with Indians eligible for Federal services. The responses indicated a desire for more tribal operation or involvement, but with continuing heavy emphasis on operation in accordance with or under State school regulations and policy.[8]

Most comments on direct tribal operation referred to taking over BIA operated schools. Two stressed quality of teaching and extra help for students who needed it with Federal funding to assist public schools.

Heavy use, with general satisfaction, is made of State employment services. Use is also made of the BIA Employment Assistance Program, which is considered important by the larger Federal tribes.

Tribal leaders also recognize that States and counties are heavily involved in foster home placement of Indian children and in judicial, prevention and enforcement services for Indians.

Even with the above recognition of the part State and local governments have in servicing Indian communities, most of the Federal tribes responding considered the Federal Government the most important of the three governmental levels.

Complaints against present servicing agencies (local, State, or

---

[7] *Indian Organization Questionnaire,* op. cit.

[8] Bureau of Indian Affairs statistics indicate that in 1971 there were 232 public school districts with Indian membership on the school boards totaling 631 Indian board members. For example, the Tuba City elementary and high school board has an Indian majority as does the Whiteriver elementary school

Federal) seem to be generally based on what the respondents considered unsatisfactory performance.

The responses indicated an interest in increased Indian involvement either through direct operation of activities that affect their lives (e.g., schools, law and order) or effective participation in co-operation with others in such operation. Several respondents reported the value of State Indian commissions and some wanted this activity strengthened in their States.

No "assimilation" philosophy was generally expressed; rather recognition of the validity of Indian groups and governments (when large enough to have them) was stressed. However, there was the additional recognition that such Indian groups, their neighbors (county and city or town groups), the State and Federal Governments must work effectively together when appropriate to reach the goals of the Indian communities.

The majority of the respondents, especially the larger groups, seemed to see no major difficulty in the four systems of government working together to resolve problems as they arise.[9]

TRIBAL GOVERNMENTS

Tribal organizations exercise governmental powers within the limits of Federal law on many Indian reservations. Some are organized under the Indian Reorganization Act (IRA), some are traditional, and some have developed ordinances and practices recognized as controlling but not under the authority of IRA. The powers exercised may include the right to choose their form of government, determine membership, regulate internal conduct including domestic relations, tax and collect taxes, appropriate funds, and administer justice for their own members.[10]

Many State enabling acts and constitutions include provisions that the State in question disclaims jurisdiction over Federal Indian reservations within their boundaries.[11]

---

[9] *Indian Organization Questionnaire,* op. cit.

[10] See William A. Brophy and Sophie D. Aberle, *The Indian, America's Unfinished Business,* Report of the Commission on the Rights, Liberties, and Responsibilities of the American Indian (Norman, Okla.: University of Oklahoma Press, 1966), pp. 24–61. Also see Albert E. Kane, "Jurisdiction Over Indian Reservations," *Arizona Law Review,* Spring, 1965, for a review of tribal government and tribal authority. Also see ch. II for discussion of IRA constitutions and corporate charters.

[11] The New Mexico enabling act (36 Stat. 557), June 20, 1910, states: ". . . the people inhabiting said proposed State do agree and declare that they forever disclaim

Meeting Colorado River Tribal Council, 1971. Seated from left to right: Harry Patch, Gladys Townsend, Bill Alcaida, Marjorie Scott, Adrian Fisher, Veronica Murdock, Tony Martinez, Dwight Lomayestewa and Dean Welch.

(Photo: *Parker Pioneer.*)

Thus, within many States and their political subdivisions are separate units of Indian government which are not subject to State authority, except as authorized by the Federal Government.

From the time of Chief Justice John Marshall's description of Indian tribes as "domestic dependent nations" in 1831 [12] Indian tribes have been described variously as "municipal corporations," "political sovereigns," as having a "status higher than States," and as "separate political communities." [13] Since the time of Chief Justice Marshall tribal sovereignty has eroded and tribes are no longer sovereign in the traditional sense. Indian tribes recognized by the Federal Government as being under its jurisdiction will be considered here as "distinct political societies" within our Federal system.

Historically, there has been a devolution from Federal to State services, even for federally recognized Indians.[14] Many Indians now

all right and title to . . . all lands lying within said boundaries owned or held by any Indian or Indian tribes the right or title to which shall have been acquired through or from the United States or any prior sovereignty, and that until the title of such Indian or Indian tribes shall have been extinguished the same shall be and remain subject to the disposition and under the absolute jurisdiction and control of the Congress of the United States. . . ." See also Arizona (36 Stat. 569); Oklahoma (34 Stat. 267–268; 280); Utah (28 Stat. 107–8); North Dakota, South Dakota, Montana, and Washington (25 Stat. 676).

[12] Cherokee Nation v. Georgia, 30 U. S. (5 Pet.) 1 (1831).

[13] See Kane, op. cit., pp. 237–238.

[14] See Chapter III.

are serviced totally by their State and local governments and have no special Federal services.[15] The Menominees, for example, are now a Wisconsin county for governmental purposes. This raises the question of the future of separate Indian governments as "distinct political societies" within our Federal system. Can tribal governments be absorbed into the normal State and local government framework?

It is difficult to conceive of the Navajo tribe, with 120,000 members and a land area the size of West Virginia, voluntarily giving up governmental authority over its land and people. Since the tribal land and population is in parts of three States, the route taken by Menominees would not result in a single unit of government as it did in Wisconsin. Another possibility would be to carve the 51st State out of Arizona, New Mexico, and Utah for the Navajos. This would provide a "Navajo" government within the normal framework of our Federal system. Tribes totally within a State that wish to retain their own governmental institutions would probably use the Menominee format or develop some other arrangement with the State.

As indicated, the majority of tribal leaders where they now have tribal governments seemed to see no major difficulty in the Indian governments working with local, State, and Federal Governments to resolve problems as they arise. Indian leadership, where Indian government exists at present, seems to think only in terms of continuance of such Indian government.

In view of Indian attitude and the responsiveness of the Federal and State Governments to Indian policy desires, there would seem to be little question but that Indian governments will continue to exist for as long as the Indian communities involved want them. Although this may be largely contingent on the continuation of the "trust" status of Indian land [16] there seems to be little reason to believe that such "trust" status will not continue for as long as desired by the Indians concerned.[17]

---

[15] See Chapter VI.

[16] See Chapter VI.

[17] The non-Indian population might not support continued trust status for a wealthy Indian group over an extended period of time. However, various State governments are experimenting with a possessory interest tax which, if held legal by the courts, may erode the tax protection provided by trust land and therefore take the pressure off eliminating trust status, as such, even for a wealthy Indian group.

INDIAN POWER

The American people, and other peoples around the world, romanticize the free, outdoor, independent and self-reliant Indians of early America. Indian names, food, and culture have enriched the American heritage. And the Nation tends to have a guilt complex concerning the treatment of the original Americans. Up until recently, the power of public response to Indian needs has been largely manipulated by non-Indians in such organizations as the Association on American Indian Affairs,[18] and individuals working with Indian organizations such as James Curry, when he was counsel for the National Congress of American Indians; special surveys (especially the Meriam survey in 1928); and by persons in pivotal positions in the Congress and the Federal executive establishment, such as John Collier as Commissioner of Indian Affairs.

However, Indian leadership and action is becoming more sophisticated and effective. "Red Power" is a recently coined phrase. It is not used much by the traditional Indian leaders on Federal reservations. It comes from those whom reservation Indians would term the "militants," largely urban oriented.[19] Some of them participated in the Poor People's March on Washington in 1968.

Though the Indians related to Federal reservations do not accept the slogan "Red Power" (and its militant tactics) its members are exercising more and more power through normal channels in their States and in the Nation. There has been a steady growth in the power of tribal councils and Indian leadership in the tribes as they become more involved in decisions that have an impact on the lives of their constituents. Better qualified leaders are running for office and getting elected. Intertribal organizations are increasing; at present there are 17 of them. The United Tribes of North Dakota, for example, are a potent force in that State. The Alaska Federation of Natives was vigorous and effective in preparing a Native position and in lobbying for enactment of the Alaska Native Claims legislation.[20]

---

[18] The present president is Roger Ernst, a former Assistant Secretary in the Interior Department with responsibility for Indians. The Association had its greatest influence during the time of Oliver LaFarge, the author, who was president for a number of years before and after World War II.

[19] Vine Deloria, Jr. (several years ago), Clyde Warrior (deceased), Mel Thom and others, well described in Stan Steiner, op cit. which has a chapter on "Red Power".

[20] For example, they employed: Arthur Goldberg, former Justice of the Supreme

President Nixon signing bill returning to the Taos Pueblo approximately 48,000 acres of land and Blue Lake, December 15, 1970. Front row-left to right: Secretary of Interior Rogers C. B. Morton; Mrs. LaDonna Harris; Senator Fred Harris; John Rainer, Chief Indian Member, National Council on Indian Opportunity and member of Taos Pueblo; Quireno Romero, Taos Governor; James Mirabal, Taos Pueblo. Standing: Paul Bernal, Interpreter, Taos Pueblo; Juan de Jesus Romero, Cacique, Taos Pueblo.

(Photo: White House.)

The tribes in the southeast have banded together to improve their bargaining power with Federal agencies and educational institutions such as universities. The Indians of Arizona have formed the Indian Development District of Arizona, funded by Economic Development Administration (EDA). The presently organizing tribal chairman's association may be another step forward in influence.

The National Congress of American Indians (NCAI) has had its ups and downs, but the Indians have learned a great deal of organizational and lobby "know how" from its operation. Indians have far greater influence than their number would lead one to suspect. They beat the conservationists, the sportsmen, the Forest Service, New Mexico's senior Senator, and Sen. Henry Jackson, Chairman of the Senate Committee on Interior, on transfer of title of Blue Lake from the Forest Service to the Taos Pueblo in New Mexico in 1970.[21]

Indian writers such as Scott Momaday and Vine Deloria, Jr., and leaders such as Robert L. Bennett former Commissioner of Indian Affairs, keep the public aware of the Indian and his future.[22]

Unless the militants create a backlash, the strong public support for Indians will continue and Indians will in large measure have the power to use such support constructively or otherwise. If a State or the Federal Government tries a major Indian policy move without consultation and agreement on the part of the Indians, the Government is likely to be stopped dead in its tracks and the policy not implemented. No State imposed State law and order on an Indian reservation under authority of P.L. 280 without the consent of the Indians concerned, even before 280 was amended to require such consent. The 1970 proposed rotation of Superintendents and Area personnel, announced without what the Indians considered adequate consultation, has not worked largely because of Indian opposition.

The time is ripe for Indian leadership to play a dominant role in initiating public Indian policy. The chances are good that if the

---

Court; Tom Clark, former Attorney General; and Edward Weinberg, former Solicitor of the Department of the Interior to help them develop and present their case for Alaska Native Claims.

[21] P.L. 91–550, December 15, 1970, (84 Stat. 1437). The President and the Interior Department backed the Indians.

[22] Scott Momaday, *A House Made of Dawn* (New York: Harper & Row, 1969); Vine Deloria, Jr., *Custer Died for Your Sins* (New York: The Macmillan Co., 1969).

Swearing in of Indian members of National Council on Indian Opportunity by Commerce Secretary Maurice Stans, September 1, 1970. Left to right: Joseph C. Vasquez, Apache Sioux; Earl Old Person, Blackfeet; John Rainer, Taos Pueblo; Harold Shunk, Yankton-Sioux; B. Frank Belvin, Choctaw; Secretary Stans; Betty Mae Jumper, Seminole, and Martin Seneca, Jr., Seneca.

(Photo: U.S. Department of Commerce.)

Indians can achieve an effective national pressure group they will play such a role. In any event, even without a unified solidarity, individual leaders, such as many of the present chairmen of Indian tribes, will have considerable innovative impact on Indian policy affecting their communities.[23]

Evidence of the Indian's greater leverage is seen in governmental policy, structure, and procedure.

Indian representatives have a voice at the highest level in the Federal Executive Branch. One half of the members of the National Council on Indian Opportunity are Indian; and other members are cabinet rank; the chairman is the Vice President.[23A]

---

[23] e.g., Zuni developing a plan for their reservation, getting cooperation from all agencies (Federal and State), and taking over much of the BIA function on the reservation; Warm Springs employing their own consultants and moving ahead in timber and tourist enterprises; Navajo enticing industry onto the reservation as well as operating an $18 million a year tribal government, etc.

[23A] The present Indian members serving until September 1972 are: John C. Rainer (Taos), Dr. B. Frank Belvin (Choctaw), Mrs. Laura Bergt (Eskimo), Mrs. Betty

As we have seen, Indians are also planning their individual reservation programs with technical assistance from Federal agencies, such as BIA, Indian Health Service (IHS), and the Department of Housing and Urban Development (HUD), as well as assistance from consultants the tribes employ. The tribes then collaborate in the development of the BIA budget in support of the tribal programs and it is hoped they can be kept informed as to action on the budget as it proceeds through the Area Office, Central Office, Department, Office of Management and Budget, and the President's budget message, and action in the Congress.

State Governments have recently recognized Indian influence and leadership, and the States' inherent responsibilities to their Indian citizens, through statutes, executive orders, and special services to Indians. Indians have increased access to Governors and other State officials as a result.[24] States also recognize that separate cultures can exist together in harmony and are seeking Indian participation in achieving such accommodation as necessary to achieve this along with self-sufficiency.

With some exceptions, State funded Indian activities, such as Indian affairs commissions, are frequently an expression of intention rather than fundamental action (Maine and Texas are obviously exceptions). Indian commissions and their staffs are poorly funded, though many of them do excellent work with what resources they have. State activities for Indians that have impact are frequently supported by Federal funds, such as Johnson-O'Malley funds for an Indian student program and Labor funds for the State employment service. State law and order has earned Indian antagonism in some instances due to poor service (in large measure the result of inadequate funding).

Nevertheless, official statements of responsibility for Indian citizens in State law and executive orders are big steps forward and provide a philosophy and policy base for future constructive action.

The tribes and the neighboring communities and counties recog-

---

Mae Jumper (Seminole), Earl Old Person (Blackfeet), Harold W. Shunk (Yankton-Sioux), Martin E. Seneca, Jr., (Seneca), and Joseph C. (Lone Eagle) Vasquez (Sioux-Apache). The cabinet officers are: The Secretaries of Interior; Agriculture; Commerce; Labor; Health, Education and Welfare; Housing and Urban Development; and the Director of the Office of Economic Opportunity.

[24] See Chapter VI.

nize the desirability of considering a logical area for economic development, which often includes Indian and non-Indian communities. The stage has been set for expansion in this type of activity as Indian sophistication and careful use of Indian influence increases, and as neighboring communities develop an awareness of the mutual advantages of cooperative action.

Partly as a result of the increased effectiveness of tribal leadership—but also as a result of the general revolution in attitudes towards minorities, economic, social and political institutions—the current President and immediate past President have highlighted the Indian American in Presidential messages and proposed legislation.[25]

INDIAN CULTURE AND ADAPTATION

Many Indians have adjusted to the non-Indian culture to the extent that they compete successfully—economically, socially, and politically—and many of these have retained those portions of their Indian culture and tradition that they find useful.

Many others, however, on reservations and in city slums, have not made this adjustment. What is Indian culture? Before the white man, there were many different Indian cultures, often warring with one another, with different languages and different customs. Indian culture changes with time as do all cultures. The destruction of game, elimination of wars between tribes, and concentration of Indians on reservations changed the Indian's way of life. The traditional Indian is often pictured sitting on his horse gazing into the sunset—the horse was unknown to the Indian until it was introduced by the Spanish. Sheep, which are often considered the traditional economic mainstay of the Navajos, were also introduced by the Spanish. The pickup truck is replacing the wagon; the snow-go is replacing the dog sled. Radio and TV sets are everywhere. These changes have a subtle impact on many phases of Indian life. Shifting from horse and wagon and from dog sled to gasoline powered vehicles require a different family economy. Cash is needed for gas, whereas natural grass and fish were available for horses and dogs. Some Indians have gone to the city to get cash income; but more and more employment opportunities are being sought for the reservation.

---

[25] See Chapter V.

Often there are different stages of acculturation in the same Indian community or family. But the Indians can, and many do, retain those portions of their traditional culture which they still find useful for enrichment of their lives.

Many ethnic groups in this country retain traditional customs—marriage ceremonies, social activities (e.g. folk dances), crafts, language and historical heritage from their ancestors as a part of their personal identification. Yet, they also have accommodated themselves to the economic, social, and governmental systems generally prevailing in the country so as to be self-sufficient. The Indians seem to be moving in the same direction.

ASPECTS OF SELF-DETERMINATION AND ITS IMPLEMENTATION

A key policy is "self-determination." This has not been defined in detail in any official statement. It is a concept that has been expressed from time to time in the past. The "removal" and "reservation" policies in the 19th Century initially involved the concept of the Indians running their own affairs in Indian country. Later, the philosophy of the Indian Reorganization Act (IRA) included tribally elected governments which would administer the affairs of their respective tribes. Tribal corporations were an option open to tribes under IRA which made it possible for tribes to finally determine many actions without the approval of the Secretary of the Interior. Commissioner John Collier also stressed the importance of individual plans for each reservation. In 1952 Commissioner Dillon Myer enunciated the principle of consultation but also presented the following alternatives to tribes: (1) if they considered BIA a handicap he was willing to recommend termination of BIA's trusteeship; (2) if a tribe wanted a modification of the trusteeship arrangement the BIA was willing to work out details; and (3) if a tribe desired to assume some of the responsibilities of BIA, without termination, BIA was prepared to work out an appropriate agreement with the tribe. As the Commissioner put it: [26]

> This statement constitutes, in effect, a standing offer by the Bureau to work constructively with any tribe which wishes to assume either full control or a greater degree of control over its own affairs.

---

[26] Commissioner of Indian Affairs, *Annual Report*, 1952.

Reservation community planning by Indian reservation residents and Indian participation in Federal budgeting at the reservation level have been described earlier in this chapter. Such planning and budgeting provide the major and most important process through which Indian self-determination can be achieved. It is not a new thought, as has been pointed out. But its implementation is not simple. Implementation requires that resources be made available in accordance with long-range plans and goals of the individual reservations. The specific program projects provided for in annual budget requests of Indian and non-Indian governmental agencies involved must relate to such long-range plans and goals. This has not happened.

How can this concept be made to work?

There seems to be unanimous agreement that individual reservation plans and goals make sense. One suggestion is to have the Indian budget of various Federal and State agencies on the same geographic base as the Indian reservation plans and tied into these plans. The relationship between plans and yearly increments toward the long-range goal would be easy for all to see—the Indians affected, as well as the executive and legislative branches of the Federal and State governments. Appropriations could be made on the same geographic basis and would facilitate knowledge of the specific aspects of the long-range plan that would be accomplished by the annual appropriation.[27]

For this concept to work, it would have to be agreed to by the Indian communities concerned, the Executive (Interior Department and the President's Office in the case of the Federal Government) and the Appropriation Committees of the Federal and State Governments. Since change is difficult, obtaining this agreement may be a major task in itself. A pilot effort with five to ten reservations might be a logical first step.

Full adoption of this approach probably would have an impact on BIA structure. One possible option would be for the Central Office to have regional coordinators as the primary organizational breakdown, with an advisory group of functional specialists. At

---

[27] This is not a suggestion for numerous appropriations in a technical sense. All BIA appropriated funds could be in one appropriation, but the justification material would be on a reservation basis rather than functional basis as at present. Followup and accountability would be on a reservation result rather than a generalized across-the-Nation functional result. It has been pointed out that this fits in with the concept of block grants and local determination of the use of funds.

First presentation of Zuni Comprehensive Development Plan concept by Zuni Pueblo Governor Robert E. Lewis, Bureau of Indian Affairs Auditorium, 1967.
(Photo: U.S. Department of the Interior, Bureau of Indian Affairs.)

present functional specialists are the primary groups and they run national functional programs such as education and forestry. The suggested reorganization would deemphasize functional control from Washington and emphasize integrated, related planning and execution in each individual Indian community. This would provide reservation Indian communities the opportunity for maximum impact on the planning and execution of plans affecting their future. Other approaches may be possible for the supporting organizational arrangement.

Through the development of community plans and goals the Indians can point the way for the kind, quantity, and quality of development they desire. Through consultation with the reservation Superintendent and local representatives of other Federal and State agencies they can indicate reasonable annual projects and the money and resources necessary to achieve a specific portion of the community long-range plan. The Zuni Pueblo, the Gila River Community, and some other reservations have defined long-range plans. Their problem has been to get necessary annual implementation of segments of the program incorporated in Federal and State budgets.

One of the components of each reservation's plans could be proposed changes in the delivery system, such as tribal assumption of specific functions like the operation of a school (under a school board in accordance with State law or by contract with the BIA). The contract option is available also for many other service activities such as law and order, plant maintenance, road construction and maintenance, and general welfare assistance. The projected timing of any such assumption of responsibility by the tribe and any necessary preliminary steps such as training of personnel, should be indicated in the plan with a tentative time table.

Zuni provides an example of the "take over" of supervision of BIA agency personnel on the basis of a 1834 statute. Former BIA personnel now function largely as a part of the Zuni Pueblos' Indian government. Basic trust responsibility for trust land and trust funds, of course, cannot be turned over to the Indians by the Secretary of the Interior without specific statutory authority.

President Nixon proposes to put the ability of a tribe to take over functions on a legislative basis. The executive draft of the bill provides that if a tribe decides to take over any BIA or IHS function, the two agencies concerned have no choice but to turn the function over along with the funds to perform the function. The proposed legislation also provides for retrocession of the responsibility to BIA or IHS if the tribe so decides. There are certain restrictions. The Secretary is charged with monitoring the tribe's performance on a function taken over and funded by the Federal Government. The reports and records of the tribal program are to be open for review by the General Accounting Office and the Secretary. If the rights, safety, health, or welfare of the individual Indian are endangered or there is gross negligence or mismanagement of Federal funds, the Secretary of the Interior may reassume control, after appropriate notice and hearing, for such time as he deems necessary. In other words, the tribes may take over the operation but the Federal Government retains the responsibility.[28]

Contracts with tribes, discussed under "Policy Options," include requirements and controls to assure performance of the function for which a contract is made.

An important underlying factor is attitude. For maximum self-determination the Indians must be willing to plan for their future in the form of long-range goals and specific plans to meet these goals. They must also be willing to work out the specific annual programs and projects for budget purposes that fit into the long-range plan and which are reasonable in the eyes of the Executive and the Congress. And they must have at least the necessary minimum resources to allow their representatives to spend adequate time on these basic self-determination activities which may require BIA or other funding for tribes without funds for such staff time.

On the other hand, the attitude of Federal and State Government representatives must be one of providing maximum help and assistance, in response to tribal request, in achieving the tribes' goals and specific sub-projects related to such goals.

Some have equated self-determination as final authority to select Federal officials who administer BIA or other governmental programs for Indians. This is related only in a peripheral way to the fundamentals of self-determination as discussed above. The basic aspect is determining the goal and the timing of implementation. Who carries out the goal in accordance with the Indian designed reservation plan is a relatively minor matter as long as it is done effectively. The Secretary, who is responsible for trust resources and expenditure of appropriated funds (unless relieved of this responsibility by specific statutory provisions) must bear the final responsibility for personnel appointments and the performance of such appointees, as well as Indian performance in carrying out functions under contract.

Nevertheless, Indian tribes have generally had a great deal more latitude and opportunity to be more "self-determining" than they

---

[28] Executive Proposal No. 32, transmitted by the Secretary of Interior, April 1, 1971, "To Provide for the assumption of the control and operation by Indian tribes and communities of certain programs and services provided for them by the Federal Government and for other purposes."

have used. Only three tribes used the IRA corporate device described in the discussion on the Indian Reorganization Act in Chapter II. Less than 50 percent of the tribes have organized under IRA. Few took advantage of Commissioner Myer's offer described earlier in this section. Few have taken advantage of the opportunity to contract for important services such as education.

Why have not Indians exercised maximum self-determination? Several reasons have been advanced:

—Lack of Indian resources, both in funds and trained personnel.

—The way BIA is organized.

—The non-Indians in BIA oppose it.

—The paternalistic attitude of some BIA employees—to administer rather than be a service agency.

—The fear on the part of some employees of losing their jobs if they encourage and assist in tribal "take over."

—The general wariness of Indian groups of the implications of a "take over" action.

—The tradition of depending on the agency staff or what might be termed a Bureau-Indian culture.

—The traditionalist attitude of some Indians and satisfaction with a subsistence existence in the reservation economy.

In spite of all these possible factors, in the past BIA functions have been transferred to the tribe or the States (local control) when the Indians were willing—witness the tremendous transition in education and other fields described in earlier chapters. In fact, and at least in part due to some of the above factors, one of the main fears of the federally eligible Indian is that BIA and the Federal and State Governments may try to go faster in this direction than he wants to go or is prepared to go.

The writer has no way of scientifically demonstrating which of the reasons advanced above are important or how they might rank in priority. But he does believe Indian resources, readiness in the way of training and experience, and attitudes (including Indian attitudes toward Indian tradition and the State and Federal instrumentalities) are important. These factors need to be faced and plans made to meet them through the reservation planning process by the Indians, if they so desire.

Some individuals put great weight on alleged "paternalistic attitudes" on the part of BIA employees as a negative factor. The belief that the trained professional can do the job (whatever it may be, such as education or road construction) better than if the Indian community endeavored to perform the service for itself may result in Bureau field staff influencing Indian attitudes against planning or taking over the delivery of service.

Others say that fear of job loss is an incentive for BIA employees to subtly oppose real reservation programing under Indian leadership as well as any proposals to take over the service functions by the tribes. The author has not seen much evidence that supports these two allegations, but others believe they are important.

If "paternalism" and "fear of losing job" are considered important problems by the Indians, there may be at least two options for a solution. First, the reservation program could call for "grants" or "contracts" covering the various programs desired. Under a "grant" or "contract" the funds would go directly to the tribe and it would hire tribal employees and consultants whose incentive would be to carry out the assignment the way the Indians wanted it.

Secondly, if President Nixon's "take over" legislation is passed, this would provide another avenue of resolving this issue.

The degree to which either of these procedures would be utilized would have a direct impact on BIA structure, and numbers and kind of personnel. If all functions were primarily funded through "grants" or "contracts" the organization would be focused on "grant" and "contract" processing. Most action personnel would be tribal employees or personnel of corporations or groups under contract with the tribe. This is obviously an option open to Indian groups if they wish to pursue it. Legislation would be required for "grants" for many BIA functions but "contracting" is available now. If a major segment of the Indian community is interested in the "grant" approach the author believes that both State and Federal governments would be responsive, especially if early pilot projects were well administered.

Complete "self-determination" is the lot of very few, if any, individuals or groups in any organized society as there are many constraints on resources and conflicting economic and social pressures with which to contend. "Self-determination" on a subsidy basis and with a legally designated trustee is of necessity somewhat circumscribed as general tax revenues and statutory legal responsibilities are involved. However, as indicated, Indians as well as the rest of society, rarely exercise to the maximum all available options.

This analysis presents the writer's view on subject matter and procedure involved in Indian self-determination. These subjects and procedures have tremendous potential for expansion. Reservation planning and implementation through a geographically based budget would facilitate coordination of all efforts and is discreet enough to provide understandable and digestible indication of progress toward each reservation's goal.

Although the author believes the above, a touch of philosophical reminiscence may be in order.

When he first joined the Bureau of Indian Affairs in 1950, he was all fired up with the potential of effective action by the BIA helping Indians make real progress. In discussing this matter with a former administrative officer at that time, the administrative officer's comment was "The Indians will proceed at their own pace and what BIA does or does not do will not have much impact." This shook the author and he was inclined to discount this analysis. However, when one reviews the wild swings in Federal and State policies towards Indians, the frequent changes in policy priorities, and the ruptures that occur with changes in administration, it is easy to see that in this environment the only relatively stable factor has been the Indian community. They never know what to expect next from the Great White Father. What the administrative officer was saying is that the Indians have been controlling and will continue to control what they accept from the non-Indian society. Indians will determine their pace of adjustment. As pointed out in this study, and by other students of the subject, the Indians have to want to change, want to obtain an education, or want to operate a motel before there is any chance that these things will happen in any given reservation community situation. Effective educational, community, or economic development personnel suggest alternatives, sow ideas, stimulate, and "lead without seeming to lead." With Indian motivation, great leaps forward are possible.

CHAPTER ELEVEN

SUMMARY AND CONCLUSIONS

Looking over the historic sweep of Indian policy gives perspective on the Indian-State-Federal relations of today. Present responsibilities, services, attitudes and actions are based on the colorful, changing, and sometimes tragic events of the past.

The two historic policies of "assimilation" and "separation" are reflected in the development of educational programs and the remnants of the reservation system.

The frontal attack on Indian society and governmental institutions during the Allotment Act period of the 1880's and 1890's left its scars. The reversal of policy under the Indian Reorganization Act of the 1930's and the termination drive in the 1950's are both the basis for many tribal, State, and Federal attitudes and activities today.

The original assumption of full responsibility for relations with Indians by the Federal Government has been modified over the years. The attempt to snuff out tribal governments and Indian culture in the latter part of the last century has been reversed and increasing responsibilities are being placed on tribal governments.

Along with this, the Citizenship Act of 1924 made Indians the responsibilities of their respective States. State services to Indians have also been increasing, and States are developing a more positive view of their responsibilities to their Indian citizens. Reallocation of initiatives and responsibilities among tribal, State and Federal Governments is still in process. The revolutionary movements of our time have and will continue to affect Indians and may drastically rearrange these relationships.

Indians recognize the importance of State services and in general desire to work with local, State and Federal Governments toward a solution to their problems, but believe continued Federal responsibility for trust land, funding, and other services are still very essential.

Indians and the various governmental levels recognize that

Indian motivation, desire and action are the most crucial ingredients in Indian progress.

The two basic needs of Indian communities are education and employment. With education and an opportunity to work to their full potential, Indians could move rapidly toward economic self-sufficiency.

Indians are involved in the policy process with the Federal and State Governments, through local reservation planning, as members of Federal and State executive and legislative branches, as members of school boards, as members of boards of directors of Indian enterprises. Further involvement comes through lobbying with the Congress and State legislatures, and through participation in court actions affecting Indian rights.

Indians are going to college in increasing numbers and gaining experience in business and the professions. This trend will increase in geometric progression and the impact of sophisticated, able young Indians will provide the cutting edge for rapid change in the years ahead.

There is increasing recognition that the Federal system is also changing. States are no longer as independent as they used to be. In the past, the States and localities often did not give fair treatment to individuals—especially poor people and ethnic minorities. As described by Publius, "States rights" have now become "rights of first refusal." [1] If a State does not serve all of its citizens fairly the Federal Government will step in. National goals must be a unifying force, but there is need for the leeway of local option. This is evolving generally and for Indian government in particular. Indians see the need for improving their local governments which are afflicted by the same problems as other local governments. One of the comments of South Dakota's Coordinator of Indian Affairs was that tribes should be encouraged to "adopt more responsible forms of government" incorporated under Federal or State law, so that "Indian leaders . . . learn to work with State agencies, private enterprise, and, more important, make their own decisions." [2] And they are increasingly seeking to modernize their governing documents [3] and taking on important responsibilities.

[1] Publius, *New Federalist Paper #1*, duplicated, no date, but of recent origin.

[2] Vernon L. Ashley, Coordinator of Indian Affairs, response to Governors' Interstate Indian Council questionnaire.

[3] Nineteen tribes have proposed constitutional amendments either being reviewed by the BIA or being voted on by their memberships. Forty nine other tribes are

Truly effective local government, however, requires an adequate economic base and an ability to generate a good percentage of its own revenue.

To achieve maximum cooperation and support from the States, intertribal organizations could play an increasingly important role. Not only could they pressure the States for more service and higher quality service, but they can also work on the Federal Government for any necessary assistance to the States to provide the resources for effective action. State Indian activity is at a germinal stage—both on the part of the States' Indian citizens and the States themselves. Indian leadership and organization can play a decisive role in this development.[4]

Nationally, the Indians are experienced participants, and will continue to increase their effectiveness in dealing with the Executive Department and the Congress.

Indian leadership sees the advantages of Indian, local, State and Federal cooperation to achieve objectives. It will move to increase effective cooperation. In those States and localities in which the Indians constitute a significant voting bloc they have considerable leverage. In other situations, through effective public relations, they can accomplish seemingly impossible tasks. This is because the general public is concerned and wants to help.

The author believes that a consensus of Indian views on reservation objectives is already existent in many reservations and if appropriate teamwork can be developed among these communities and the local, State and Federal Governments, progress can be greatly facilitated. A high priority implementation of the concept of reservation planning and geographical budgeting by Indians would result in a large degree of actual "self-determination" through Indian determination of what programs would be carried out and how they are to be executed in their communities. The Executive and Legislative reviews and appropriations would primarily control the rate of progress consistent with funds available

---

considering changes and discussing possibilities with representatives of BIA. In the last month, three tribes adopted constitutional changes which have been approved by the Secretary.

Information from the Branch of Tribal Operations, BIA, July 19, 1971.

[4] The National Congress of American Indians (NCAI) recognizes this. "There are state funds and state programs which need to be looked into. Urban Indians are not getting their share of city services. NCAI would certainly support them in seeing they get a fair share of the pie." American Indian Press Association, Washington, D. C. M151, undated (1971).

under Executive and Legislative appropriation ceilings. Within the limits of available funds, Indians in large measure would direct and control the steps taken to reach their reservation objectives in those instances where they chose to follow this concept.

This proposal for action based on reservation plans and geographical budgets requires consistent support and followup over a period of time. Consistent support and followup have not occurred in the past, but I believe it can happen in the future. Indian leadership and governmental officials must agree on the basic concept and follow it through for a reasonable period. Action for the future should include:

Indian leadership on the reservations, the Federal executive, and the Congress should work out an agreement to coordinate all Federal aid and assistance through the use of separate long-range plans and goals for each reservation that desires to do so, and implement such programs with specific annual programs reflected in tribal and Federal agency budgets. Such budgets should be coordinated and integrated for the reservation and specific amounts should be specified for each reservation (geographical basis) in the budgeting and appropriation process. This would be a change from the present functionally oriented budgets and appropriations.

Reservation Indian leadership should increasingly take the lead in reservation planning and in specifying the content of the annual budget requests of Federal and State agencies for each reservation. BIA and other government personnel and private consultants should provide expertise, point out alternatives, and offer other assistance as desired by the Indian leadership in carrying out these important functions.

Federal funds should be provided those reservation tribes which do not have sufficient resources to support a minimum planning and budgeting function.

The Indians and the States should see to it that the Governors' Interstate Indian Council becomes an effective instrument for action—or abandon it for a more effective procedure. It cannot be effective without a minimum support staff to perform or coordinate necessary studies, prepare alternative policies for consideration, and provide followup and continuity. State and regional Indian groups should work closely with States to achieve maximum service.

The Congress should respond to current Indian requests to repeal HCR 108 (termination policy) and adopt a policy statement based on "Indian involvement" and "consent" and "support" for federally recognized Indians for as long as necessary, with no reference to "scheduling" progress or "cessation of services."

The above recommendations are primarily concerned with basic long run policy. In the short run, Indian, State, and Federal leaders should analyze the sum total of Indian community needs and their relationships to non-Indian community needs in the same geographic economic areas. Since two main needs of Indian groups are education (including training) and jobs, consideration should be given to assigning a priority to Indian communities to attack these two challenges on a crash basis. Doubling or tripling education funds for Indian children might be in order on the education front. A crash emergency employment program might be explored with Indians on the job front. It could be done fast, and might greatly assist in accomplishing the ultimate Indian community goals in a more expeditious fashion. It would also provide, as Schifter has pointed out, a pilot program which might be informative on possible broader applications for the economy as a whole.

With reservation planning as the base, the American Indian and all Americans can move forward together in building stronger communities, more viable States, and a Nation proud of its Indian heritage and Indian participation.

ppendix

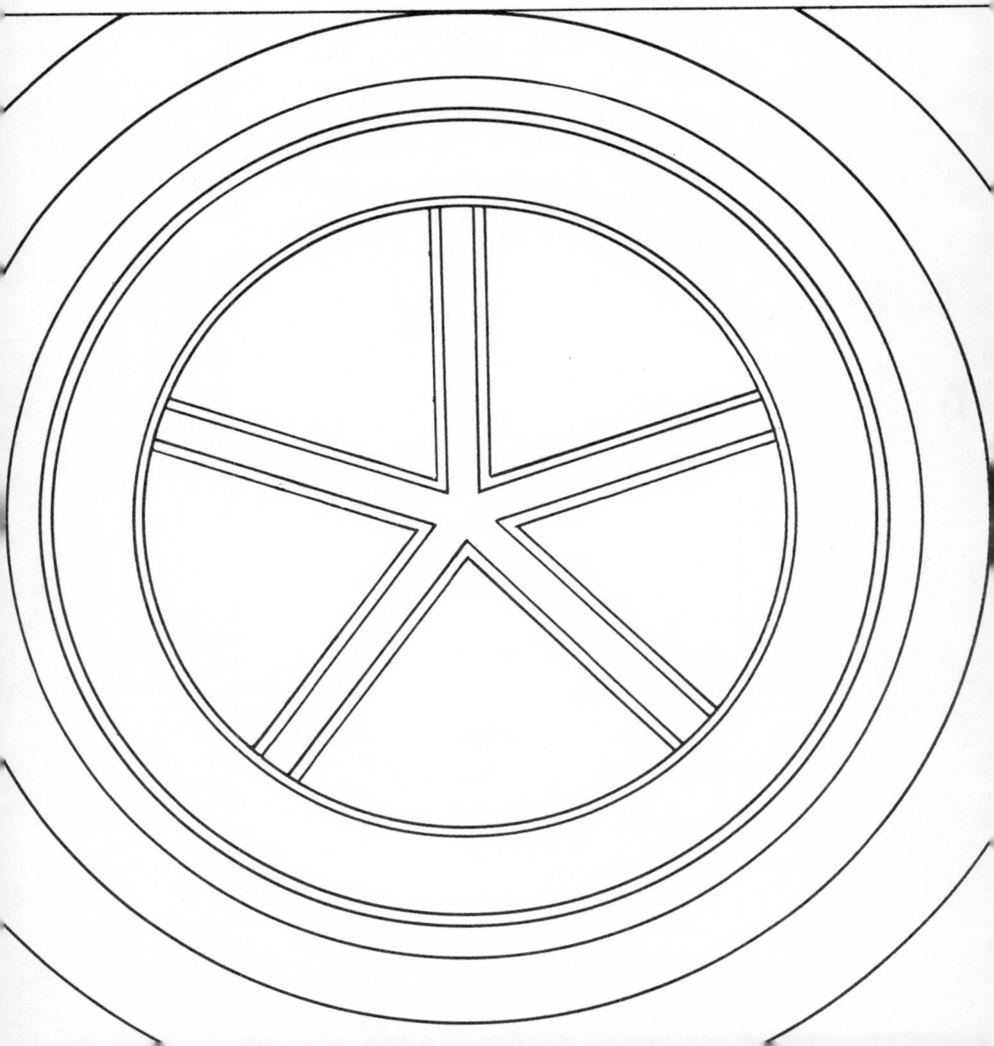

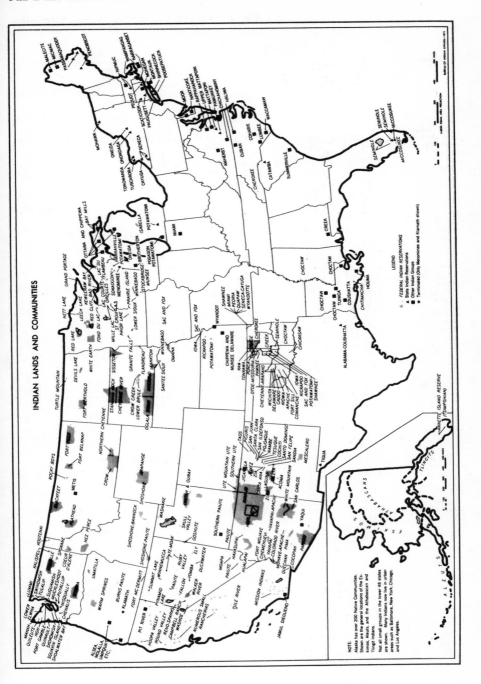

INDIAN LANDS AND COMMUNITIES

LEGEND

FEDERAL INDIAN RESERVATIONS
△ State Indian Reservations
● Other Indian Groups
✚ Terminated (Only Menominee and Klamath shown)

NOTE:
Alaska has over 200 Native Communities. Shown are the general locations of the Eskimo, Aleut, and the Athabascan and Tlingit Indians.

Not all small groups in the lower 48 states are shown. Many Indians now live in urban areas such as Baltimore, New York, Chicago, and Los Angeles.

175

APPENDIX B

Table 1.—Indian Population, Land, Education,

States	Population Total Population (All races) 1970 Advanced Census Report	Indian Population Total 1970 Census	Percent Indian	Federal Indian Areas March 1970 BIA	Percent State Responsibility	Land (Acres) Federal Trust June 30, 1970 Tribal	Allotted	State Reservation
U. S. Total or Number of States	203,184,772	827,091	.41	477,458	42.27	39,642,412.09	10,697,621.58	237,582.70
Alabama	3,444,165	2,514	.07	------	100.	------	------	-----
Alaska	302,173	51,528	17.05	56,795 [2]	0 [3]	87,635.70	18,003.77	-----
Arizona	1,772,482	95,812	5.41	115,002 [2]	0 [3]	19,363,995.73	259,269.28	-----
Arkansas	1,923,295	2,041	.11	------	100.	------	------	-----
California	19,953,134	91,018	.46	6,984	92.33	460,927.73	75,405.65	-----
Colorado	2,207,259	8,836	.40	1,764	80.04	750,110.64	4,969.50	-----
Connecticut	3,032,217	2,222	.07	------	100.	-----	-----	804.00
Delaware	548.104	656	.12	------	100.	-----	-----	-----
Florida	6,789,443	6,719	.10	1,286	80.86	79,014.06	-----	104,800.00 [4]
Georgia	4,589,575	2,455	.05	------	100.	-----	-----	-----
Hawaii	769,913	1,126	.15	------	100.	-----	-----	-----
Idaho	713,008	6,687	.94	5,121	23.42	413,161.20	373,796.09	-----
Illinois	11,113,976	11,413	.10	------	100.	-----	-----	-----
Indiana	5,193,669	3,887	.07	------	100.	-----	-----	-----
Iowa	2,825,041	2,992	.11	514	82.83	4,115.00	-----	-----
Kansas	2,249,071	8,672	.39	2,594	70.09	1,966.49	24,484.57	-----
Kentucky	3,219,311	1,599	.05	------	100.	-----	-----	-----
Louisiana	3,643,180	5,366	.15	268	95.01	262.23	-----	-----
Maine	993,663	2,195	.22	------	100.	-----	-----	22,600.00
Maryland	3,922,399	4,258	.11	------	100.	-----	-----	239.40
Massachusetts	5,689,170	4,475	.08	------	100.	-----	-----	120.00
Michigan	8,875,083	16,854	.19	1,026	93.92	7,875.51	9,242.19	-----
Minnesota	3,805,069	23,128	.61	11,023	52.34	682.731.51	51,977.20	-----
Mississippi	2,216,912	4,113	.19	3,127	23.98	17,381.37	1.00	-----
Missouri	4,677,399	5,405	.12	------	100.	-----	374.53	-----
Montana	694,409	27,130	3.91	22,592	16.73	1,791,862.62	3,355,988.99	-----
Nebraska	1,483,791	6,624	.45	2,499	62.27	17,178.21	44,341.52	-----
Nevada	488,738	7,933	1.62	4,697	40.79	1,061,182.18	79,125.86	-----
New Hampshire	737,681	361	.05	------	100.	-----	-----	-----
New Jersey	7,168,164	4,706	.07	------	100.	-----	-----	-----
New Mexico	1,016,000	72,788	7.16	76,835 [2]	0 [3]	6,141,752.27	681,154.02	-----
New York	18,190,740	28,330	.16	------	100.	-----	-----	103,719.00
North Carolina	5,082,059	43,487	.86	4,766	89.04	56,433.57	-----	-----
North Dakota	617,761	14,369	2.33	13,948	2.93	151,697.41	692,227.02	-----
Ohio	10,652,017	6,654	.06	------	100.	-----	-----	-----
Oklahoma	2,559,253	97,731	3.82	81,229	16.89	58,872.60	1,337,124.69	-----
Oregon	2,091,385	13,510	.65	2,835	79.02	517,698.34	167,974.85	-----
Pennsylvania	11,793,909	5,533	.05	------	100.	-----	-----	-----
Rhode Island	949,723	1,390	.15	------	100.	-----	-----	-----
South Carolina	2,590,516	2,241	.09	------	100.	-----	-----	600.00
South Dakota	666,257	32,365	4.86	29,707	8.21	2,041,086.41	2,693,543.29	-----
Tennessee	3,924,164	2,376	.06	------	100.	-----	-----	-----
Texas	11,196,730	18,132	.16	------	100.	-----	.16	3,243.30
Utah	1,059,273	11,273	1.06	5,999	46.78	2,215,909.90	55,088.19	-----
Vermont	444,732	229	.05	------	100.	-----	-----	-----
Virginia	4,648,494	4,904	.11	------	100.	-----	-----	1,457.00
Washington	3,409,169	33,386	.98	15,845	52.54	1,875.933.77	583,452.31	-----
West Virginia	1,744,237	808	.05	------	100.	-----	-----	-----
Wisconsin	4,417,933	18,924	.43	6,862	63.74	66,198.80	81,958.96	-----
Wyoming	332,416	4,980	1.50	4,140	16.87	1,777,428.84	108,117.94	-----
Washington, D.C.	756,510	956	.13	------	100.	-----	-----	-----

[1] Number of States.
[2] Alaska, Arizona, and New Mexico show more Indians in Federal service area than the 1970 Census totals for the State. BIA has not had a chance to review all pertinent data and review its service population figures.
[3] Some Indians are undoubtedly in urban areas and not receiving service from BIA. Complete Census detail not yet available to determine the number.
[4] Florida has also committed another 143,620 acres for Indian use bordering on the state reservation. The State has also dedicated three small parcels of land along the Tamiami Trail.
[5] Some Chitimachas in Federal school, included in Mississippi total.
[6] Maine has State reservation schools for elementary pupils on the reservations. These totals are the only students that Maine funds specially because they are Indians. All other Indians in the State are in the public schools on the same financial basis as any other children. The Maine figure for "public schools" and "other schools" are not included in totals.
[7] Figures only for Eastern Cherokee; do not cover Lumbees, the most numerous Indian group, none of whom are eligible for Federal schools.
[8] Figures only for federally recognized groups. Other Indians are State or private responsibility.

176

Law and Order and Other Services, 1970

Indian Commission or Equivalent	Director or Coordinator	Director's Staff	Federal Schools	Public Schools	Other	Tribal	State	Federal	Agencies and Field Offices	Hospitals and Facilities
	Special State Organization		Indian Education (5–18 year olds in school)			Law & Order (Jurisdiction)			BIA	IHS
17[1]	16[1]	14[1]	47,922	127,596	10,942	14[1]	45[1] X	16[1]	28[1]	19[1]
--	--	--		* All			X			
--	--	--	7,245	13,212	411	--	X	--	9	16
X	X	4	17,824	19,747	3,957	X	--	X	15	18
				All			X			
--	Pt. Time	--	--	All	--	--	X	--	12	--
--	--	--	65	622	18	X	--	X	3	1
--	--	--	--	All	--	--	X	--		
			--	All			X			
X	--	--	124	258	0	--	X	--	2	--
--	--	--	--	All	--	--	X	--		
X	--	--	73	1,569	58	X	X	X	2	3
--	--	--	--	All	--	--	X	--	2	--
			61	All			X			
X	X	--	44	152	5	--	X	--	1	--
--	--	--	--	1,196	0	--	X	--	2	1
--	--	--	--	All	--	--	X	--		
--	Comm.	10	--	All[5]	--	--	X	--		
				121[6]	213[6]		X			
--	--	--	--	All	--	--	X	--		
X	X	3	--	All	--	--	X	X		
X	X	3	23	2,995	207	X	X	X	3	3
--	--	--	1,237	263	14	X	--	X	1	1
				All			X			
X	X	2	769	8,274	939	X	X	X	10	8
X	X	1½	44	737	92	--	X	--	1	1
X	X	2	125	1,675	20	X	X	X	1	2
--	--	--	--	All	--	--	X	--		
X	X	2	8,733	20,377	1,855	X	X	X	13	12
X	X	4	--	All	--	--	X	--	1	--
--	--	--	1,155	533[7]	32	--	X	X	1	1
X	X	2	3,459	3,409	1,119	X	--	X	5	3
				All			X		1	
X	X	3	1,102	35,278	89	--	X	--	24	15
--	--	--	55	1,200	47	X	X	X	4	2
--	--	--	--	All	--	--	X	--		
--	--	--	--	All	--	--	X	--		
--	--	--	--	All	--	--	X	--		
X	X	2	4,347	5,167	1,553	X	X	X	8	10
--	--	--	--	All	--	--	X	--		
X	X	25	--	All	--	--	X	--	1	--
X	X	4	1,023	1,407	101	X	X	X	2	1
--	--	--	--	All	--	--	X	--		
--	--	--	--	All	--	--	X	--		
--	--	--	334	6,537	242	X	X	X	6	4
--	--	--	--	All	--	--	X	--		
--	--	--	--	1,947[8]	--	--	X	--	1	--
X	--	--	80	1,041	183	X	--	X	1	1
--	--	--	--	All	--	--	--	--	1	--
								Total	133	103

Federal trust land as of June 30, 1970, from Annual Report of Indian Land, BIA.
State reservation land figures from the States concerned.
Special State organization from answers to GIIC questionnaire by the States.
Indian Education statistics from "Statistics Concerning Indian Education" Fiscal Year 1970, BIA. (Figures do not total as Winnebago omitted from source and included here). Figures do not cover all Indians in public schools even in States listed, but are only figures reported by BIA.
Law and Order jurisdiction from information compiled by Branch of Judicial, Prevention and Enforcement Services, BIA, by telephone conversation with areas, June 1970.
BIA agencies, BIA Directory, October 1970 (includes area-wide offices, Indian agencies, independent irrigation districts, independent boarding schools, field employment assistance offices, industrial development offices.) Does not include over 200 schools under supervision of agencies. Does include Sherman, Phoenix, Haskell, Carter Seminary, Seneca Indian School, Chemawa, Chilocco, Riverside, Eufaula, Jones Academy. For example, there are 69 BIA schools in Alaska and only Mt. Edgecumbe and Wrangell schools are included in the above count.
Indian Health Service Hospitals and facilities, from information submitted by IHS.

177

TABLE II—State Attendance at Meetings
(also NCIO State Meeting,

	St. Paul	Salt Lake City	Oklahoma City	Helena	Phoenix	Carson City	Sun Valley	Santa Fe	Sheridan	Oklahoma City	St. Paul
		1950		1951	1952	1953	1954	1955	1956	1957	1958
	March 14	May 12	Dec. 7–8	Dec. 10–11	Dec. 5–6	Oct. 27–29	Sept 30 Oct 1–2	Oct. 5–7	Aug. 6–7	Oct. 24–26	Oct. 9–11
Alaska											
Arizona		x		x	x	x	x	x	x	x	x
California		x	x	x	x	x	x	x			x
Colorado					x			x	x	x	
Florida											x
Idaho		x	x	x	x	x	x		x	x	x
Iowa											
Kansas										x	x
Maine											
Michigan											
Minnesota	x	x	x	x	x	x	x	x	x	x	x
Mississippi											
Montana	x	x	x	x	x	x	x	x	x	x	x
Nebraska		x	x				x	x			x
Nevada					x	x	x		x	x	
New Mexico	x	x	x	x	x	x	x	x	x	x	
New York											x
North Carolina											
North Dakota	x	x	x	x	x	x	x	x	x	x	x
Oklahoma	x	x	x	x	x	x	x	x	x	x	x
Oregon		x	x	x	x	x	x	x	x	x	x
South Dakota	x	x	x	x	x	x	x	x	x	x	x
Texas							x	x	x	x	
Utah	x	x	x	x	x	x	x	x	x	x	x
Washington	x	x	x	x	x	x	x	x	x	x	x
Wisconsin	x	x		x	x		x	x	x	x	x
Wyoming		x			x	x	x	x	x		x
Illinois											
Navajo Nation											
Ohio											
Virginia											
Total	9	15	12	13	16	14	17	16	16	16	17

**of the Governors' Interstate Indian Council
1969, Lake Tahoe)**

Sylvan Lake S.D.	Palm Springs	Missoula	Phoenix	Boise	Denver	Santa Fe	Tulsa	Reno	Wichita	Rapid City	Tulsa	Total	1969 L. Tahoe NCIO
1959 Sept. 22–24	1960 Nov. 13–15	1961 Aug. 13–16	1962 Oct. 14–17	1963 Sept. 22–25	1964 Sept. 23–26	1965 Aug. 9–11	1966	1967 Oct. 18–20	1968 Sept. 25–27	1969 Sept. 10–12	1970 June 11–13		
					x	x	x	x		x	x	6	x
		x	x	x	x	x	x	x	x	x	x	19	x
		x		x	x	x	x	x	x	x		16	x
				x	x		x	x	x	x	x	11	x
				x		x	x	x			x	6	x
		x	x	x	x	x	x	x	x	x	x	19	x
		x		x	x	x	x	x	x			7	x
		x	x		x	x	x	x	x	x		9	x
									x			1	x
										x	x	2	x
		x	x								x	14	x
											x	1	x
		x	x	x	x	x	x	x	x	x	x	21	x
			x								x	7	x
				x			x	x	x	x	x	11	x
			x	x	x	x	x	x	x	x	x	19	x
		x	x	x	x	x	x	x	x	x	x	11	x
							x	x	x	x		4	x
		x	x	x	x	x	x	x	x	x	x	21	x
		x	x		x	x	x	x	x	x	x	20	x
		x	x	x	x	x	x	x	x	x		19	x
		x	x	x	x	x	x	x	x	x	x	21	x
			x	x	x	x	x	x	x	x	x	13	x
		x	x	x	x		x	x			x	18	x
		x	x	x	x	x	x	x	x	x	x	21	x
		x	x	x	x	x	x	x	x	x	x	19	x
		x	x	x	x	x	x	x	x			15	x
													x
													x
													x
													x
		16	16	18	19	18	22	22	20	19	20	351	31

TABLE III—Termination Legislation
Based on Policy of H. Con. Res. 108 of August 1, 1953
(Listed Alphabetically)

Tribe	Date of Act	Date of Termination	Tribal Membership	Tribal Land (Acres)
Alabama-Coushatta Tribes of Texas	6/23/54 (68 Stat. 768)	7/1/55	450 (est.)	3,200
California Rancherias and Reservations	8/18/58 (72 Stat. 619) 8/11/64 (78 Stat. 390)	35 rancherias as of 6/30/69	1,107	4,315.5
Catawba Indians of South Carolina	9/21/59 (73 Stat. 592)	7/1/62	631 (final roll)	3,388
Klamath Tribe of Oregon	8/13/54 (68 Stat. 718)	8/13/61	2,133 (final roll)	862,662
Menominee Tribe of Wisconsin	6/17/54 (68 Stat. 250)	4/30/61	3,270 (final roll)	233,881
Ottawa Tribe of Oklahoma	8/3/56 (70 Stat. 963)	Proclamation deferred until claim settled*	630 (final roll)	0
Paiute Indians of Utah	9/1/54 (68 Stat. 1099)	3/1/57	232 (est.)	42,839
Peoria Tribe of Oklahoma	8/2/56 (70 Stat. 937)	Proclamation deferred until claim settled*	640 (final roll)	0
Ponca Tribe of Native Americans of Nebraska	9/5/62 (76 Stat. 937)	10/27/66	442	834
Uintah & Ouray Ute Mixed Bloods of Utah	8/27/54 (68 Stat. 868)	8/27/61	490 (final roll)	211,430
Western Oregon Indians (60 bands)	8/13/54 (68 Stat. 724)	8/18/56	2,081 (est.)	3,158
Wyandotte Tribe of Oklahoma	8/1/56 (70 Stat. 893)	Deferred by disposition of cemetery	1,157 (final roll)	94.36
Totals			13,263	1,365,801.86

*Although tribal claims determination has delayed formal termination of trusteeship of these tribes, it has been completed in most respects and tribal members are no longer receiving Bureau aid.

Table IV—Funds Paid to States for Indian Education by Bureau of Indian Affairs, Fiscal Year 1970

State	Total Amounts (Johnson-O'Malley contracts)	Number of Students
Alaska	$ 2,594,000	2,851
Arizona	3,668,843	14,322
California	25,300	--
Colorado	182,427	733
Florida	28,000	216
Idaho	395,000	1,496
Iowa	113,000	152
Kansas	48,000	134
Minnesota	796,500	2,680
Mississippi	5,250	19
Montana	577,987	4,287
Nebraska	282,000	741
Nevada	141,500	1,593
New Mexico	2,197,487	12,620
North Dakota	441,200	1,639
Oklahoma	1,015,000	16,081
South Dakota	1,197,000	4,058
Utah	11,223	16
Washington	560,000	4,823
Wisconsin	326,500	1,269
Wyoming	70,000	217
Peripheral Dormitories	1,716,069	2,134
Totals	$16,392,286	72,081

Table V.—Metropolitan Areas with 500 or More Indians

The 1970 Census, Table 67, "Race of the Population for Areas and Places," provides the following population figures for "Standard Metropolitan Statistical Areas":

	Percent	Number
White	86.49	120,578,729
Negro	12.03	16,770,610
Indian	.22	307,867
Japanese	.36	505,522
Chinese	.29	405,546
Filipino	.21	289,781
All other	.40	560,756
Total	100.00	139,418,811

Of the 827,091 Indians reported in the Census, 307,867 (37%) live in "Standard Metropolitan Statistical Areas." This metropolitan Indian group, however, is less than one quarter of one percent (.22) of the total metropolitan population.

Those "Standard Metropolitan Statistical Areas" with 500 or more Indians are:

Arizona
Phoenix   11,159
Tucson   8,837

Arkansas)
Oklahoma)
Fort Smith   3,812

California
Anaheim ⎫
Santa Ana ⎬   3,920
Garden Grove ⎭
Bakersfield   2,039
Fresno   2,144
Los Angeles ⎫
Long Beach ⎬   24,509
Modesto   686
Oxnard ⎫
Ventura ⎬   1,150
Sacramento   3,559
Salinas ⎫
Monterey ⎬   1,139
San Bernadino ⎫
Riverside ⎬   6,378
Ontario ⎭
San Diego   5,880
San Francisco ⎫
Oakland ⎬   12,011
San Jose   4,048
Santa Barbara   1,008
Santa Rosa   1,623
Stockton   1,218
Vallejo ⎫
Napa ⎬   1,263

Colorado
Colorado Springs   639
Denver   4,348

District of Columbia
Washington, D. C. ⎫
Maryland ⎬   3,300
Virginia ⎭

Florida
Ft. Lauderdale ⎫
Hollywood ⎬   664
Miami   1,085
Pensacola   517

Tampa ⎫
St. Petersburg ⎬   811

Georgia
Atlanta   893

Hawaii
Honolulu   996

Illinois
Chicago   8,996

Indiana
Gary   504
Indianapolis   767

Iowa
Sioux City, Iowa, ⎫
          Nebr. ⎬   865

Kansas
Topeka   981
Wichita   1,977

Louisiana
New Orleans   885

Maryland
Baltimore   2,553

Mass.–R. I.
Boston   2,132
Providence ⎫
Pawtucket ⎬   909
Warwick ⎭

Michigan
Detroit   5,683
Flint   635
Grand Rapids   1,311
Lansing   772

Minnesota-Wisc.
Duluth-Superior   1,781
Minneapolis ⎫
St. Paul ⎬   9,852

Missouri
Kansas City   2,402
St. Louis, Mo., Ill.   1,931

Montana
Billings   1,063

Great Falls	1,509	*Oregon*	
Nebraska		Eugene	764
Lincoln	531	Portland-Wash.	4,011
Omaha-Iowa	1,401	Salem	1,104
Nevada		*Pennsylvania*	
Las Vegas	1,131	Phila., N.J.	3,631
Reno	1,926	Pittsburgh	847
New Jersey		*South Dakota*	
Newark	1,214	Sioux Falls	591
Paterson ⎫		*Texas*	
Clifton ⎬	655	Dallas	5,022
Passaic ⎭		El Paso	576
New Mexico		Ft. Worth	1,610
Albuquerque	5,839	Houston	3,215
New York		San Antonio	975
Buffalo	5,775	*Utah*	
Rochester	1,446	Ogden	511
New York, N.Y.	12,160	Provo ⎫	613
Syracuse	2,458	Orem ⎭	
North Carolina		Salt Lake City	2,005
Charlotte	850	*Virginia*	
Fayetteville	3,199	Norfolk ⎫	851
Greensboro ⎫		Portsmouth ⎬	
Winston Salem ⎬	1,169	Richmond	635
High Point ⎭		*Washington*	
Ohio		Seattle ⎫	9,496
Cincinnati, Ohio, ⎫	797	Everett ⎭	
Ky.-Ind. ⎭		Spokane	1,988
Cleveland	1,750	Tacoma	3,343
Columbus	661	*Wisconsin*	
Oklahoma		Appleton-Oshkosh	1,434
Lawton	3,343	Green Bay	1,695
Oklahoma City	13,033	Milwaukee	4,075
Tulsa	15,519		

SUMMARY OF POLICY STATEMENT AND RESOLUTIONS, 1969 MEETING, GOVERNORS' INTERSTATE INDIAN COUNCIL

The Policy Statement and Resolutions adopted at the 1969 meeting (Report of the Twenty-Second Annual Meeting, Governors' Interstate Indian Council (GIIC), Rapid City, S. Dak., September 10–12, 1969) give a flavor of the current thinking of the Council. The analysis that follows concentrates on the Council's view of the Federal-State-Indian relationships, and what the respective responsibilities of each should be.

EDUCATION

Education is a responsibility at all levels. After stressing the importance of education "to the development of each individual's capacity to meet his responsibilities to himself and his community", the statement emphasized the necessity for ". . . the support of parents and their assumption of responsibility for development in their children of acceptable standards for personal advancement, their use of educational work opportunities, the assumption of moral and social obligations and the preservation of traditional cultural values."

Education of Indian students could be improved by:
1. New and expanded individual Indian student guidance services by existing school systems.
2. Adequate financial support from Federal sources until each State, on an individual option basis, can finance the education of Indian students.
3. Continued research into the high dropout of Indian students from school, with specific recommendations as to how this loss of human resources can be best corrected.
4. Cooperation among Tribal Councils, local public school officials, officials of State Departments of Education, and the Bureau of Indian Affairs (BIA), in developing opportunities for all pupils, Indian and non-Indian, not only for formal education, but also for further training after leaving school.
5. A continuing preschool program to meet the needs of this age group is urged.
6. More college scholarships are fundamental to Indian development.

Although a majority of Indian school children are in public schools, the Council supports the historical theme of adequate Federal support until each State is able to finance the education of its Indian students. The underlying assumption appears to be eventual State operation and support of public schools for Indian children. Cooperation among tribal councils, local governments, State Governments, and the

Bureau of Indian Affairs (BIA) for formal education and training after leaving school is highlighted. In another part of the policy statement special emphasis is placed on each State Government cooperating with the BIA on adult education and vocational training.

ECONOMIC DEVELOPMENT

The Council endorsed economic development and employment of Indian people on reservations to the fullest potential. "Technical branches of the Federal and State Governments should provide efficient services in the development of the economic potential of the reservations."

Further, "the Bureau of Indian Affairs in cooperation with Indian Tribes, local non-Indian communities and State and county industrial development organizations should work together to develop job opportunities for Indian people through the utilization of reservation resources and by attracting suitable industries to the area."

The Council endorsed the use of Department of Commerce funds for reservation development, but noted that "numerous economic planners" were "meeting with Indian reservations" and "yet none or at best, very few projects are actually planned or initiated", and resolved "that each governor having small reservations investigate with Economic Development Administration (EDA) and BIA to determine clear-cut objectives or goals, and also to align economic development services to Indians under either BIA or the appropriate State agency through 'cross funding' by using Department of Commerce funds."

Here the Council views it to be the responsibility of both the State and Federal Governments to work with tribes and suggests that the governors take the lead in assigning coordination responsibility for planning and encouragement of industry on small reservations. Large reservations could deal directly with EDA and other fund sources.

HEALTH

"Cooperative relationships among tribal governments, governmental health agencies and the medical profession for developing and coordinating health services for Indian people" should be emphasized.

The Council also requested the Department of Health, Education, and Welfare (HEW) ". . . to study and propose a new system of Indian Health Services that would allow the Indian patient medical services at the nearest facility of his choice" as "some Indian people would prefer to use the same medical service as other citizens." Here again is emphasis on a cooperative approach by Indians, State, Federal Government, and the profession involved, with the implied eventual objective of Indian health services being administered in the same manner as for other citizens. Federal financing is still a key aspect, otherwise they would not have to worry about HEW adjusting its program.

ADULT EDUCATION AND VOCATIONAL TRAINING

The Council urged ". . . that each State Government provide its Indian communities with all information on Federal and State aid available to them" for adult education and vocational training, and "each State Government should cooperate with the Bureau of Indian Affairs."

The Council recognized adult and vocational education as important in "alleviation of sub-standard economic conditions in Indian communities", but was positive in stating that these programs were supplemental to elementary, secondary, and higher education programs.

TERMINATION OF FEDERAL OR STATE SUPERVISION

The Governors' Interstate Indian Council believes that no plan or proposal to terminate Federal or state supervision over any Indian tribe, band or reservation should be considered which does not have the understanding and acceptance of tribal authorities, their constituents, State executive, legislative and judicial branches, Federal agencies and other political subdivisions concerned. Such understanding should include all factors; economic, social and political, which affect the governmental levels involved.

The above reflects a concern over possible State termination as well as Federal.

WELFARE SERVICES TO INDIANS

There is particular need for more adequate child welfare services to be developed in cooperation with tribal, State and Federal Governments. It is the responsibility at each level of government to make certain that information regarding public welfare services is available to Indian people and that they also are aware of restrictions in the programs. It is a particular responsibility of tribal governments to keep informed regarding public welfare services and to help individual Indians to take advantage of such services.

INDIAN TREATIES

The Governors' Interstate Indian Council recognizes the existence of Indian treaties entered into in good faith by the several tribes and the United States Government or State Governments. These treaties constitute moral and legal obligations which must be recognized by the Federal Government and State Governments. Federal or State programs which adversely affect any treaty rights, whether water, land or mineral, or cause an adverse impact on tribal development policies should be given full consideration in the light of existent treaties. In addition, such programs of Federal or State Governments should respect and honor the provisions of all treaties applicable to both parties, granting the right of Indian tribal members to give final approval to programs which might tend to violate treaty provisions.

COORDINATION OF INDIAN PROGRAMS

The Council recognized the seeking of funds from all Federal sources by State-wide Indian Community Action Program (CAP) Agencies and "the resultant amassing of government service outside of state government" resulted "in greater bureaucracy and red tape that is frustrating and confusing to all concerned. . . ." Pointing out that ". . . there is great educational value in local Indian program management" the Council resolved that ". . . each represented governor take appropriate administrative action or recommend legislation to allow each state Indian Commission or other appropriate coordinating state agency to assume all

Indian program approval, except approval on those services currently maintained by and within the Bureau of Indian Affairs or Indian Health Service, and, large tribes with Indian Community Action Programs." Such commission or other appropriate State agency was to work "intimately and directly with each local Indian group."

EXPANSION OF INDIAN ELIGIBILITY FOR FEDERAL GRANT-IN-AID

The Council pointed out that ". . . There has been a reluctance of the Federal agencies to budget programs for some states who have assumed various services to their Indian reservations" and that certain grant-in-aid agencies "made vague distinctions between Federal and non-Federal Indians which affected the eligibility of those state Indians for Federal assistance." It was recommended that grant-in-aid programs be reviewed and modified to make non-Federal Indians eligible, and that the Governors work through their congressional delegations for appropriate legislation "to assure elimination of these distinctions."

GENERAL POLICY VIEWS

The Council believed that closer "cooperation and coordination" was needed among Federal, State, and local agencies concerning services, facilities, planning and development for Indians. It emphasized that at least one of each State's three delegates "be a member of the administrative staff of the respective Governor's office" for most effective implementation by States of council actions. The Council also went on record that

. . . Indians should be full participants in the decision-making processes which affect their lives and futures. To this end, the Council endorses the assignment of increased decision-making powers to Tribal governing bodies.

NOTE:
The GIIC as an organization has evolved. To emphasize the importance of effective communication with the States, policy was revised in 1965 to provide for three delegates from each member State—with one of them to be an Indian and another to be a member of the Governor's staff. This formula was reemphasized in 1969. The Council has also moved toward more Indian participation and involvement. The members indicated in 1966 that in the past, they had spent too much time listening to Federal representatives explain programs without very much discussion and involvement on the part of participants. In 1966, Raymond Nakai, Chairman of the Navajo Tribe, made the keynote address. In addition, tribal leaders were on panels and responsible for various aspects of the program. Since then, Indian representatives have been much more active. However, on balance, the Council seems to lack continuity and effectiveness as now constituted and operated.

LIST OF TRIBES AND
DRAFT LEGISLATION SUBMITTED BY
MR. ZIMMERMAN IN 1947

CLASSIFICATION OF TRIBES SUBMITTED TO COMMITTEE

In responding to the request of the Senate Committee on Post Office and Civil Service, Acting Commissioner William Zimmerman, Jr. submitted a list of tribes in three groups: Group 1 could be released immediately from Federal supervision; Group 2 in 10 years; and Group 3, indefinite time.[1]

GROUP 1
Flathead
Hoopa
Klamath
Menominee
Mission
New York
Osage
Potawatomi
Sacramento
Turtle Mountain (conditionally)

GROUP 2—10 YEARS
Blackfeet
Cherokee
Cheyenne River
Colville (subject to restoration of ceded lands)
Consolidated Chippewa
Crow (special legislation)
Fort Belknap
Fort Peck (irrigation and power)
Fort Totten (no resources)
Grand Ronde (no resources)
Great Lakes (no resources)
Northern Idaho
Quapaw (in part, Wyandotte, Seneca)
Taholah, Tulalip (consolidation, in part)
Tomah
Umatilla

Warm Springs
Wind River (Shoshone only)
Winnebago (Omaha still predominantly full-blood)

GROUP 3
Cheyenne and Arapaho
Choctaw
Colorado River
Consolidated Ute (claims recoveries)
Crow Creek
Five Tribes (Oklahoma policy and legislation)
Fort Apache
Fort Berthold
Fort Hall
Hopi
Jicarilla
Kiowa
Mescalero
Navajo
Pawnee
Pima
Pine Ridge
Quapaw (in part)
Red Lake
Rocky Boy
Rosebud
San Carlos
Sells
Seminole

[1] *Hearings on S. Res. 41, Post Office and Civil Service Officers and Employees of the Federal Government* (Washington, D.C.: 80th Cong., 1st sess., U.S. Senate, 1947), pt. 1, p. 547.

Shawnee
Sisseton
Standing Rock (re State's ability)
Taholah, Tulalip (in part)
Tongue River
Truxton Canyon
Uintah and Ouray

United Pueblos (if submarginal lands
are added to reservation and if
franchise granted, then perhaps in
class II)
Western Shoshone
Wind River (Arapaho only)
Yakima

Zimmerman, as requested, also submitted drafts of sample legislation involving three alternate routes for termination.[2]

INCORPORATION PROPOSALS

The Klamath, Osage, and Menominee proposals provided for incorporation and the transfer of functions performed by the Bureau to the tribe. Each proposal was different due to different tribal situations, but each proposal provided for tribal consent before incorporation was effective. All three proposals were for Federal charters, and the Secretary of the Interior retained some responsibilities as spelled out in the drafts. The Klamath charter provided for the transfer of tribal trust property to the corporation, but prohibited sale of trust land to other than members of the Tribe and only with the consent of the Secretary. The corporation could acquire allotted land if the allottee and the Secretary concurred. Enrolled members received stock certificates in the corporation; adult members could sell their certificates, but not to any white person. The corporation was to have a life of 50 years.

Since the primary resource of the Osage Tribe was oil, each member's voting strength in the corporation was to be determined by his percentage of ownership interest in oil (headright interest). The corporation would administer the mineral estate and its operating expenses could be taken from lease income. The Interior Department could inspect the books and property, and if misuse was discovered, the matter would be reported to the U. S. District Attorney for action in Federal Court. There was no time limitation in this charter.

The Menominee charter placed authority in the corporation to manage the Tribe's resources, including the operation of the Menominee Indian Mills, the primary source of tribal and individual income. The corporation was not prohibited from selling tribal land but could "prevent" its sale without the consent of the Tribe. This is a broader authority than that proposed for Klamath. In managing its assets, the corporation was authorized to negotiate with Federal, State, local governments, eleemosynary institutions, or other corporations. Stock certificates could only to go to other members of the Tribe. All trust lands, including lands purchased after incorporation, were to be held in trust, ". . . inalienable and nontaxable for a period of 50 years." Any corporation salary in excess of $2,500 per annum "may be reviewed by the Commissioner of Indian Affairs", and bonds for corporate officials would be in such amounts as specified by the Commissioner.

The Commissioner of Indian Affairs continued to be responsible for the sustained yield management of the Menominee forests.

The Secretary, with a 90-day notice, could revoke the Menominee charter if the conditions leading to the notice were not corrected in the 90-day period.

---

[2] Ibid., pp. 544–547, with discussion following.

STATE CONTROL

The two "State control" proposals had different approaches. A Joint Indian Welfare Board was proposed for California composed of two Indians (appointed by ten governors from a list submitted by the "organized California Indians") , two State officials, and one Federal representative appointed by the Secretary of the Interior. This board would provide some services needed by Indians, including protection of property, except those indicated in the following paragraph; administer the California judgment fund; and finance its work from State and Federal contributions and from available judgment funds.

Law enforcement would be transferred to the State and counties; present Indian lands in trust status would be retained for a definite period (not specified) . Cooperatives under State or Federal law would be authorized by the joint board to manage tribal lands. Allottee lands could be administered by such cooperatives if desired by the allottee. Fee patents of trust allotments had to have approval of the joint board; the allottees waived right "to any special Federal Indian gratuity services for himself and family" upon application for and receipt of fee patent. "Organized tribes and groups may make contributions to counties and school districts in lieu of taxes while land remains in trust." The proposal was based on the requirement of approval of both the Congress and the California legislature.

For North Dakota the Commissioner proposed a contract (based on legislation to be obtained and Indian approval) between the Federal Government and the State providing for:

Payment of $224,688 annually for 10 years by the Federal Government to the State in lieu of taxes on Indian trust property.

Reduction of Federal payment would be made in appropriate ratio as Indian trust property became taxable.

Transfer Federal facilities (school buildings, etc.) to the State.

Provision of all necessary governmental services to Indians by the State (e.g., health, education, welfare, law and order, resource services, roads) .

Preparation of a plan for presentation to the Congress by the Bureau and North Dakota which provides "for the administration of affairs of Indians of North Dakota or for the discontinuation of State or Federal administration." If no agreement reached, the contract could provide for the continuation of administration by the State.

Approval of sale of trust land by a committee consisting of a State appointee, a BIA appointee, and one Indian ex-officio from the appropriate reservation.

Administration by the State of all trust land transactions and services for all transactions not involving land going out of trust.

Examination of State records by BIA and authorization for amendment or discontinuance of the contract by the Congress at any time before the expiration of 10 years.

INDIVIDUAL TERMINATION

The draft presented to the Committee authorized the Secretary to require an Indian applicant for a patent-in-fee to waive all special services as an Indian; and authorized the tribe to adopt regulations, which, when approved by the Secretary, would require the applicant to relinquish all membership and property rights in the tribe. The Indian receiving a patent-in-fee under the above conditions would receive a certificate indicating that he ". . . shall have all the benefits of and be subject to the laws, both civil and criminal, of the State. . . ." [3]

---

[3] Ibid. The Senate Committee apparently lost interest in these proposals when Mr. Zimmerman pointed out that there might not be any significant savings to the Federal Government if these proposals were adopted. Ibid., pp. 566–568.

HOUSE SELECT COMMITTEE COMMENTS ON EDUCATION, LAW AND ORDER, AND RELATIONS TO STATES, 1944[1]

As the Committee saw it, Indian education had the following inadequacies:[2]

(a) Irregular and indifferent school attendance on the part of many Indian children; (b) inferior and impossible home conditions to which many Indian children are compelled to return after school hours and during the summer vacation; (c) courses of study which fail either to equip an Indian child to practice, successfully, a vocation or to inspire and equip him to seek higher education; (d) a tendency in many reservation day schools to "adapt the education to the Indian and to his reservation way of life" rather than to "adapt the Indian to the habits and requirements he must develop to succeed as an independent citizen earning his own way off the reservation"; (e) inadequate opportunity for Indian students to secure standard high-school education and training in junior and senior colleges or universities so that the Indian can develop talented leaders of his own race and so that able Indian students can enter the professions or secure advanced vocational training.

The Committee recommended upgrading instruction to the general non-Indian level, compulsory school attendance, scholarships to encourage higher learning, and commented on the general goal of education:[3]

The goal of Indian education should be to make the Indian child a better American rather than to equip him simply to be a better Indian. The goal of our whole Indian program should be, in the opinion of your committee, to develop better Indian Americans rather than to perpetuate and develop better American Indians. The present Indian education program tends to operate too much in the direction of perpetuating the Indian as a special-status individual rather than preparing him for independent citizenship.

Then the Committee tackled the way to achieve this goal.[4]

The Indian Bureau is tending to place too much emphasis on the day school located on the Indian reservations as compared with the opportunities afforded Indian children in off-the-reservation boarding schools where they can acquire an education in healthful and cultural surroundings without the handicap of

---

[1] *Report, No. 2091, Pursuant to H. Res. 166, a Resolution Creating a Select Committee of the Indian Affairs Committee to Make an Investigation to Determine whether the Changed Status of the Indian Requires a Revision of the Laws and Regulations Affecting the American Indian* (Washington, D. C.: 78th Cong., 2nd sess., U. S. House of Representatives, December 23, 1944).

[2] Ibid., p. 8. It is interesting to note the criticism of curricula oriented to Indian culture; today the criticism is *on the opposite tack.*

[3] Ibid., p. 9.

[4] Ibid., p. 9.

having to spend their out-of-school hours in tepees, in shacks, with dirt floors and no windows, in tents, in wickiups, in hogans, or in surroundings where English is never spoken, where there is a complete lack of furniture, and where there is sometimes an active antagonism or an abysmal indifference to the virtues of education.

If real progress is to be made in training the Indian children to accept and appreciate the white man's way of life, the children of elementary school age who live in violently substandard homes on reservations should be encouraged to attend off-the-reservation boarding schools where they can formulate habits of life equipping them for independent citizenship when they reach maturity.

The Committee visited both day schools and off-reservation boarding schools and was impressed with the boarding schools, especially as a means of working effectively[5] ". . . in the direction of educating the Indian to acquire ambitions and attitudes above the level of ordinary reservation life."

Commissioner Collier had informed the Committee that the[6] ". . . . Indians are the most rapidly increasing population in the United States." And the Committee commented that the country could not afford delay in adopting policies ". . . which will incorporate this rapidly growing group into our society on a self-supporting and self-respecting basis . . ." becoming ". . . independent American citizens of Indian descent."

The Committee also directed its attention to substituting State administration for Federal:[7]

Finally, your committee recommends that careful consideration should also be given the possibility of gradually shifting from Federal to State administration such features of the Indian Service as education, health, extension service, and law enforcement. Where this is done, the Federal Government should appropriate the money required to fulfill its obligation to the Indian but the administration of these services could be left to the States in which the Indians live with real economy to the Federal Government and with appreciable improvement in the results. In Minnesota, for example, the education of the Indian children is now largely handled on this basis with highly satisfactory and encouraging results.

We also recommend that careful study be given by State and Federal law-enforcement agencies as to the wisdom and practicability of moving toward concurrent jurisdiction in all matters of law enforcement including game laws, health and sanitation provisions, and compulsory school-attendance legislation.[8]

Congressman Gilchrist in the minority report went even further:[9]

Most of the States, and in fact all of them which have large Indian populations, are too prone and too anxious to pass the buck to the Federal Government. Such States want the Federal Government to foot the bills for a hundred things that the State government and local authorities ought to pay. I observed

---

[5] Ibid., p. 10. The Committee also recommended " . . . that copies of all elementary courses of study and of all textbooks used by the Indian educational service be placed on file with the House Committee on Indian Affairs, so that continuing attention can be given to the development of more appropriate training for young Indian children."

[6] Ibid., p. 11. Later in the Report the Committee states: "We feel competent Indians should be encouraged to leave the reservation and to earn their living as independent citizens, free from all contacts with the Indian Bureau." Ibid., p. 16.

[7] Ibid., p. 14.

[8] Ibid., p. 17.

[9] Ibid., pp. 20-21.

many instances of this on the trip which I made with the other members of the subcommittee. In the final end the Federal Government should not be required or expected to pay the expense of the upkeep of the Indians or their food, clothing, or hospitalization and education except as the Federal Government pays for such things in other cases and for white and other people. The Indians can never be assimilated into the body politic of white men while the Indians are mendicants and while the States expect them to remain such. The local authorities have a responsibility in this regard which should not be placed on the Federal Government. States and local authorities have many duties which are commonly exercised by them on behalf of white people, and we should look forward to the time when this same kind of supervision will be given by local people to Indians. This cannot be done at once, but it is an object toward which we should strive.

In defense of their position the States say "Oh, the Federal Government is guardian of the Indian." This is a mere slogan. There is no statute which makes the Federal Government such a guardian.

HOOVER COMMISSION[1]
RECOMMENDATIONS
AND MINORITY REPORTS

The Commission recommended:

... that, pending achievement of the goal of complete integration, the administration of social programs for the Indians should be progressively transferred to State governments.

The States should receive appropriate recompense from Federal funds until Indian taxes can help carry the load. The transfer to the States should be accompanied by diminishing activities by the Bureau of Indian Affairs.

The Commission stressed "creative Federalism":[2]

The Commission recommends that all agencies concerned with Indian affairs, including State and local governments, should take part in comprehensive planning of programs to carry out this policy.

Three Commissioners took issue with the majority. Vice Chairman Dean Acheson pointed out that the recommendations went beyond reorganization and improved efficiency:[3]

We are to integrate the Indian, remove "surplus" Indians from Indian lands, put the lands into private, individual, or corporate ownership, remove tax exemption, and, as soon as possible, merge the Indian, his life and lands with those of the people of the State where he resides, subject entirely to State jurisdiction.

These recommendations seem to me beyond our jurisdiction. If they are said to fall within it because they abolish functions of the executive branch, it is equally true that they change substantive legislative policy established by the legislative branch. We have neither the right nor the duty to enter this field. On occasion common sense may tell us not to draw too fine a line.

But, for me, this is not such an occasion. I have not the knowledge nor the time, in view of the vast amount of material before this Commission, to acquire it, to pass judgment whether the policy recommended is wise, just, and understanding. Recollections of the painful history which surrounds the cases of the Cherokee Nation v. The State of Georgia (5 Peters I) and Worcester v. Georgia (6 Peters 534) make a novice in this field pause before endorsing a recommendation to assimilate the Indian and to turn him, his culture, and his means of livelihood over to State control.

---

[1] Commission on Organization of the Executive Branch of the Government, *A Report to the Congress on Social Security, Education, and Indian Affairs*, March 1940.

[2] Ibid., p. 65. The Commission recommended transfer of the Bureau of Indian Affairs (BIA) to a new Department proposed as the successor to the Social Security Agency "pending discontinuance of all specialized Indian activity on the part of the Federal Government." p. 71.

[3] Ibid., pp. 77–78.

Commissioner James H. Rowe, Jr., agreed with Acheson and also questioned moving the Bureau of Indian Affairs (BIA) land functions from Interior.[4]

Commissioner James Forrestal was concise:[5]

> The task force on Indian Affairs and the Commission members in this report adopt the policy that assimilation is the first step in the solution of "The Indian Problem." Without any consideration of those who opposed the forced assimilation of the Indian and in disregard of the fact that a controversial matter of substantive Congressional policy is involved, this step is boldly taken and most of the recommendations are contingent upon a policy of assimilation. I feel that this Commission, established as it was to examine into the organization of the executive branch of the Government, lacks both the competence and authority to make this basic policy decision. I, therefore, dissent from this report and that of the task force.

---

[4] Ibid., p. 79.
[5] Ibid., p. 80.

SUMMARY OF
INDIAN MESSAGES OF
PRESIDENTS JOHNSON AND NIXON

PRESIDENT JOHNSON'S INDIAN MESSAGE

The great interest of Secretary Stewart L. Udall in Indians, the fact that Commissioner Robert L. Bennett was an Indian himself and took the role of advocate, and President Lyndon B. Johnson's personal interest in the underprivileged resulted in two confidential Presidential task forces on Indians and a Presidential Message on Indians to the Congress.[6]

The President proposed an end to the "old debate about 'termination'" and a "policy of maximum choice for the American Indian: a policy expressed in programs of self-help, self-development, and self-determination."

To strengthen Federal leadership a Presidential Executive Order on the same day established the National Council on Indian Opportunity, chaired by the Vice President, with cabinet heads and prominent Indian leaders as members.

He endorsed the Bureau's efforts to establish a kindergarten program and the Office of Economic Opportunity (OEO) Head Start program; the improvement of curriculum and establishment of Indian school boards; increased grants for higher education; improved health programs, emphasizing community participation; a doubling of appropriations for vocational training; increased funding for Indian roads; and a doubling of funds for Indian housing.

He noted the pending Indian Bill of Rights and urged the Congress to complete its action, which it did in April 1968.[7]

The Indians located in urban centers were recognized as having "urgent needs for education, health, welfare, and rehabilitation services, which are far greater

---

[6] White House Task Force, 1966, Dr. Walsh McDermott, Chairman. See *Washington Post*, February 13 and 14, 1968.

Task Force on Indians, 1967, Lee C. White, Chairman. See, Alvin M. Josephy, Jr., *The American Indian and the Bureau of Indian Affairs*, February 24, 1969. A report for President Nixon, which discussed both of the Johnson Task Force reports.

"The Forgotten American," The President's Message to the Congress on Goals and Program for the American Indian, March 6, 1968.

[7] 82 Stat. 73.

Titles II through VII relate to Indians. In addition to providing an Indian Bill of Rights, this act directed the development of a model code governing Courts of Indian Offenses, modified P.L. 280 concerning civil and criminal jurisdiction over Indian reservations by States to require Indian consent for such jurisdiction to be taken by the States, provided for retrocession of jurisdiction by the State, gave consent to the States to amend their State constitutions or statutes to remove any legal impediments to the assumption of civil or criminal jurisdiction, provided that if the Department of Interior had not acted on employment of legal counsel by a tribe within 90 days approval will be assumed, and specified an updating of documents concerning Indian law and treaties.

than that of the general population." These needs ". . . can be met through Federal, State, and local programs." The new Council on Indian Opportunity was charged with studying the urban problem and reporting on actions needed.

Concerning Alaska Native Claims the President recommended prompt action by the Congress to provide Natives title to the lands they occupy, rights to hunting and fishing, and compensation for land taken from them.

The President concluded his message with the following words:

> The program I propose seeks to promote Indian development by improving health and education, encouraging long-term economic growth, and strengthening community institutions.

> Underlying this program is the assumption that the Federal government can best be a responsible partner in Indian progress by treating the Indian himself as a full citizen, responsible for the pace and direction of his development.

> But there can be no question that the government and the people of the United States have a responsibility to the Indians.

> In our efforts to meet that responsibility, we must pledge to respect fully the dignity and the uniqueness of the Indian citizen.

> That means partnership—not paternalism.

> We must affirm the right of the first Americans to remain Indians while exercising their rights as Americans.

> We must affirm their right to freedom of choice and self-determination.

> We must seek new ways to provide Federal assistance to Indians—with new emphasis on Indian self-help and with respect for Indian culture.

> And we must assure the Indian people that it is our desire and intention that the special relationship between the Indian and his government grow and flourish.

> For, the first among us must not be last.

> I urge the Congress to affirm this policy and to enact this program.

PRESIDENT NIXON'S INDIAN MESSAGE
Preelection Statement

In a preelection statement Richard Nixon pledged the following:

1. Recognition of the special responsibilities of the Federal Government to the Indian people.

"Termination of tribal recognition will not be a policy objective and in no case will it be imposed without Indian consent."

"We must recognize that American society can allow many different cultures to flourish in harmony and we must provide an opportunity for those Indians wishing to do so to lead a useful and prosperous life in an Indian environment."

2. Respect for the right of self-determination of the Indian people and encouragement of their "participation in planning their own destiny."

3. Opposition to any effort ". . . to transfer jurisdiction over Indian reservations without Indian consent."

4. Full support for the National Council on Indian Opportunity.

5. Consultation with Indian people before programs under which they must live are planned.

6. Encouragement of increasing authority and responsibility by Indian people over programs affecting them such as:

    a. Independent school boards for each Bureau of Indian Affairs (BIA) school, funded at Government expense.

    b. Tribal operation of reservation law and order programs and road construction and repair activities.

    c. Contracts for operation of school buses and school lunch programs providing for Federal funding.

7. Encouragement of the economic development of Indian reservations by:

    a. Training for both on and off reservation employment.

    b. Economic incentives to private industry for reservation activity.

    c. Recognition of special development problems of smaller reservations.

    d. Development of the recreation and tourist potential of Indian reservations.

8. Improvement of health services to Indian people.[8]

President Nixon's Indian team reemphasized many of the above policies after assuming office.[9]

Message to the Congress

In his Indian Message to the Congress, July 8, 1970, the President again affirmed that the policy of forced termination was wrong and gave three reasons:

The special relationship between the Federal Government and the Indians is the result of "solemn obligation" such as treaties and formal and informal agreements. "To terminate this relationship would be no more appropriate than to terminate the citizenship rights of any other American."

In those instances of completed termination the ". . . practical results have been clearly harmful. . . ."

Thirdly, the threat to the special relationship posed by possible termination has created "apprehension among Indian groups" and "has had a blighting effect on tribal progress" and "has often worked to produce . . . excessive dependence on the Federal government."

The "excessive dependence" means that the Indian community may be "almost entirely run by outsiders who are responsible and responsive to Federal officials in Washington, D. C., rather than the communities they are supposed to be serving."

This, then, must be the goal of any new national policy toward the Indian people: to strengthen the Indian's sense of autonomy without threatening his sense of community. We must assure the Indian that he can assume control of his own life without being separated involuntarily from the tribal group. And we must make it clear that Indians can become independent of Federal control without being cut off from Federal concern and Federal support.

Rejection of Termination

The President then asked the Congress to pass a Concurrent Resolution which would "repeal the termination policy as expressed in House Concurrent Resolution

---

[8] Statement by Richard M. Nixon, 450 Park Ave., New York, N. Y., September 22, 1968.

[9] See, for example: Address by the Vice President, National Congress of American Indians, October 8, 1969, Albuquerque, N. M. "This Administration *opposes* termination. This Administration *favors* the continuation of the trust relationship and the protection of Indian lands and Indian resources."

    Remarks of Secretary of the Interior, Walter J. Hickel, NCAI, same date. "We are not a pro-termination Administration."

    Address by Commissioner of Indian Affairs Louis R. Bruce, National Congress of American Indians, Albuquerque, N. M., October 9, 1969. The Commissioner accepted appointment with the commitment "that this administration was not going to become a termination administration and that I would have the fullest high-level cooperation in my efforts to reorganize the Bureau of Indian Affairs."

108 of the 83rd Congress and "explicitly affirm": the right of tribes to continued existence; recognize "that cultural pluralism is a source of national strength"; assure tribes that the United States would "continue to carry out its treaty and trusteeship obligations to them as long as the group themselves believed that such a policy was necessary or desirable"; and guarantee that Indian groups could "assume control or responsibility for government service programs . . . and still receive adequate Federal financial support."

The Right to Control and Operate Federal Programs

Another new policy announced in this message: ". . . it should be up to the Indian tribe to determine whether it is willing and able to assume administrative responsibility for a service program which is presently administered by a Federal agency." (Legislation was not forwarded at the time of the message but was submitted shortly thereafter). Under this program the President hoped that the tribes and the Government agencies would cooperatively work out such transfers, but if they did not agree, ". . . the final determination should rest with the Indian community." This program was "voluntary," it could involve parts of programs, and the Indians would have the "right of retrocession."

Technical assistance would be made available by the Federal Government "to help local organizations successfully operate these programs." Funds for locally administered programs would be "on equal terms with similar services still administered by Federal authorities."

The proposed "legislation would apply only to services which go directly from the Federal Government to the Indian community."

Federally funded services ". . . which are channeled through State or local governments could still be turned over to Indian control by mutual consent."

Importantly, the President provided flexible employment practices in operating activities for which they assumed control. The Indians "could employ local people or outside experts. If they chose to hire Federal employees who had formerly administered these projects, those employees would still enjoy the privileges of Federal employee benefit programs—under special legislation which will also be submitted to the Congress."

Restoring the Sacred Lands Near Blue Lake

Legislation accomplishing this objective should be promptly enacted. "Such action would stand as an important symbol of this government's responsiveness to the just grievances of the American Indians."

Indian Education

Indians should be able to control and operate their schools, and the President designated the Vice President to establish a special subcommittee of the National Council on Indian Opportunity (NCIO) made up of Indian educators ". . . selected by the Council's Indian members." This subcommittee ". . . will provide technical assistance to Indian communities wishing to establish school boards, will conduct a nationwide review of the educational status of all Indian children. . ., and will evaluate and report annually on the status of Indian education, including the extent of local control." The objective of this subcommittee ". . . should not be self-perpetuation but the actual transfer of Indian education to Indian communities."

The President directed the Secretary of the Interior ". . . to make every effort to ensure that Johnson-O'Malley funds which are presently directed to public school districts are actually spent to improve the education of Indian children in these districts."

Economic Development Legislation

Under this heading the President proposed legislation that would increase the Revolving Loan Fund from "approximately $25 million to $75 million" and provide "loan guarantees, loan insurance and interest subsidies to encourage *private* lenders to loan more money for Indian economic projects" up to an aggregate amount of $200 million.

Legislation authorizing 99 year leasing for all tribes was urged and the Secretary of Interior was "directed to play an active role in coordinating" additional comprehensive economic development plans such as the Pima-Maricopa and Zuni plans.

More Money for Indian Health

The President said he would request an allocation of an additional $10 million for Indian health for the current fiscal year and would expand efforts "to train Indians for health careers."

Helping Urban Indians

The President directed the Office of Economic Opportunity to lead the joint efforts of OEO, Health, Education, and Welfare, (HEW), Labor, Housing and Urban Development (HUD), and Commerce in the support of "seven urban Indian centers in major cities which will act as links between existing Federal, State, and local service programs and the urban Indians." After learning from these projects he hoped "to expand our efforts as rapidly as possible."

Indian Trust Counsel Authority

The President called on the Congress "to establish an Indian Trust Counsel Authority to assure independent legal representation for the Indians' natural resource rights" and to avoid the conflict inherent in the present situation with Interior and Justice having to "advance *both* the *national* interest in the use of land and water rights *and* the *private* interest of Indians in land which the government holds as trustee."

Assistant Secretary for Indian and Territorial Affairs

The recommendation of legislation to establish a new position of Assistant Secretary for Indian and Territorial Affairs "represents an elevation of Indian affairs to their proper role within the Department of the Interior. . . ."

Relationship of Indian Welfare to Other Programs

The message cites valuable efforts of the Office of Economic Opportunity (OEO) in Indian matters and urges the Congress to appropriate the full amount requested for OEO.

The welfare reform proposals such as the Family Assistance Plan and the Family Health Insurance Plan relate to the Indian problem. "It is estimated, for example, that more than half of all Indian families would be eligible for Family Assistance benefits and the enactment of this legislation is therefore of critical importance to the American Indian."

SUPPLEMENTARY
STATE MATERIAL

For the reader who wishes to explore State activity in more detail as well as review specific examples of the meshing of Indian, Federal, State, and local activity, the following supplementary materials may be helpful.

1. provides quotes and statements of philosophy from State statutes, executive orders, or statements of officials.

2. indicates the funding of State commissions and staffs.

3. outlines some of the circumstances encountered in the 26 States with no special organization or services for Indians, particularly in the six of these States (Alaska, Iowa, Louisiana, Mississippi, North Carolina, and Oregon) with federally recognized Indians. The Oregon discussion includes an analysis of the termination and present status of the Klamath Indians. The critical Alaskan situation is also presented.

4. describes briefly the programs in four States—Colorado, Connecticut, Virginia, and Wisconsin—that provide some special services for Indians, but which do not have a specially labeled Indian activity such as an Indian commission. An analysis of the Menominee Indian termination and present circumstances is included in the Wisconsin discussion.

3. and 4 provide, in effect, a more detailed analysis of ten States having both federally eligible and non-eligible Indians and widely varying conditions. These examples illustrate the numbers of Indians served by the State and Federal Governments and the mix of programs in such services in more specific terms than in the general discussion.

1. ADDITIONAL ILLUSTRATIONS OF STATE PHILOSOPHY CONCERNING THEIR INDIAN CITIZENS

Montana states ". . . it is the legislative policy of this state that the best interests of the Indians will be served by the fostering of a program which is designed to establish and place our Indian citizens in a position whereby they will be able to take their rightful place in our society, and assume the rights, duties and privileges of full citizenship. . . ." Montana believed it ". . . necessary that a state office of the coordinator of Indian affairs be established so that the problems of the Indians of Montana can be approached and reconciled from a state level in cooperation with the United States of America. . . ." [1]

In South Dakota, the State Commission of Indian Affairs was ". . . established to consider and study living conditions among the Indians residing within the state, with the purpose in view of establishing a method of absorbing the Indian people

---

[1] Ch. 319, 82–2701, Session Laws 41st Legislative Assembly, State of Montana.

into the economy of the state." Commission studies were to cover the fields of education, employment, housing, betterment of living conditions, medical care, hospitalization, and promotion of the general welfare of the Indian people.[2]

The purpose of Florida Indian legislation ". . . is to protect the Seminole Indians of Florida against undue and unnecessary hardships during these difficult years of transition from their ancestral culture to the culture of the white man's civilization and to aid said Indians to obtain independence as a tribe and as individuals." [3]

Minnesota sounds a warning. In reviewing the Minnesota Legislature's 20 year history of Indian policy, it was pointed out that in 1951, a State Senate committee reported that ". . . the administration of social programs for Indians should be progressively transferred to State Governments and that the states should receive appropriate recompense from Federal funds until Indian taxes can help carry the load." [4]

This was appropriate for the philosophy of the time that resulted in the passage of House Concurrent Resolution 108 and Public Law 280. The 1951 report also stated: ". . . that progressive measures to integrate the Indian into the rest of the population is the best solution to the Indian problem." The 1969 report comments that such attitudes "have proven to be a major factor in slowing the Indian's progress toward a better life." This is in part due to the difference between the Indian and non-Indian viewpoint. "While proud of being an American (as his service in our armed forces testifies) he is also proud of being an Indian. While striving for health, education, housing, and employment, he also seeks development of his Tribal resources and expression of his heritage: language, dance, history, etc." [5]

Therefore, the Minnesota Commission recommends that State agencies responsible for law enforcement, education, welfare, and other functions extend full and equitable use of these services to Indians, and at the same time "place emphasis on outreach programs that recognize the Indian as an Indian and that facilitate his participation and achievement." Employment of Indian personnel by State agencies is one way, the Commission points out, to increase ". . . an agency's ability to relate to the Indian community." [6]

The former Deputy Commissioner of the Maine Department of Indian Affairs emphasizes the point that Indians will have to determine their own destiny: "The future of the Maine Indian population rests in their own hands if the non-Indian agencies (Federal, State, and private) could lend assistance and give the needed monies." He continues: "There should be no unilateral action on the part of non-Indians to improve Indian conditions. The situation will be changed only through determined efforts on the part of the Maine Indians." [7]

This concept is endorsed by North Dakota, whose 6 year plan states: "While many see the complete assimilation of Indian communities into state and local structures as 'The Mission' in Indian affairs, this cannot be a serious statement of mission until the Indian people themselves desire such assimilation." [8]

---

[2] Ch. 1–4 South Dakota Compiled Laws, 1967, Ch. 65.0801.

[3] Ch. 285.07, Florida Statutes.

[4] Introduction, Report of the Minnesota Indian Affairs Commission, 1969.

[5] Ibid.

[6] Ibid.

[7] Michael R. Crawford (Indian), in response to Governors' Interstate Indian Council Questionnaire, April 1970; comments compiled in *State Directory, State Organization and Activities for Indian Citizens*, by Theodore W. Taylor, December 1970. (Draft for Review and Correction).

[8] A 6 year plan (July 1, 1967 to June 30, 1973) for the North Dakota Indian Affairs Commission, adopted December 12, 1967. The Governor is the Chairman of the Commission in North Dakota.

The North Dakota philosophy is to provide "technical and moral support to Indian individuals and groups . . . as they seek to develop their own goals . . ." and seek to achieve those goals. To assist Indian people in "achieving a full, meaningful, and productive life" the North Dakota Commission seeks to develop ". . . working relationships of mutual respect between Indian citizens and the various units of government. . . ." [9]

The North Dakota Legislature expressed the policy of the State "to cooperate fully with tribal councils" and urged all agencies of the State and its political subdivisions "to give all possible encouragement and assistance to tribal councils in developing to the fullest their political, economic, judicial, artistic, social, and cultural resources." [10]

The composition of Indian commissions reflects the need for recognition of the Indian viewpoint. In setting up the Indian Commission in Nebraska, the Governor noted that it had been requested by Indians and that the basic proposal had been formulated by a group of Indians, and that the Commission was distinctive in that its membership was entirely Indian. The Governor expressed the hope that the Commission ". . . will be a vehicle whereby the Indians of the State of Nebraska will be able to work together to solve many of their common problems." [11]

The New York long-range program is ". . . to help Indians to help themselves by providing them with the same services as are available to other groups. . . ." New York also recognizes cultural diversity, indicating that by assisting Indians to take their rightful place in the community it will also make it possible for the Indians ". . . to make their cultural contributions to the community." [12]

Texas has assumed the responsibility through its Commission for Indian Affairs for the development of the human and economic resources of the Alabama-Coushatta reservation and the Tigua Indian community and to assist the tribal councils in making the communities self-sufficient. [13]

The philosophy of involving Indians is achieving results. In New Mexico many Indians are serving on boards and commissions. [14] Indians are serving on school boards of public schools and in the New Mexico State legislature.

The Director of the Department of Economic Opportunity in Nevada, who is also a member of the Governor's cabinet, is an Indian. [15]

The Chairman of the Nevada Indian Affairs Commission pointed to some of the difficulties of State initiative in the Indian field: [16]

". . . when state government does show a willingness to provide better delivery of a particular service, private organizations or Indians themselves accuse the state of either meddling in Indian business or seeking to serve a state ulterior

[9] Ibid.

[10] Senate Concurrent Resolution No. 25, 41st Legislative Assembly of North Dakota, passed Senate February 28, 1969; passed House March 12, 1969.

[11] Governor's statement on signing Executive Order establishing the Commission, April 7, 1970. On May 13, 1971, Nebraska provided statutory authority for its Indian Commission in Legislative Bills 904 and 904A.

[12] The Indian Today in New York State, (6th ed., Albany: Director of Indian Services, New York State Department of Social Services, October 15, 1969.)

[13] Ch. 276, H.B. 654, as approved May 23, 1967, Texas statutes.

[14] In New Mexico Indians serve on State boards and commissions dealing with the following: alcoholism, the American revolution bicentenial; children and youth; economic development; health planning; human rights; Indian affairs; judiciary; law enforcement; drug abuse; and motion picture industry promotion.

[15] Alvin James.

[16] Frank Durham, Chairman, in response to Governors' Interstate Indian Council questionnaire of April 1970.

motive of eliminating trust land or worse yet—spreading rumors to the effect that the state desires 'termination'." He continues: "There is much the State can do *and is willing to do at every level*. The time has come for innovative approaches. . . ."

In summary, a review of the evidence indicates that most of these States recognize officially in statutes, executive orders, or statements by officials that Indians are an integral part of the State's citizenry. The objective of State policy in most instances is to assist Indian citizens to adjust to the surrounding culture. This is in cooperation with tribal governments and Federal agencies when they are involved. Although some policy statements seem to emphasize the historical theme of assimilation of the Indians into the non-Indian culture, most States recognize that the Indian has his own culture and that the degree of adjustment will be determined in large measure by Indian groups and individuals. States such as Montana and Michigan stressed the need for State policy and State agencies to be concerned with all Indian citizens of the State, as in both instances there were numerous Indians not receiving special services from the Federal Government, while others were receiving such services.

States also agree on the value and necessity of Indian participation in governmental actions that impinge on Indian life. Indians are beginning to participate on public school boards, State elective offices, and on State boards and commissions. Indians in these States have a strong voice on the State Indian commissions.

2. FUNDING OF STATE COMMISSIONS AND STAFFS

Per diem for commission members varies: from no per diem or actual expenses, to specific ceilings of $10 to $25 a day. Some States have a limitation on the number of days for meetings and the number of meetings in 1 year. Travel allowances vary from nothing to actual expenses; automobile mileage rates, when specified, were 9 cents or 10 cents a mile.

The salaries of the executive directors or coordinators varies from $9.7 to $15 thousand per year. Some individuals who have Indian concerns as a part of their total responsibility have higher annual salaries.

State funds for operating commissions and coordinators' offices vary from $1.3 to $270 thousand. Some States have sizeable capital expenditures as well. Eight States have budgets in the $20 to $40 thousand range. These State funds are amplified by Federal and private funds in many instances.[17]

3. STATES WITH NO SPECIAL ORGANIZATIONS OR SERVICES FOR INDIANS (including a special analysis of the Klamath Indian situation)

Of the 26 States with no special organizations or services for their Indian citizens based on their Indian ancestry, 20 have no "Federal" Indians—that is, no Indians for whom the Federal Government accepts special responsibility because of their Indian status.

Twenty States of This Group with No Federal Indians

These 20 States are characterized by a relatively small indigenous Indian population (preliminary 1970 Census counts):

---

[17] Not all respondents provided fiscal information.

Alabama, 2,514; Arkansas, 2,041; Delaware, 656; Georgia, 2,455; Hawaii, 1,126; Illinois, 11,413; Indiana, 3,887; Kentucky, 1,599; Maryland, 4,258; Massachusetts, 4,475; Missouri, 5,405; New Hampshire, 361; New Jersey, 4,706; Ohio, 6,654; Pennsylvania, 5,533; Rhode Island, 1,390; South Carolina, 2,241; Tennessee, 2,376; Vermont, 229; and West Virginia, 808. Although Hawaii does not have special arrangements for American Indians it does have such arrangements for descendants of the Polynesians who inhabited the islands before the advent of Captain Cook.

Illinois Indian population is primarily in Chicago and represents 115 tribes from all over the Nation. Many of Maryland's Indians are Lumbees in Baltimore, originally from North Carolina. Cleveland has a considerable number of Ohio's Indian population and many of the Cleveland Indians are from other States.

The Indians in these 20 States are theoretically, at least, integrated into the structure of our Federal system in the same manner as other citizens.

The Bureau of Indian Affairs (BIA) has Employment Assistance offices in Chicago and Cleveland as well as in other States. These offices help orient reservation Indians who apply for training and placement on a job. These offices receive them when they come to the city, help locate housing, help them enroll in training, and help them find a job after training. The living and training costs during the training period for both the trainee (and his family, if he has one) are borne by the Bureau of Indian Affairs (BIA).

The situation in Massachusetts is illustrative. At Gay Head, Mass. each member of the Wampanoag group was given a lot and a cottage in 1870. The number of Wampanoags is decreasing, now being slightly under 100. Each family that is still there has its own cottage and lot, pays real estate and other taxes, votes in elections, is serviced by the public schools, and is under the jurisdiction of the Town Government. Most of the children finish high school, some go on to higher education. Because of lack of opportunity at Gay Head many young people move to locations with better economic opportunity. Many of the adult Indians are engaged in the trades and odd jobs. Very seldom is any Indian family of that area with able-bodied members on public assistance.[18]

An Indian reservation of 227.5 acres was established within the Massachusetts Freetown—Fall River State Forest (Ch. 384, Acts of 1939) and authorization given to the Commissioner of Natural Resources to establish a museum at his discretion. The museum was never established as no criteria or overall plan of development has been forthcoming from the Indians, even though the Division of Forests and Parks has made several attempts to get the Indians to propose a plan.[19]

No Indians live on the reservation. There are no special programs or services for Indians, as such, in the State.

In 1927, the Grafton Reservation was set aside for the Hassanamisco Tribe in the State of Massachusetts. This reservation now consists of 11.9 acres, has one resident, and is not taxed.[20]

Six States of This Group With Federal Indians

The six States of this group—Alaska, Iowa, Louisiana, Mississippi, North Carolina, and Oregon—which have some federally recognized Indians have diverse situations.

---

[18] Information from Luther Madison, Gay Head Town Hall, Telephone Conversation 1–26–71. Letter of January 18, 1971, from Henry Lee, Assistant Secretary to the Governor.

[19] See letter of January 18, 1971 from Henry Lee and enclosed memorandum from Director, Division of Forests and Parks.

[20] Ibid.

Alaska

General

Alaska is different from other States in several respects. Although federally recognized, most Natives do not have reservations. A majority of the Natives live in some 200 Native villages, and approximately 30 percent live in urban centers with 2,000 or more total population (1970 Census). They are considered as full-fledged citizens of the State and are legally eligible to receive all of the services provided by the State Government in the same manner as other State residents. However, the Federal Government has massive inputs into Alaska programs and the Bureau of Indian Affairs (BIA) and the Indian Health Service (IHS) still provide direct services to many Natives. The basic BIA program in Alaska is education. There is also considerable funding for social services.

In fiscal year 1970, 21,857 Native children were 5 to 18 years of age. Of these 13,212 (60 percent) were in public school, 7,245 (33 percent) in Federal schools, 411 (2 percent) in other schools, and 989 (5 percent) not in school or unknown.[21]

The BIA paid full costs for the operation of the Federal schools, and also paid the State approximately $2.6 million for support of Indian pupils in public schools.[22] Under an agreement with the State, BIA schools are being transferred to the State as rapidly as the State and the Natives concerned agree. Grants for tuition costs are provided as necessary.

Alaska, in cooperation with BIA, is currently implementing a program of regional high schools. This program will allow Alaskan Native high school students who presently must attend BIA boarding schools in Alaska, Oregon, and Oklahoma to remain in Alaska near their home communities.

Alaska is also different in that a higher proportion (17 percent) of its total population is Native (51,528 Natives; 302,175 total population) than is the case in any other State. Thus the various divisions of the State Government have a considerable number of Natives in their constituency. This is especially true of those State departments and agencies oriented toward rural programs (Rural Development Agency, Rural Areas School Service Project, Division of State Operated Schools, and the Regional Schools Division).

Those State programs in the fields of health and welfare have a heavy Native load, up to 50 percent of the total in some instances. Although many of these programs receive Federal funding, some have partial or full State funding, and they are administered by State agencies.

Alaska Native Land Claims and Oil Pipe Line

The Alaska Natives and the State of Alaska urgently needed a solution to the Native land claims, which came with the signing into law of 85 Stat. 688 on December 18, 1971. The act of May 17, 1884, providing for civil government in Alaska, reserved to the Congress the determination of the manner in which land title to Natives would be given. In 1969 the Department of the Interior put a "freeze" on transfer of Federal land [23] which continued until the land claim was settled.

The Governor of Alaska set three "landmark" goals: settlement of Native land claims, building the pipeline from Prudhoe Bay to Valdez, and the creation of an economic development policy for Alaska.[24]

---

[21] Appendix A, Table I, *Statistics Concerning Indian Education* (Lawrence, Kans.: Bureau of Indian Affairs, Haskell Indian Junior College, FY 1970).

[22] 1971 Budget Justification, Bureau of Indian Affairs (BIA).

[23] Public Land Order 4582.

[24] *Tundra Times*, January 13, 1971.

All of these goals are important to the Natives. Said the Governor: [25]
> First we must achieve, with the help of the Congress, a just settlement of the Native Land Claims. **** There will be no progress without it.

The Alaska Native Claims act provides Alaska Natives with 40 million acres of land in fee simple title, $462.5 million in Federal appropriations, and $500 million in mineral royalties. The Alaska Federation of Natives accepted the terms of the bill prior to the President's signature.

The Natives of Alaska are also very concerned about the proposed trans-Alaska pipeline system from the North Slope to Valdez. The Natives want assurance that they will be a part of, and share in, the economic growth that such a development would bring. They, as well as the conservationists, the State, and Interior, are also concerned about the pipeline's impact on the environment, including its effect on caribou migration. Most of the length of the proposed pipeline would be on land owned by the United States and claimed under aboriginal title by Alaskan Natives. However, near the southern terminus the route would be in the vicinity of several settlements, two of which are predominantly Native.

Several proposals for expediting construction of the pipeline have been made such as creation of a transportation corridor along the pipeline route. The settlement of the Alaska Native Claims will be a factor in the decision on the pipeline. It is clear that the Native, the State, the Federal Government and private interest groups all have a stake in pending policy matters related to the settlement of the Native land claims and possible construction of the Alaska pipeline.

Iowa

Most of Iowa's Indians (2,992) receive governmental service from the State and localities. However, approximately 500 Mesquakie Indians (Sac and Fox Reservation) are federally recognized. They have a small amount of trust land (3,476 acres). In the past, BIA has operated a small school and currently has a small contract for foster care of Indian children. In 1970, out of a total of 224 children 5 to 18 years of age, 61 attended Federal boarding schools at other locations, 152 attended public school, 5 attended other schools, and 6 were not in school.

Iowa was scheduled to receive $113 thousand from BIA school funds for support of Indians in public school in 1970.

Iowa has exercised jurisdiction over the Sac and Fox Reservation since 1948, except for offenses defined by laws of the United States.[26]

In 1968, Iowa assumed civil jurisdiction over the Sac and Fox Reservation as authorized by P.L. 280.[27]

Most governmental services for the Sac and Fox come from the State and the locality.

Louisiana

Of the 5,366 Indians in the State, only 268 Chitimacha Indians are recognized by the Federal Government; they have 262 acres of tribal trust land. The other Indian groups—for example, Choctaws, Tunicas, Houmas, and Coushattas—are not recognized by BIA but the Public Health Service is considering a domestic water and sewerage program for some of the other groups.[28]

---

[25] Ibid.
[26] 62 Stat. 1161.
[27] 67 Stat. 588.
[28] Telephone conversation, John Gordon, Superintendent, January 13, 1971.

Such governmental services as most of Louisiana's Indians receive have been from State and local sources. The Federal Government operates a day school with a 1971 enrollment of 44 Chitimacha students. Seven Chitimachas also attend the Choctaw boarding school at Pearl River (Mississippi). The Chitimachas are also eligible for post high school scholarships, and for health and hospital services if they go to Indian Health Service (IHS), Choctaw facility in Mississippi.

During calendar year 1970 the Choctaw Agency has worked closely with the Chitimachas in the development of a constitution and bylaws. These tribal documents will provide a basis for land use and assignment and provide guidelines for tribal enrollment.

In July 1970, the Coushattas, Tunicas, Houmas, and Chitimachas marched on the State capital in Baton Rouge to dramatize their economic and social needs.[29]

This apparently indicates the Indians' recognition that primary services and help must come from the State and localities, and that they hope the State will recognize this, too, and do something about it.

Mississippi

Of Mississippi's 4,000 Indians (4,113), approximately 3,000 Choctaws are recognized by the Federal Government. The Federal Government provides schools, social services (including general assistance and foster home care for children), adult training, employment assistance, forestry and land use advice, law and order, and maintains an agency near Philadelphia, Miss.

Of the 1,585 Choctaws 5 to 18 years of age, 1,237 are in Federal schools (there are two elementary boarding schools, one combination elementary and high boarding school, and three elementary day schools), 263 in public schools, 14 in other schools, and 71 not in school. In 1970, $5,250 was paid by the Federal Government to the State for Indian children in public schools.[30]

The tribe owns approximately 17,400 acres held in trust by the Secretary of the Interior and there is only one acre of individually owned trust land. The largest area of tribal land, 11,400 acres, is in Neshoba County, the rest of the acreage is scattered in seven other locations.

Law and order is a responsibility of the Tribe and the Federal government; the State exercises no jurisdiction over tribal land.

North Carolina

North Carolina is the home of 43,487 Indians with a heavy concentration in Robeson County. In 1885, the State recognized the people of Robeson County as Croatan Indians, "on the theory of descent from Raleigh's lost colony of Croatan." [31] The State provided separate schools as the Croatans refused to go to Negro schools and were not permitted in white schools. These people are of mixed Indian and white blood.[32] In 1911 the State changed these peoples' designation to "Indians of Robeson

---

[29] Ibid.

[30] Ibid.

[31] Frederick W. Hodge, *Handbook of American Indians North of Mexico* (Washington, D.C.: Bureau of American Ethnology, 1907), Bulletin 30, p. 365. Hodge regarded this theory as baseless. However, Clifton Oxendine, in a Masters thesis (1934) at George Peabody College for Teachers supports the theory.

[32] Hodge, op cit. See also Calvin L. Beale "American Triracial Isolates," *Eugenics Quarterly*, December 1957, pp. 187–196.

County," and in 1913 to "Cherokee Indians of Robeson County" but without privileges, rights or immunities of the Eastern Band of Cherokee Indians.[33]

In 1956, the Congress of the United States designated the Indians of Robeson County to be the Lumbee Indians of North Carolina.[34] The statute specifically provided that the Lumbees were not eligible for any services performed by the United States for Indians because of their status as Indians. They remain solely under State jurisdiction. The statute also referred to tribal legend, distinctive appearance and manner of speech, and the frequency of certain family names such as Oxendine. Locklear, Chavis, Drinkwater, Bullard, Lowery, Sampson, and others, also found on the roster of the earliest English settlement, and concluded there was considerable reason to the proposition that these Indians could trace their origin to a mixture of colonial and Indian blood.

Approximately 5,000 (4,766) Cherokees, nestled in the Smoky Mountains at Cherokee, N. C., are recognized by the Federal Government. The Cherokee Reservation has approximately 56,400 acres of tribal trust land. A full-fledged BIA agency is maintained, carrying out school, forestry, welfare, land use, employment assistance, industrial development and other programs. Of the 1,789 children 5 to 18 years of age, 1,155 attended Federal, 533 attended public, 32 attended other schools, and 69 were not in school in fiscal year 1970. The BIA did not subsidize Indian education in the public schools.

By a succession of treaties ending with Treaty of New Echota in 1835 (7 Stat. 478) the tribe "surrendered all right to any lands in North Carolina" and the tribe agreed to move west of the Mississippi.[35] Heads of families who desired to become citizens of the States involved and who were qualified to take care of themselves and their property were not required to move to lands beyond the Mississippi, according to one provision of the treaty. Others fled to the hills and were not rounded up by the troops supervising the removal. In 1838, it was estimated that between 1,100 and 1,200 had remained, and were in an anomalous status. They were no longer members of the Cherokee Tribe, had no land, and no right of self-government. They were subject to the laws of North Carolina. They continued to occupy some of their traditional lands, and eventually the Federal Government purchased lands, gave permission for them to remain permanently in North Carolina (as did the State), and directed the Secretary of the Interior to assume some responsibility.[36]

In 1889, North Carolina gave the Cherokees a corporate charter, and the Federal Government transferred title of the Cherokee land to this corporation, where it remained until it was re-conveyed to the United States in 1925. During this period taxes were paid on this land to North Carolina from tribal funds in the treasury.[37]

In 1931, a Federal court commented that the Federal Government had promoted the welfare of the Cherokees through providing land, schools, adult education, health and hospital services, and the like, but that "North Carolina has afforded them few of the privileges of citizenship." [38]

North Carolina provides law and order for the reservation although a Federal court has held that the State and the Federal Government have concurrent jurisdic-

---

[33] North Carolina Laws of 1913, Ch. 123.

[34] 70 Stat. 254.

[35] U. S. v. Wright, et al., No. 3176, Circuit Court of Appeals Circuit, October 12, 1931.

[36] 15 Stat. 228.

[37] U. S. v. Wright, op. cit.

[38] Ibid.

tion, the State deriving its authority from the 1835 Treaty of New Echota and the Federal Government from its position as guardian and protector of the Cherokees.[39]

Oregon

Although Oregon has no special organizational arrangements or services special to Indians, the State was very active in considering its responsibilities toward its Indian citizens in the 1950's. Of the approximately 13,500 (13,510) Indians in Oregon, only 2,650 (2,653) are in tribes receiving special services from the Federal Government.

Klamath Indians

Oregon is the home of the Klamath Tribe (Klamath, Modoc, and Snake Indians) whose relationship with the Federal Government was terminated in 1961.[40] Removal of the Federal trusteeship had been requested by groups of the tribe. At the time of termination there were 2,133 members, 862,662 acres of tribal land and 104,322 acres of allotted land. Much of the tribal land was forested and the tribal lands and properties were appraised at $90,791,123, for pro rata share of approximately $43,500. Under the terms of the termination legislation, adults were given the option of choosing for themselves and their children whether to convert their respective interests in the tribal assets to cash or continue to hold such interests in common under State law. Seventy-eight percent elected to withdraw from membership and take their pro rata shares in cash. Twenty-two percent either chose to continue their membership or indicated no preference and were considered to have remained in the tribe. In both cases, the Indians came under State law and no longer received special services from the Federal Government because of their Indian status.

A portion of the tribal properties was sold and the proceeds distributed to the withdrawing members. The terminal legislation provided for sale of timber and marsh at the appraised price. In the case of timberlands the sale of virtually all of those lands was to be conditioned on sustained yield management, under conditions prescribed by the Secretaries of the Interior and Agriculture. The proportionate share of the timber area for the withdrawing members that was considered desirable to be retained in sustained yield production was divided into 11 units. One of the 11 sustained yield units was purchased by a private company; the other ten units were acquired by the Federal Government (Agriculture). The marshlands were acquired by the Federal Government (Interior) for a wildlife refuge.

The title to the property of the remaining group (the 22 percent who chose to remain with the tribe and not sell their portion of the tribal assets) was transferred to a bank for operation in accordance with a Management Trust Agreement, approved by the Secretary of the Interior.[41]

The bank was to produce an income for the Indians from the management of these properties and pay out such income in annual dividend payments.[42]

---

[39] Imprisonment of Frank Joseph McCoy, Civ. No. 1547, U. S. Dist. Ct., Eastern Dist., N. C., Raleigh Div., September 4, 1964, cited as 223F Supp. 409 (1964).

[40] Act of August 13, 1954, 68 Stat. 718, with five amendments. A group of Western Oregon Indians has also been terminated, P.L. 588, August 13, 1954.

[41] Property consisted of approximately 144,500 acres—134,960 acres of forest lands, 8,523 acres of farm and grazing lands, and 1,002 acres of marsh land. Bureau of Indian Affairs (BIA) files.

[42] Averaged $1,500 annually for each of the 473 full shares for the first 10 years. BIA files.

The Management Trust Agreement provided that the beneficiaries may elect to terminate the trust at the end of each 5 year period. After the first 5 years they voted to continue. At the end of the second 5 years (1969) 57 percent favored termination.[43]

The forest lands must first be offered for sale to the Secretary of Agriculture under the terms of the 1958 amendment to the Act.

A BIA summary prepared in 1969 stated: [44]

> Sampling survey made by the BIA early in 1966 indicated some slight improvement in certain economic and social areas. Termination did not create an exodus from the reservation. Klamaths, in general, either remained on their lands within the reservation area or moved to predominantly non-Indian communities or rural areas in the general vicinity of the reservation. Greater proximity to schools, churches and social activities was doubtless a factor in the change of residence. Assimilation in terms of participation in non-Indian social organizations, such as P.T.A., civic groups, and service clubs, is not taking place at any discernible or significant rate. Inference is that Klamaths continue as an ethnic segment in these areas, particularly in the larger communities. Some members already living in some of the coastal and surrounding cities, had moved there for economic and social reasons. But, like others in our society, some were living in the slum or ghetto areas and the payment of their shares did not serve to improve their existing conditions. Some counties particularly those in the vicinity of the former reservation and some of the larger cities, have expressed the view that a goodly number of the withdrawing members have dissipated their funds and are now heavily dependent on welfare assistance.

The State's congressional delegation [45] was active in the Klamath legislation. The State legislature favored termination, but also wanted to protect the Indians, the forest, and the economy of the area. Others also were interested in this problem.[46]

---

[43] The trustee bank has indicated it may take 5 years to sell the assets and distribute the money to the beneficiaries. BIA files.

[44] BIA files.

[45] Senators Morse and Neuberger; Congressman Ullman.

[46] See Senate Memorial No. 1. "Amending the Klamath Termination Act," *Hearings, Subcommittee on Indian Affairs* (Washington, D. C.: 85th Cong., 1st sess., U. S. House of Representatives, February 11, 12, and 13, March 21, 1957), pp. 14–15.

A. Harvey Wright, *Data on Termination of Federal Supervision over Klamath Indian Reservation* (Salem, Ore.; Oregon Department of Education, 1956).

"Report on the Effects of Withdrawal of Federal Supervision of Klamath Indian Tribe," *Hearings Before the Subcommittee on Indian Affairs, June 18 and August 13, 1965 at Washington, D. C.; November 3, 1965 at Spokane, Wash.; November 4 and 5 Nespelem, Wash., on the Colville Termination* (Washington, D. C.: 89th ong., 1st sess., U. S. House of Representatives, Committee on Interior and Insular Affairs), Serial No. 89–23.

Theodore Stern, *The Klamath Tribe; a People and Their Reservation* (Seattle: University of Washington Press, 1965).

"Klamath Voluntary Withdrawal Act," Hearings Before the Subcommittee on Indian Affairs, on H. R. 3402 (Washington, D. C.: 83rd Cong., 1st sess., U. S. House of Representatives, Committee on Interior and Insular Affairs, July 30, 1953), Serial No. 8.

"Amendments to the Klamath Termination Act of 1954," *Hearings Before the Subcommittee on Indian Affairs on S. 2047* (Washington, D. C.: 85th ong., 1st sess., U. S. Senate, Committee on Interior and Insular Affairs, October 2 and 4, 1957), pt. 1.

"Klamath Indian Tribe—Termination of Federal Supervision," *Hearings Before the Committee on Interior and Insular Affairs and Its Subcommittee on Indian Affairs* (Washington, D. C.: 84th Cong., 2nd sess., U. S. Senate, Committee on Interior and Insular Affairs, May 21 and October 18, 1956).

Other Groups

The Federal Government recognizes the following Oregon groups:

TABLE 1—SERVICES FOR FEDERALLY RECOGNIZED INDIANS, OREGON, 1970

| Reservations | Population [4] | Trust Land [1] (acres) | | | Education [2] | | Law and Order [3] | | |
		Tribal	Individually Owned	Federal	Public	Other	Tribe	State	Federal
Warm Springs (Warm Springs, Wasco and Paiute)	1687	483,499	80,814	31	955	7	X		X
Burns Colony	150	--	11,786	--	51	--		X	
Umatilla (Umatilla, Walla Walla, and Cayuse)	966	15,896	70,371	24	245	40		X	

[1] *Annual Report on Indian Lands*, 1970, BIA.
[2] *Statistics Concerning Indian Education*, 1970, BIA.
[3] *Law and Order Summary*, June 1970, BIA.
[4] *Indian Reservation Population*, March 10, 1970, BIA.

The above groups receive direct services from BIA, IHS and other Federal agencies, as appropriate, but as indicated in the above table, education is primarily provided by State public schools and law and order for Umatilla and the Burns Colony is a State function.[47]

There are 34 acres of tribal land at Celilo Village and the Federal Government owns 9 acres of Celilo fishing sites used by the Indians. The Burns Paiute colony has 11,000 acres of individually owned trust land; and there are 6,250 acres of individually owned trust land called the Dalles Unit. The Federal Government also operates the Chemawa Boarding High School in Salem, Ore.

Summary

These 26 States have a total Indian population of 186,079. Of the number, 63,038 are recognized for service by the Federal Government. If Alaska, with its 51,528 Natives is excluded, of the 134,551 Indians in the other 25 States only 11,510 are recognized and receive any direct services from the Federal Government. The remaining 123,041 receive whatever service they get from the States and localities. As we have seen, Alaska is moving in the direction of complete State takeover, but with continued Federal funding as required.

4. STATES WITHOUT SPECIAL ORGANIZATIONAL ARRANGEMENTS BUT WHICH DO HAVE SPECIAL PROGRAMS OR SERVICES FOR INDIANS (including a special analysis of the Menominee Indian situation)

The States of Colorado, Connecticut, Virginia, and Wisconsin do not have a

---

[47] 67 Stat. 588.

special Indian office or activity labeled for Indians as a group. They do, however, provide their Indian citizens some extra help.

Colorado

Colorado has approximately 9,000 (8,836) Indians. The majority of them are in Denver, where the only special Federal activity for Indians is employment assistance for those coming from federally recognized reservations under the BIA training and employment program.

Colorado points out that the Assistant Director, Commission on Community Relations, Denver, has provided information and services to the Indian community of Denver. A technical assistant in the State Office of Economic Opportunity spends 10 percent of his time on increasing economic opportunity for Indians through such programs as: Headstart, Community Alcoholism Program, Legal Aid, Neighborhood Youth Corps, Work and Training Program.[48]

A full-time consultant on Indian matters in the Department of Employment tries to see that federally funded training programs assist in the training and placement of Indians. Special assistance for Indians includes: transportation for job interviews; special counseling on skills, dress, etc.; and home visits by counselors.

There is a full-time consultant on Indian affairs in the Colorado Department of Education.

Ft. Lewis College, Durango, has approximately 200 Indian students from 42 different tribes, and provides a "summer pre-college course." This course not only gives help in registration procedure, study habits, tips on social behavior and campus living, but provides extra help sessions for individuals in academically weak areas.

Up until 1971 Colorado provided tuition-free education for any qualified Indian at Ft. Lewis.[49]

Following are data on the two federally recognized groups of Indians which comprise about 23 percent of the Indians in Colorado:

TABLE 2—SERVICES FOR FEDERALLY RECOGNIZED INDIANS, COLORADO, 1970

Reservation	Population [4]	Trust Land [1] (acres)		Education [2]			Law and Order [3]		
		Tribal	Individually Owned	Federal	Public	Other	Tribe	State	Federal
Southern Ute	690	302,081	4966	2	286	7	Tribal-Federal		
Ute Mountain	1359 Colo.	448,029		63	336	11	Tribal-Federal		
	N.M.	107,520							
	Utah	2,329	9459						

[1] *Annual Report on Indian Lands*, 1970, BIA.
[2] *Statistics Concerning Indian Education*, 1970, BIA.
[3] *Law and Order Summary*, June 1970, BIA.
[4] *Indian Reservation Population*, March 10, 1970, BIA.

---

[48] Many other States do this, too, but did not report a breakdown of effort for their Indian communities.
[49] Sec. 124–14–12, Colorado Revised Statutes, 1963.

It will be noted that education is under public schools for the most part. The Federal Government operates no Indian schools in Colorado, but allotted Colorado $182,427 for the education of Indian children in 1970.

Connecticut

Connecticut has a little over 2,000 (2,222) Indians and operates a small State program. The Welfare Department "is charged with the supervision and maintenance of four small reservations that were set aside for descendants possessing at least one-eighth Indian blood of the Schaghiticoke, Eastern and Western Pequot, or Golden Hill Tribes. At present, we have 14 qualified Indians residing on our reservations and 7 of these are receiving public assistance from the Welfare Department," says the Commissioner of this State Department.

The Supervisory Investigator in the Welfare Department, devotes 10 percent of his time to Indian affairs, including "resources investigation and development," general care and management of all persons residing on such reservations, and general supervision of the lands and buildings on the reservations. Tribal funds are under the control of the Commissioner of Welfare and are used for carrying out his duties in accordance with the provisions of the statutes pertaining to Indians.

"Appropriations for fiscal year 1969 totaled $5,000 of which the following was spent: general assistance $1,275; medical expense $54; property repairs $1,507," according to a letter from John F. Harder, Commissioner, Connecticut State Welfare Department, May 15, 1970.

Indians residing on State reservation land do not pay property taxes, but do pay other taxes as appropriate. If an Indian family needs special help State funds may be used; for example, the State has purchased coal for one family and paid for gas heat for another. However, those that are not self-sufficient are generally on public assistance.[50]

A few Indians are affected by the special State program in Connecticut but there is no Federal program. Most Connecticut Indians are in the same category as their non-Indian neighbors and receive no special services because of their Indian status.

Virginia

Virginia's 4,900 (4,904) Indians are serviced the same as other State citizens for the most part. The Chickahominys are the largest remaining groups (estimated to be 490 in 1966) and live on both sides of the Chickahominy River in New Kent and Charles Counties. They pay taxes, vote, own their own land, and send their children to public school. The Rappahannocks, Amherst County Indians, and Upper Mattaponi are other Virginia groups. All are Virginia citizens and relate to local and State government in the same manner as other Virginia citizens.

Only two small groups, the Pamunkeys (approximately 40 persons) and the Mattaponis (approximately 60 persons) own their own reservation lands in common and receive special dispensation from the State.

These two reservations were confirmed to the Indians in 1658 by the Colonial government of Virginia. Today tribal members who reside on the reservations are exempt from State and local taxes, and their children's education is funded by the

---

[50] Telephone conversation with Edward Danielczak, Supervisory Investigator, Connecticut State Welfare Department. 1–21–71.

State in the King William County schools—including tuition, cafeteria meals, and free textbooks.[51]

Each of the two reservations has its own government in the form of a tribal council and chief. The tribes handle arrests and punishments for misdemeanors; local and State police have jurisdiction on felonies. Local and State police will take jurisdiction for misdemeanors upon invitation from the tribe or the registering of a complaint.[52]

Under a treaty between the Indians and the English Government, ratified by the Virginia House of Burgesses in 1646, in return for protection the Indians were to pay the King's Governor 20 beaver skins at the going away of the geese yearly. With present day scarcity of beaver, this tradition is still carried out with payment being a deer, geese, rabbits, or fish.

There are no federally recognized Indian groups in Virginia.

Wisconsin

General

Of the 19,000 (18,924) Indians in Wisconsin, only 7,000 (6,862) are eligible for Federal services.[53] Thus most Wisconsin Indians obtain whatever services and benefits they receive from the State and local governments. Indians are scattered throughout Wisconsin's 72 counties. The four counties with 1,000 or more Indians are:

TABLE 3—INDIANS IN WISCONSIN BY COUNTY, 1970

County	Population	
	Indian	Total
Milwaukee	3,717	1,054,063
Menominee	2,306	2,607
Brown	1,695	158,244
Outagamie	1,064	119,356

The only federally recognized group in these concentrations is the Oneida community in Outagamie and Brown counties.

The largest Indian groups are near or in metropolitan centers except for Menominee County. Brown and Outagamie Counties are to the south and west of Green Bay. Milwaukee County has the city of Milwaukee. The former Menominee

---

[51] Letters to T. W. Taylor from: Gerald L. Baliles, Assistant Attorney General, State of Virginia, dated September 3, 1970; and J. G. Blount, Jr., Assistant Superintendent Administration, Virginia State Board of Education, August 11, 1970. There were only 4 Pamunkey and 12 Mattaponi resident children attending the King William County Schools during the 1970–71 school year.

[52] Telephone conversations by T. W. Taylor with: Chief Tecumseh D. Cook, Pamunkey, October 5, 1970; and Chief Curtis L. Custalow, Sr., October 6, 1970. Chief Cook indicated that Pamunkeys vote in State elections. Chief Custalow indicated that Mattaponis living on the reservation did not generally vote in State elections, although he thought they could so vote if they chose.

[53] The exception is any Indian with 25 percent Indian blood may be eligible for a scholarship grant for higher education from BIA.

Reservation became Menominee County in 1961. Most of the federally recognized Indians are in the northern part of the State.[54]

Even for those groups with Federal eligibility (primarily those with land held in trust by the Federal Government) the major functions of Government are performed by the State, e.g., education and law and order. The last BIA school was closed in 1948. The following table illustrates the State involvement in services for Indians with Federal eligibility.

TABLE 4—SERVICES FOR FEDERALLY RECOGNIZED INDIANS, WISCONSIN, 1970

Tribes	Population⁴	Trust Land¹ (acres)		Education²			Law and Order³		
		Tribal	Individual	Federal	Public	Other	Tribal	State	Federal
Chippewa Tribes									
Bad River	441	8,703	33,058		X			X	
La Courte Oreilles	760	3,945	26,434		X			X	
Lac du Flambeau	893	29,090	15,315		X			X	
Red Cliff	363	5,126	2,145		X			X	
Sakaogon (Mole Lake)	133	1,694			X			X	
St. Croix	327	1,715	515		X			X	
Oneida	1,948	2,109	466		X			X	
Potowatomi	219	11,266	400		X			X	
Stockbridge-Munsee	479	2,250			X			X	
Winnebago	1,353	300	3,626		X			X	
Total	6,862⁵	66,199	81,959	0	1,947⁶	0	0	10	0

¹ *Annual Report on Indian Lands*, v970, BIA.
² *Statistics Concerning Indian Education*, 1970, BIA.
³ *Law and Order Summary*, June 1970, BIA.
⁴ Indian Reservation Population, March 1970, *Annual Report on Indian Lands*, Bureau of Indian Affairs, June 30, 1970.
⁵ The figure for Winnegabo includes 54 Indians in Minnesota; these have been subtracted from the total.
⁶ Total school children, Great Lakes Agency, all in public school, fiscal year, 1970.

Wisconsin has a positive attitude toward its Indian citizens and has accepted responsibilities transferred from the Federal Government. The State maintains that it has objectively assessed Indian needs unfilled by the Federal Government or the State and attempted to devise State remedies. These efforts have not been sufficient, however, and the Federal Government has had to come to the State's aid in the case of the terminated Menominees.

A brief description of some of the State's relation to its Indian citizens will demonstrate Wisconsin's approach.[55]

---

[54] Many members of federally recognized tribes may be in the urban areas, but unless they return to the reservation they are not eligible for special Federal services execpt for higher education grants.

[55] Most of the description which follows is excerpted from the *Handbook on Wisconsin Indians* (Madison, Wisc.: Governor's Commission on Human Rights, 1966).

Education

The State used Johnson-O'Malley funds ($326,500 in 1970) to reimburse local school districts "with as much money per Indian child living on non-taxable land as that district taxes itself per child living on taxable property. *** This policy does much to bring about attitudes favoring full acceptance of the Indian child in the community school." The State Department of Public Instruction, through the supervisors of Indian education and the assistant superintendent of public instruction, has tried to develop understanding among all professional people of the special problems Indian students face, as well as to maintain close consultation with principals, teachers, Indian students, tribal leaders, and parents. "This close consultation and continued encouragement have paid major dividends in student attendance, teacher awareness, and family support."

An Indian resident of Wisconsin of one-fourth or more Indian blood, judged to have college potential, and finishing high school in the upper two-thirds of his class, is eligible for a college scholarship which is funded jointly by the State and BIA.

The State entered into a contract in 1955 with the Federal Government to conduct an adult education program for the Menominees to help them prepare for termination.

The Department of Public Instruction has expressed the following philosophy: [56]

We do not want the Indian to 'get lost.' We merely want to extend to him the opportunities of the white man's culture as he extended to us the values of basic American Indian life. The economic sufficiency of any people depends to a large extent upon relations with others. The Indian people, by and large, recognize that they are no exception. In order to carry on successful relationships, both business and social, with his white neighbors, the Indian must mingle with them. Tribal and legal fences about the reservation must have gates that permit a two-way passage of knowledge, inspiration, and service. The public school can be and should be the biggest gate of all.

Welfare

In 1951 the State legislature passed a bill making funds available to furnish relief to needy Indians residing on taxfree land. The need for this statewide appropriation resulted from the fact that most of the Indians living on Federal non-taxable lands were located in counties which themselves were among the poorest in economic resources in the state. Thus, the counties were not able to assume the additional burden of relief to a group of citizens who made no contribution to the county property tax fund. The Division of Public Assistance administers the relief through the county welfare departments. The local agencies give to the eligible Indians at least 85 percent of the standard allowance established for recipients of social security aids; the relief may be in the form of money grants, commodities or work relief.[57]

The State welfare department also has held conferences for its social workers and Indians to help recognize problems and stimulate Indian leadership to help themselves.

The State no longer accepts Federal aid for foster home care of Indian children.

---

[56] Annual Report, *Indian Education, 1951–52.*

[57] *Handbook on Wisconsin Indians* (Madison, Wisc.: Governor's Commission on Human Rights, 1966).

"Regardless of skin color or federal wardship, the state now takes full responsibility for the care of all its dependent children." [58]

Indian children *** are placed in foster homes or in boarding homes. These homes are for the most part white because few Indian homes meet state standards for foster care.

Thirty-two Indian children were accepted for adoption in 1965, mainly in Wisconsin homes, although some of the children went to out-of-state families through the sponsorship of the Child Welfare League, Indian Adoption Project.

The welfare department has also been assigned special responsibilities for the Menominees. In 1964, the department was made responsible for providing assistance grants and loans to Menominees so that they would have a reasonable alternative to assigning their bonds over to private individuals when they needed loans. A State appropriation of $1 million was made available for this purpose. [59]

Each member of the Menominee tribe was issued at termination a $3,000 bond carrying a 4 percent annual interest payment as the individual share in the Menominee Enterprises. These bonds became negotiable in 1964.

The 1964 legislation also made possible public assistance aids (such as social security, old age assistance, etc.) to Menominees who would not be considered eligible if they had negotiable bonds. To administer the bill, the Division of Public Assistance maintained a staff of three trained social workers in Menominee County for over a year and a half. Menominees borrowed against the bonds using the money to repay medical bills, to improve their houses and to buy cars for needed transportation to job sites. The loans and grants were charged against the bonds. As of May 1966, the $1,000,000 fund for this purpose was almost entirely expended.

Using Federal funds, the Menominee County Welfare office employs four Menominee homemakers to work closely with individual families to bring improvements in the standards of living. [60]

Law and Order

The State exercises civil and criminal jurisdiction over all reservations. The Wisconsin Handbook states: [61]

. . . the Attorney General is concerned with the protection of the Indians as citizens of the state and, also, as a special group of citizens who because of their heritage and history require additional care to ensure their equal treatment.

Other Activities

The State departments work with Indian groups on white pine blister rust control, 4-H, home economics, forest management plans, and employment.

The State Department of Conservation allows the town of Lac du Flambeau to carry on a netting and fish transfer program and permits the taking of suckers for food during the spring netting operations. The legislature gave the Conservation Commission authority over the harvesting of wild rice, primarily for the protection of the Indians and help insure a lasting supply of rice. The Menominee Enterprises submits a forest management plan for the approval of the Commission.

Special, direct health services by the State Board of Health have been provided

---

[58] Ibid.
[59] Ibid.
[60] Ibid.
[61] Ibid.

in Menominee County. In other areas the county public health nurses, district sanitarians and nutrition consultants work with Indian and other clients.

The State Highway Commission works with the Bureau of Indian Affairs by aiding in construction and supervision of county highways and town roads within the reservations, and in securing rights-of-way through Indian land. "In 1965 the legislature established an emergency work program ($300 thousand) in Menominee County for the purpose of providing immediate and necessary employment for the Indians . . . and for the necessary improvement of county and town highways in the county."

The Governor's Commission on Human Rights has had membership on the Menominee Study Committee and has "aided and encouraged Indians and non-Indians alike to meet together to work in solving the varied social and economic problems which Indians face." This Commission initiated the Stockbridge-Munsee arts and crafts project.

The Wisconsin Employment Service has brought to areas of concentrated Indian population all the services of a regular employment office. (Main problem: no job opportunities for the unemployed in Menominee County.)

The State Department of Resource Development works with the Great Lakes Inter-Tribal Council and BIA to bring more industry into Indian communities.

The University of Wisconsin has had an active interest in Wisconsin Indians.

Wisconsin's vocational schools are available to Indians; in fact, Indian vocational students receive special assistance of $20 a week.

Indian Leadership

The *Handbook on Wisconsin Indians* [62] points out that "A freshening wind of leadership from among the Indians themselves has generated a broad interest in discovering these forgotten citizens and in acknowledging responsibility toward them." Indian young people in greater numbers [63] are finishing high school and going on to college. Indian groups have housing authorities and are endeavoring to attract new industry to their land areas. Many Indians are living and working in non-Indian communities.

Former Governor Warren P. Knowles put it this way: [64]

> A relatively small group among us, our Indian citizens are a vital, direct link with the history of this great land. Their residence here has been far longer than ours, their appreciation of the beauty and resources of this region is greater than ours, and as we seek to preserve our wild life and streams, our fields and forests, the Indians have much to teach us. Furthermore, with increasing educational and economic opportunities, the Indians are taking an ever more important part in our common life. They live and work in our cities as well as our rural regions, but by maintaining their ancient love of the land, their kinship with the natural world, they remind us of values we tend to lose in the fast pace of modern life.

The Menominee Indian Story

The termination of Federal responsibilities for Menominee Indians is an important part of this study, as it illustrates some of the problems encountered in

---

[62] Ibid.

[63] Forty-nine were assisted by Federal-State grants in 1970.

[64] Governor Knowles—Foreword to *Handbook on Wisconsin Indians*, op. cit.

across-the-board transfers of functions from the Federal Government to State Government as compared with a function-by-function approach described in Chapter III.[65]

Wisconsin and the Menominees face tough challenges. Although the Menominees, the State, and the Executive and Legislative branches of the Federal Government all supported the Menominee Termination Act of 1954,[66] there were second thoughts on the part of all participants, except for the Federal Congress, prior to the effective date of termination. Even the Congress delayed the original effective date from 1956 to 1961.

Upon termination, two entities were established by State law in place of the Menominee Tribe: Menominee Enterprises, Inc. to which was transferred all tribal land, the forest, and the sawmill; and Menominee County, with the same boundaries as the previous reservation, which inherited governmental responsibilities. The 1970 census indicates 2,607 residents in Menominee County of which 2,306 are Indians. The dependence of the county at that time on one basic activity—the exploitation of the forest through the sawmill—was the reason for the second thoughts on the desirability of termination in 1961.

Corporation income bonds were issued to members of the Tribe to represent the capital value of the previous annual stumpage payments made to each member of the Tribe. Payment of interest on these bonds ($3,000 value each) was to approximate the former stumpage payments.

Thus, the Menominee Enterprises had two financial loads to carry over and above its operating expenses: interest on the bonds and real estate taxes for support of Menominee County government.

Menominee Enterprises has had rough going. Only in three years since 1962 has the Enterprise shown a net profit. However, those three occasions happened during the last 4 years.[67]

General Economic Condition: In 1961, Menominee County had a population of about 2,500, was one of the poorest counties in the State in terms of assessed value, and in 1960 reported that over 90 percent of the families had an income of less than $1,000 per family.

This general poverty and the knowledge that the forest and the mill would be hard pressed to support all governmental services through taxes as well as pay interest on the bonds, led the State to provide for a combination of town and county governments and for the servicing of Menominee County by the court and school systems of Shawano County.

Federal assistance for education was reduced from $220,000 in 1962 to $88,000 in 1965 and added to the county's burden.[68]

State assistance to the county through regular formula was received. In addition, the State gave Menominee two additional grants in 1964: $17,525 for a part of the county's share of welfare costs; and $80 thousand for treatment of tuberculosis.

Although income to families improved somewhat by 1965, the ever increasing tax load, reducing Federal aids, and interest payments on bonds threatened disasterous consequences for both the county and the corporation.

---

[65] See also the discussion of the Klamath Tribe in Oregon, appendix H–3.

[66] 66 Stat. 250.

[67] "Report of Menominee Indian Study Committee," vol. VIII, *Report of Wisconsin Legislative Council,* 1969, p. 18.

[68] "The Status of the Termination of the Menominee Indian Tribe," prepared by BIA in 1965. Requested by the House Committee on Appropriations. Text appeared in the *Congressional Record,* March 30, 1965, pp. 6312–17. It also appears in "Menominee County Aid," *Hearings on S. 1935,* (Washington, D. C.: 89th Cong., 1st sess., U.S. Senate, Subcommittee on Employment and Manpower, 1965), pp. 318–29.

Therefore, with the support of the Department of the Interior, in 1966 the Congress authorized $1.4 million for HEW to pay to Wisconsin over a 4 year period: education ($600 thousand), welfare ($400 thousand), and health and sanitation ($400 thousand). The act [69] also authorized an additional $450 thousand to complete the construction of sanitation facilities in Menominee County.[70]

The Dilemma: Because a close look at the Menominee situation indicated limited resources to support an independent county, in 1959 the Wisconsin legislature had asked the Congress to postpone termination.[71]

The Department of the Interior, too, had foreseen this difficulty, and in 1961 had recommended to the Congress that the effective date of termination be delayed so that Federal funds especially for Menominee Indians would not come after termination of the trust. The Congress did not see fit to follow these recommendations.[72]

So the "terminated" Menominees have received special Federal funds—somewhat of a contradiction in terms.

Special State Review: In 1959 the State provided that when the Termination Act became operative, the former reservation would receive county status. This status was to be reviewed by the legislature in 1965. If the 1965 legislature did not repeal the act creating Menominee County it would continue until July 31, 1969.[73] This deadline was extended to December 1, 1969. If the act was not repealed after review by the 1969 legislature, it would become final.

The 1969 Report of the Menominee Indian Study Committee, which was reviewed by the 1969 legislature, projected improvement in economic activity and the tax base for the county—from approximately $21 million in 1969 to $43.4 million in 1974.[74]

The basis for this increase is the recreational development proposed for the county. The "Lakes of the Menominees" land development was estimated to increase the residential tax base by approximately $18.5 million.[75]

A Visitor Destination Center, near Keshena, was initiated in 1969 [76] and will include resort oriented facilities such as a 200 room hotel, meeting and convention rooms, gift shop, nature awareness and cultural centers, logging camp area, and a museum.

Wolf River in Menominee County is an area of great scenic and natural beauty. It is federally protected under the Wild and Scenic Rivers Act and has great potential as a tourist attraction.[77]

Conclusions of the Study Committee: On the basis of the foregoing and the potential for additional development, including expansion and improvement of the forest industry, the Menominee Indian Study Committee recommended that Menominee "retain its status as Wisconsin's 72nd County." [78]

---

[69] 80 Stat. 903.

[70] These funds were appropriated over a 4 year period, the last payment being made in fiscal year 1970. Telephone conversation with Mr. Arthur J. Amadeo of IHS budget office, January 25, 1971.

[71] "The Status of the Termination of the Menominee Tribe," op. cit.

[72] Ibid.

[73] Laws of 1959, Ch. 259, A.42.

[74] "Report of Menominee Indian Study Committee," Wisconsin Legislative Council, January 1970, p. 22.

[75] This recreational development was proposed by Ernst and Ernst, in a study funded by the Economic Development Administration (EDA) in 1967. Menominee Enterprises entered into a partnership with N. E. Isaacson and Associates, Inc., in July 1968, for the development of the project. Ibid.

[76] EDA project No. 06–1–00653.

[77] 82 Stat. 906.

[78] "Report of Menominee Indian Study Committee," op. cit. p. 39.

The legislature took no action and Menominee County continues.

Present Situation: Although welfare costs in the county have increased from approximately $49.7 thousand in 1965 to $80 thousand in 1968, the cash income per family seems to be improving. With the projected development and its related jobs these family income figures should improve.

Welfare costs indicate a major increase in Aid for Dependent Children and medical assistance.[79]

If the proposed recreational and land developments proceed as projected, the economic situation at Menominee should improve. In any event, the Menominee experience indicates the concern of the State, as well as the Federal Government, in working out a viable solution to the county's difficulties.[79A]

Summary

In these four States with a total of 34,886 Indians, 75 percent receive primary services from the States and localities. Only 25 percent (8,626) receive some services from the Federal Government.[80]

---

[79] Ibid., p. 27.

[79A] The Menominee Tribe is pushing legislation to repeal termination (June 1972).

[80] South Carolina has a 600 acre State reservation for the Catawba Indians. There are 60 residents, land is held in common, and land is not taxed. The children go to public schools. Letter to writer from Martin Hardin, February 19, 1971. Telephone conversation with Donald Williams, pastor of Mormon church on the reservation, May 20, 1971.

CONFLICTING ATTITUDES ON THE ALLOTMENT ACT OF 1887 (24 Stat. 388)

Arguments by those favoring the Act in the 1880's were: the Act would provide the land base and the incentive for the Indians to become self-supporting farmers and citizens of the Nation; Indian land held in common was not intensively used and it was difficult to protect from white encroachment, which led to bitter and bloody conflicts and threatened the loss of *all* tribal land to whites; development and civilization of the Nation was desirable and surplus Indian land should be sold so that it could be developed; the more aggressive Indians exploited their brethren by using large areas of commonly owned land with no payment of rent to the other owners.

"Friends of the Indian" organizations supporting the proposal included the Women's National Indian Association, the Indian Rights Association, and the Lake Mohonk Conferences from 1883 to 1887.

The Bureau of Indian Affairs, the Secretary of Interior, John Wesley Powell, Director of the Bureau of American Ethnology, the Board of Indian Commissioners, and the President, were in favor.

Some Indians favored allotment, probably with "a hope that patents in fee would protect them against white inroads upon their lands and against the danger of removal by the government." [81]

Opponents of the Act made the following points: Indians were not agriculturists and the basic premise that they would become independent farmers and integrate into the society around them was false; the proposal was a scheme by the "land hungry" to appropriate Indian land. For example, the minority report of the House Indian Affairs Committee in 1880 accused: [82]

> The real aim of this bill is to get at the Indian lands and open them up to settlement. x x x If this were done in the name of greed, it would be bad enough; but to do it in the name of humanity, and under the cloak of an ardent desire to promote the Indian's welfare by making him like ourselves, whether he will or not, is infinitely worse.

Desire for land was a factor, but in the author's opinion public servants and friends of the Indians had other compelling motives. Many Indians, being largely

---

[81] D. S. Otis, Professor at Columbia University, "History of the Allotment Policy", *Hearings on H. R. 7902*, pt. 9, Committee on Indian Affairs (Washington, D.C.: 73rd Cong., 2nd sess., U. S. House of Representatives, 1934), p. 443.

[82] Ibid., p. 434. Many students of Indian history lay primary emphasis on land pressures. See, for example, Theodore H. Haas, "The Legal Aspects of Indian Affairs from 1887 to 1957," *The Annals of the American Academy of Political and Social Science*, May 1957, p. 12–13. See also D'Arcy McNickle, op. cit., p. 1; John Collier, *Indians of the Americas* (New York: W. W. Norton, 1947), pp. 214–216.

subsisted by the Government, lived near the agency. Large portions of their land were unused. White settlers moved into the vacuum, sometimes not knowing that it was Indian land. Agency staffs were small; the expulsion of trespassers was difficult. Secretary of the Interior Carl Schurz, in 1881, pointed out that feeling against the Utes was running high in Colorado and allotment was the only device that saved a portion of their lands.[83]

It must be kept in mind that the settlement of the Indians in severalty is one of those things for which the Indians and the government are not always permitted to choose their own time. *** Nobody will pretend that the Utes were fully prepared for such a change in their condition. ***But nothing short of it would have saved the Ute tribe from destruction, and averted a most bloody and expensive conflict. ***The question is, whether the Indians are to be exposed to the danger of hostile collisions, and of being robbed of their lands in consequence, or whether they are to be induced by proper and fair means to sell that which, as long as they keep it, is of no advantage to anybody, but which, as soon as they part with it for a just compensation, will be a great advantage to themselves and their white neighbors alike.

In summary, Otis stated perceptively: [84]

Implicit in this statement of Carl Schurz's is a summary of the whole Indian problem so far as Government policies are concerned. Clear is the sense of limitation and of justification. It makes understandable the entire subsequent working out of the allotment program. It was apparent that the Indian system was being smashed by the white economy and culture. Friends of the Indian, therefore, saw his one chance for survival in his adapting himself to the white civilization. He must be taught industry and acquisitiveness to fit him for his 'ultimate absorption in the great body of American citizenship.' Making him a citizen and a voter would guarantee to him the protection of the rules under which the competitive game of life was played. And it was to be hoped that he would take his place among the more skillful white players.

However, Indians did not favor agriculture and they proceeded to lease their allotments rather than farm the land themselves. Their tradition and culture proved an infertile bed for the seeds of independent farming. Otis points out that the friends of the Indians favoring the allotment system paid little attention to previous unsatisfactory experience in individualizing land ownership. The passage of the Allotment Act was an act of faith "that individual enterprise was the God-given way of civilization".[85]

---

[83] Article in *North American Review*, July 1881, cited by Otis, op. cit., p. 433.

[84] Ibid.

[85] Otis, op. cit., p. 449.

LIST OF STATE RESERVATIONS, INDIAN GROUPS WITHOUT TRUST LAND, TERMINATED TRIBES AND GROUPS
(keyed to map in pocket)

State Reservations	Numbers 1–26
Indian Groups Without Trust Land	Numbers 30–67
Terminated Tribes and Groups	Numbers 80–93

STATE RESERVATIONS

Pocket map { Symbol: Red ▲ Numbers 1–26

(Acreage and population for States concerned as of 1969.)

MAINE

No.	Reservation	Acreage	Population
	PASSAMAQUODDY Tribe		
1	Indian Township (colonially derived)	18,000	221[1]
2	Pleasant Point (colonially derived)	100	342[1]
3	PENOBSCOT Tribe (Indian Island)		
	(colonially derived)	4,500	400[1]

MASSACHUSETTS

4	NIPMUC Tribe	11.9	1
	Grafton Reservation (colonially derived)		
	Nipmuc community may consist of 2 to 300 individuals, only one of whom lives on the reservation.		
	NOTE: 227.5 acres in Freetown Forest, no residents.		

CONNECTICUT

5	PAUGUSETT, Golden Hill Reservation	1 lot	2
6	PEQUOT, Eastern Pequot Reservation	220	11
7	PEQUOT, Western Pequot Reservation (Lantern Hill)	184	2
8	SCATICOOK, Schagticoke Reservation (Kent)	400	0

---

[1] Economic Development Administration (EDA) Handbook, *Federal and State Indian Reservations* (Washington, D. C.: Department of Commerce, 1971).

MICHIGAN

No.	Reservation	Acreage	Population
8A	POTAWATOMI of the Huron Community	120	157

NEW YORK

IROQUOIS—largely State supervised;
Federal consent required for
alienation of land; some Federal
programs available.

No.	Reservation	Acreage	Population
13	CAYUGA NATION, members live on Cattaraugus Reservation	0	303
9	ONEIDA NATION OF NEW YORK, non-reservation tax exempt land	358	120
10	ONONDAGA NATION, Onondaga Reservation (includes some Oneida)	7,300	1,110 Onondaga 470 Oneida
11	ST. REGIS BAND OF MOHAWKS (Akwesasne)	38,390	2,229
	SENECA NATION	44,320	4,600
12	Allegany Reservation	(22,000)	(1,200 resident) [2]
13	Cattaraugus Reservation (incl. Cayuga Nation)	(21,680)	(2,400 resident) [2]
14	Oil Springs Reservation	(640)	0
15	TONAWANDA BAND OF SENECA, Tonawanda Reservation	7,549	824
16	TUSCARORA NATION, Tuscarora Reservation	5,700	647

Other New York—State supervised;
colonially derived.

No.	Reservation	Acreage	Population
17	POOSEPATUCK (Long Island)	60	100
18	SHINNECOCK (Long Island)	400	240

PENNSYLVANIA

No.	Reservation	Acreage	Population
19	SENECAS of Cornplanter Reservation State established	?	0

VIRGINIA

(colonially derived)

No.	Reservation	Acreage	Population
20	MATTAPONI Tribe, Mattaponi Reservation	382	65
21	PAMUNKEY Tribe, Pamunkey Reservation	1,075	33

SOUTH CAROLINA

No.	Reservation	Acreage	Population
22	CATAWBA Tribe, Catawba Reservation (Formerly under Federal trust and supervision) Colonially derived	600	60

---

[2] Ibid.

FLORIDA [3]

No.	Reservation	Acreage	Population
23	MICCOSUKEE Tribe of Indians of Florida (Tamiami Trail)	76,800	255
24	SEMINOLE Tribe of Florida	28,000	1,031

TEXAS

No.	Reservation	Acreage	Population
25	ALABAMA-COUSHATTA Tribe, Polk County Reservation (formerly Federal trust and supervision)	3,200	450
26	YSLETA TIGUA Community, El Paso State established lands	443	409

INDIAN GROUPS WITHOUT TRUST LAND

Pocket map { Symbol Red: ■ Number 30–67

(Population from 1966 figures for *National Atlas* prepared by Bureau of Indian Affairs unless otherwise noted.)

NOTE: Includes groups of partial Indian ancestry on the Eastern seaboard. Only the larger or better known are included. Quotation marks around name indicate the name was not derived from a specific historic tribe.

ALABAMA

No.	Reservation	Population
30	CREEK, near Atmore	545

ARIZONA

No.	Reservation	Population
31	YAQUI Indians of Arizona Pasqua Village, Tucson (federally established village)	650
	Barrio Libre, South Tucson	600
32	Guadalupe, Phoenix	550
32A	TONTO, APACHE, Payson	85

CALIFORNIA

(Only the two largest and more homogeneous historic groups are listed.)

No.	Reservation	Population
33	PIT RIVER, Alturas	100
34	JAMUL DIEGUENO, near San Diego	100

CONNECTICUT

No.	Reservation	Population
35	MOHEGAN Community, New London County	150

DELAWARE

No.	Reservation	Population
36	"MOOR" Community, Kent County	310
37	NANTICOKE Community, Sussex County	411

---

[3] In addition, Florida provides 143,000 acres of use rights.

FLORIDA

No.	*Reservation*	*Population*
37–A	Non-enrolled SEMINOLES in Tamiami Trail area eligible for membership with either of the two Florida tribes	200

INDIANA

38	MIAMI Community at Peru	93

KANSAS

39	CHIPPEWA and MUNSEE DELAWARE Community, Franklin County	43
39–A	WYANDOT Community, Wyandot County	134

LOUISIANA

40	CHOCTAW Community, La Salle Parish	41
41	CHOCTAW Community, Rapides Parish	181
42	CHOCTAW Community, St. Tammany Parish	55
43	COUSHATTA Community, Allen and Jefferson Davis Parishes	196
44	HOUMA Communities, Terrebonne and Lafourche Parishes	2,221
45	TUNICA Community, Avoyelles Parish (land evidently not taxed by State)	23

MAINE

46	MALECITE Communities, Aroostook County	517
46A	MICMAC Communities, Aroostook County	600

MASSACHUSETTS

47	NIPMUC Community, near Worcester	2–300
48	WAMPANOAG Community, Gay Head	100
49	WAMPANOAG Community, Mashpee	435

MICHIGAN

50	OTTAWA and CHIPPEWA Indians of Michigan primarily in Delta, Schoolcraft, Mackinac, and Charlevoix Counties	1,500
51	POGAGON POTAWATOMI Communities in Berian, Cass, and Van Buren Counties	637

MONTANA

52–A	Montana "Landless Indians," primarily METIS at Great Falls, Chinook, Hays, Wolf Point, and other places	1,500

NEW YORK

54	MONTAUK Community, Montauk	42

NORTH CAROLINA

No.	Reservation	Population
55	"COHARIE" Indians, Sampson and adjoining counties	3,000
56	PERSON COUNTY INDIANS, Person County	333
57	"HALIWA" Indians, Halifax and Warren Counties	2,000
58	"LUMBEE" Indians of North Carolina, Robeson and adjoining counties	31,380
59	"WACCAMAW" Communities, Columbus and Bremswick Counties	2,000

OREGON

60	Communities in Lane, Douglas, and Curry Counties (1966) ALSEA, MOLALLA, UMPQUA, and others	600

RHODE ISLAND

61	NARRAGANSET Community, Narraganset Church and Washington County (Colonially derived; formerly State supervised. Some acreage left (non-taxable) around church.)	424

SOUTH CAROLINA

61A	SUMMERVILLE INDIANS, Dorchester and Colleton Counties	250

UTAH

62	SOUTHERN PAIUTE Community, Cedar City Informally organized on Mormon Church land	162

VIRGINIA

63	CHICKAHOMINY Communities, Providence Forge and Charles City	490
64	AMHERST County Indians, Amherst County	128
65	RAPPAHANOCK Community, Caroline and King and Queen Counties	165
66	UPPER MATTAPONI, Central Garage, King William County	120

WISCONSIN

67	BROTHERTON Community, Winnebago and Calumet Counties	254

BORDER GROUPS (Not posted to map)

CANADA

MALECITE (Maine–Canada)
ST. REGIS MOHAWKS (New York–Canada)
(New York group is separately organized.)
METIS (North Dakota and Montana–Canada.
Most American Metis are enrolled with Turtle Mountain
Band of Chippewa Indians of North Dakota.)
TLINGITS and HAIDAS (Alaska–Canada)

MEXICO

KICKAPOOS Mexican reservation in state of Coahuilla—related to the Oklahoma
Kickapoos and member of that tribe. Group situated well below the border.
Mexican PAPAGOS (Arizona–Mexico)
DIEGUENOS (Baja, California) maintain some contact with Mission groups in
California.

TERMINATED TRIBES AND GROUPS

Pocket map { Symbol: red □
{ Numbers 80–93

Note: Lands no longer in trust with the Federal Government and Indians no
longer eligible for special Federal services to Indians.
See also Table III, Appendix B, for list of termination statutes.

CALIFORNIA

No.	Tribe or Group	Tribal Acres [1]	Membership [1]
	California Rancherias, 38 terminated as of 6–30–71, scattered over State, small, not posted to map	4,317	1,107

NEBRASKA

| 80 | PONCA Tribe of Nebraska 10–27–66 | 834 | 442 |

OKLAHOMA

81	OTTAWA Tribe of Oklahoma [2] (except for claims purposes)	0	630
82	PEORIA Tribe of Oklahoma,[2] has termination act, proclamation deferred, still eligible for education and health and trust property services	0	640
83	WYANDOTTE [2] has termination act, proclamation deferred, still eligible for education and health and trust property services	94	1,157

[1] At time of termination.
[2] Not shown on map as terminated.

OREGON

No.	Tribe or Group	Tribal Acres [1]	Membership [1]
84	KLAMATH Tribe of Oregon 8–13–61	862,662	2,133
85	WESTERN OREGON Indians, 60 "bands" over large coastal area. 8–18–56	3,158	2,081

SOUTH CAROLINA

No.	Tribe or Group	Tribal Acres	Membership
86	CATAWBA Tribe of South Carolina 7–1–62	3,388	631

TEXAS

No.	Tribe or Group	Tribal Acres	Membership
87	ALABAMA-COUSHATTA Tribe of Texas 7–1–55 (Polk County) Texas assumed responsibility	3,200	450

UTAH

No.	Tribe or Group	Tribal Acres	Membership
	SOUTHERN PAIUTE Indians of Utah 3–1–57	42,839	232
88	Indian Peak		
89	Kanosh		
90	Koosharem		
91	Shivwitz		
92	UINTAH and OURAY Ute Mixed Bloods 8–29–61	211,430	490

WISCONSIN

No.	Tribe or Group	Tribal Acres	Membership
93	MENOMINEE Tribe of Wisconsin 4–30–61	233,881	3,270

FEDERALLY RECOGNIZED TRIBES

No numbers on map; Alaskan villages not on map but listed here. Tribes living in more than one State are listed in each State.

Code to numbers appearing after name of tribe

1. Indian or Alaska Native organizations whose constitutions are approved by the Secretary of the Interior under Federal statuatory authority of the Indian Reorganization Act; Oklahoma Indian Welfare Act; or Alaska Native Act.
2. Indian or Alaska Native organizations whose constitutions are approved by the Secretary of the Interior or his designated representative under authority other than the Indian Reorganization Act; Oklahoma Indian Welfare Act; or Alaska Native Act.
3. Indian organizations served by the Bureau of Indian Affairs whose organizational structure is not one of the above.
4. Public Domain allotments. Individuals who reside on these lands held in trust receive Bureau of Indian Affairs services on the basis of the Secretary of the Interior's responsibility over their land.
5. Indian groups that receive assistance from the Bureau only in matters relating to the settlement of claims against the U. S. Government, such as those involving inadequate compensation for land taken in the past.

ALABAMA

Creek (5) near Atmore (no corporate land base). Only the Atmore group is considered an Indian community. Others are descendants recognized for claims purposes only, for example, "Creeks East of the Mississippi."

ALASKA

(Native Villages and Reservations) An asterisk * by name of village indicates incorporation under State law in addition to Federal organizational status.

ALASKA

Juneau Area Office

Angoon (1) *	Kluckwan (Chilkat) (1)
Craig (1) *	Metlakatla (1)
Douglas (1)	Petersburg (1) *
Haines (Port Chilkoot) (1) *	Saxman (1) *
Hoonah (1) *	Sitka (1) *
Hydaburg (1) *	Wrangell (1) *
Kake (1) *	Pelican City (3)
Kasaan (1)	Skagway (3) *
Ketchikan (1)	Tenakee Springs (3)
Klawock (1) *	Yakutat (3) *

Anchorage Agency

Atka (1)
Chanega (1) (destroyed by
  earthquake)
Kanatak (1)
Karluk (1) *
Kenaitze (1)
Nikolski (1)
Perryville (1)
St. Paul (1) *
Tatitlek (1)
Tyonek (1)
Akhiok (Alitak) (3)
Akutan (3)
Aleknagik (3)
Belkofsky (3)
Bristol Bay (3) *
Chignik (3)
Chignik Lagoon (3)
Chignik Lake (3)
Chistochina (3)
Clark's Point (3)
Copper Center (3)
Cordova (3) *
Dillingham (3) *
Egegik (3)
Eklutna (3)
Ekuk (3)
Ekwok (3)
English Bay (3)
False Pass (3)
Gulkana (3)
Iliamna (3)
Ivanof Bay (3)

King Cove (3) *
Koliganek (3)
Kokhanok (3)
Larsen Bay (3)
Levelock (3)
Matanuska (3) *
Manokotak (3) *
Mentasta Lake (3)
Naknek (3) *
Nelson Lagoon (3)
Newhalen (3)
New Stuyahok (3)
Ninilchik (3)
Nondalton (3)
Old Harbor (3) *
Ouzinkie (3)
Palmer (3)
Paulof Harbor (3)
Pedro Bay (3)
Pilot Point (3)
Portage Creek (3)
Port Graham (3)
Port Heiden (3)
Port Lions (3) *
St. George Island (3)
Sand Point (3) *
South Naknek (3) *
Sterling (3)
Togiak (3) *
Twin Hills (3)
Ugashik (3)
Unalaska (3) *
Valdez (3) *

Bethel Agency

Akiachak (1)
Akiak (1)
Grayling (Holikachuk) (1)
Kwethluk (1)
Kwigillingok (1)
Mekoryuk (1)
Napakiak (1) *
Nunapitchuk (1)
Quinhagak (Kwinhagak) (1)
Shageluk (1)
Tuluksak (1) *
Tununak (1)
Alakanuk (3)
Aniak (3)
Anvik (3)
Atmautluak (3)

Bethel (3)
Chaloonawick (3)
Chaneliak (3)
Chefornak (3)
Chevak (3) *
Churarbalik—see Russian Mission
  (Kuskokwim)
Crooked Creek (3)
Eek (3)
Emmonak (Kwiguk) (3) *
Farewell (3)
Flat (3)
Georgetown (3)
Goodnews Bay (Mumtrak) (3)
Hamilton (3)
Holy Cross (3)

Hooper Bay (3) *
Kalskag (3)
Kasigluk (3)
Kipnuk (3)
Kongigonak (3)
Kotlik (3) *
Kwinhagak—See Quinhagak
Lelida (3)
Lime Village (3)
Lower Kalskag (3)
Marshall (3)
Medfra (3)
McGrath (3)
Mountain Village (3)
Nepaimute (Napamute) (3)
Napaskiak (3)
Newtok (3)
Nightmute (3)
Nikolai (3)

Oscarville (3)
Pilot Station (3)
Pitkas Point (3)
Platinum (3)
Quinhagak (3) (also spelled
   Kwinhagak)
Red Devil (3)
Russian Mission (Kuskokwim)
   (3) (Native name is Churarbalik)
Russian Mission (Yukon) (3)
St. Mary's (3) *
Scammon Bay (3) *
Sheldon's Point (3)
Sleetmute (3)
Stony River (3)
Takotna (3)
Toksook Bay (3)
Tuntutuliak (3)

Fairbanks Agency
Fort Yukon (1) *
Inupiat (1)
Minto (1)
Point Lay (1)
Stevens Village (1)
Tanacross (1)
Tanana (1) *
Tetlin (1)
Venetie (1)
Allakaket (3)
Anaktuvuk Pass (3) *
Arctic Village (3)
Barrow (3) *
Barter Island (3)
Beaver (3)
Bettles (3)
Birch Creek (3)
Cantwell (3)
Canyon Village (3)

Chalkyitsik (3)
Circle (3)
Delta Junction (3) *
Dot Lake (3)
Eagle (3) *
Galena (3)
Hughes (3)
Huslia (3)
Kaltag (3)
Koyukuk (3)
Manley Hot Springs (3)
Nenana (3) *
Northway (3)
Nulato (3) *
Rampart (3)
Ruby (3)
Tok (3)
Wainwright (3) *

Southeast Agency
Tlingit and Haida (2)

Nome Agency
Buckland (1) *
Deering (1) *
Elim (1) *
Gambell (1) *
King Island (1) *
Kivalina (1) *
Kotzebue (1) *
Koyuk (1) *

Little Diomede (1) *
Noatak (1) *
Nome (1) *
Noorvik (1) *
Point Hope (1) *
St. Michael (1) *
Savoonga (1) *
Selawik (1) *

Shaktoolik (1) *
Shishmaref (1) *
Shungnak (1) *
Stebbins (1) *
Unalakleet (1) *
Wales (1) *
White Mountain (1) *
Ambler (3) *

Brevig Mission (3) *
Candle (3)
Golovin (3) *
Kiana (3) *
Kobuk (3) *
Northeast Cape (3) *
Teller (3) *

ARIZONA

Navajo Nation (2)   Navajo Area Office (In Arizona, New Mexico & Utah)
Papago Tribe, Papago Agency (1)
San Carlos Apache Tribe (1) San Carlos Agency
White Mountain Apache Tribe (1) Fort Apache Agency

Pima Agency
  Ak Chin Indian Community (1)
  Gila River Indian Community (1)

Colorado River Agency
  Chemehuevi Indian Tribe (1)
  Cocopah Tribe (1)
  Colorado River Indian Tribes (1)   (In Arizona and California)
  Fort Mohave Tribe (1)   (in Arizona, Calif. & Nevada)
  Quechan Indian Tribe (1)   (Fort Yuma Indian Reservation)   (Arizona & Calif.)

Salt River Agency
  Fort McDowell Mohave-Apache Community (1)
  Salt River Pima-Maricopa Indian Community (1)

Truxton Canyon Agency
  Havasupai Tribe (1)
  Hualapai Tribe (1)
  Yavapai-Apache Indian Community (Camp Verde) (1)
  Yavapai Prescott Community Association (2)

Hopi Agency
  Hopi Tribe (1)
  Kaibab Band of Paiute Indians (1)

CALIFORNIA

California Agency
  Cachil Dehe Band of Wintun Indians of the Colusa Indian Community (1)
  Covelo Indian Community (Round Valley Reservation) (1)
  Fort Bidwell Indian Community (1)
  Grindstone Indian Rancheria (1)
  Kashia Band of Pomo Indians of the Stewarts Point Rancheria (1)
  Manchester Band of Pomo Indians (1)
  Santa Rosa Indian Community (Kings County) (1)
  Susanville Indian Rancheria (1)
  Tule River Indian Tribe (1)
  Tuolumne Band of Me-Wuk Indians (1)
  Cahto Indian Tribe of Laytonville Rancheria (2)

Fort Independence Indian Community (2)
Pit River Home and Agricultural Cooperative Assn. (X-L Ranch) (2)
Alturas Rancheria (3)
Berry Creek Rancheria (3)
Big Pine Band of Owens Valley Paiute-Shoshone Indians (Owens Valley) (3)
Cedarville Rancheria (3)
Cortina Rancheria (3)
Dry Creek Rancheria (3)
El-Em Indian Colony (Sulphur Bank) (3)
Enterprise Rancheria (3)
Paiute-Shoshone Indians of the Bishop Community
    (Owens-Valley) (3)
Paiute Shoshone Indians of the Lone Pine Community
    (Owens-Valley) (3)
Lookout Rancheria (3)
Sheep Ranch Rancheria (3)
Shingle Springs Rancheria (Verona Tract) (3) (unoccupied)

Termination Pending
Upper Lake Band of Pomo Indians (3)
Big Sandy Association (3)
Hopland Nokomis Association (3)
Jackson Rancheria (3)
Likely Rancheria (no membership) (1.32 acres of cemetery remaining)
Middletown Rancheria (3) (Named in original Rancheria Act PL 85–671 but
    has made no progress toward termination.)
Rumsey Rancheria (3)
Sherwood Valley Rancheria (3)
Sycamore Valley Association (Cold Springs) (3)
Table Mountain Rancheria (3)

Terminated Since 1958

Alexander Valley
Auburn
Big Valley
Buena Vista
Cache Creek
Chicken Ranch
Chico
Cloverdale
Graton
Greenville
Guidiville
Indian Ranch
Lytton
Mark West
Mooretown
Nevada City

North Fork
Paskenta
Picayune
Pinoleville
Potter Valley
Quartz Valley
Redwood Valley
Robinson
Ruffeys
Scotts Valley
Shingle Springs (El Dorado tract)
Strathmore
Strawberry Valley
Taylorsville
Wilton

Hoopa Agency
Hoopa Valley Tribe (2)
Big Bend Rancheria (3)
Hoopa Extension (3)

Montgomery Creek Rancheria (3)
Roaring Creek Rancheria (3)

Termination Pending
Cher-ae Heights Indian Community of the Trinidad Rancheria (2)
    (Constitution revoked)
Big Lagoon Rancheria (3)
Resighini Rancheria (3) (no residents)

Terminated Since 1958

Blue Lake	Rohnerville
Crescent City (Elk Valley)	Smith River
Redding	Table Bluff

Palm Springs Office
Agua Caliente Band of Mission Indians (Palm Springs) (2)

Riverside Agency
Santa Ynez Band of Mission Indians (1)
San Pasqual Band of Mission Indians (1)
Cabazon Band of Mission Indians (2)
La Jolla Band of Mission Indians (2)
Mesa Grande Band of Mission Indians (2)
Pala Band of Mission Indians (2)
Pauma Band of Mission Indians (2)
Rincon, San Luiseno Band of Mission Indians (2)
San Manuel Band of Mission Indians (2)
Augustine Band of Mission Indians (3) (no resident members)
Barona Group of Capitan Grande Band of Mission Indians (3)
Cahuilla Band of Mission Indians (3)
Capitan Grande Band of Mission Indians (3)
Cuyapaipe Band of Mission Indians (3) (no resident members)
Inaja—Cosmit Reservation (3)
LaPosta Band of Mission Indians (3)
Los Coyotes Band of Mission Indians (3)
Manzanita Band of Mission Indians (3)
Mission Band of Indians of Campo Community (3)
Morongo Band of Mission Indians (3)
Pechanga Band of Mission Indians (3)
Ramona Reservation (3) (no members)
Santa Rosa Band of Mission Indians (3)
Santa Ysabel Band of Mission Indians (3)
Soboba Band of Mission Indians (3)
Sycuan Band of Mission Indians (3)
Torres-Martinez Band of Mission Indians (3)
Twentynine Palms Band of Mission Indians (3) (no resident members)
Viejas (Baron Long) Group of Capitan Grande Band of Mission Indians (3)

Terminated Since 1958
Mission Creek Band of Mission Indians

Colorado River Agency (Arizona)
Chemehuevi Indian Tribe (1)
Colorado River Indian Tribes (1) (in Arizona and California)
Fort Mojave Tribe (1) (in Arizona. California, and Nevada)

Quechan Indian Tribe of the Fort Yuma Reservation (1)
  (in California and Arizona)

Nevada Agency (Phoenix Area Office)
  Washoe Tribe of Nevada and California (1) (Woodfords Community)

COLORADO

Southern Ute Tribe (1) Southern Ute Agency
Ute Mountain Ute Tribe (1) (in Colorado, New Mexico & Utah)
  Ute Mountain Agency

FLORIDA

Miccosukee Tribe of Indians of Florida (1) Miccosukee Business Committee
Seminole Tribe of Florida (1) Seminole Agency

IDAHO

Northern Idaho Agency
  Coeur d'Alene Tribe (2)
  Kootenai Tribe of Idaho (2)
  Nez Perce Tribe of Idaho (2)
Shoshone-Paiute Tribes of the Duck Valley Reservation (1)
  (in Idaho and Nevada) (Nevada Agency; Phoenix A.O.)
Shoshone-Bannock Tribes of the Fort Hall Reservation (1) Fort Hall Agency

IOWA

Omaha Tribe of Nebraska (1) (in Neb. & Iowa) Winnebago Agency
Sac and Fox Tribe of the Mississippi in Iowa (1) (Sac & Fox Area Field Office)
Winnebago Tribe of Nebraska (1) (in Nebraska and Iowa) Winnebago Agency

KANSAS

Horton Agency
  Iowa Tribe (1) in Kansas and Nebraska
  Kickapoo Tribe in Kansas (1)
  Prairie Band of Potawatomi Indians (2)
  Sac and Fox Tribe of the Missouri (1) (in Kansas and Nebraska)

LOUISIANA

Chitimacha Tribe of Louisiana (1) Washington Office

MICHIGAN

Great Lakes Agency
  Bay Mills Indian Community (1)
  Hannahville Indian Community (1)
  Keweenaw Bay Indian Community (L'Anse) (1)
  Saginaw-Chippewa Indian Tribe (Isabella) (1)

MINNESOTA

Red Lake Band of Chippewa Indians (2) Red Lake Agency
Wisconsin Winnebago Tribe (1) in Wisc. and Houston County, Minn.,
  Great Lakes Agency

Minnesota Agency
  Minnesota Chippewa Tribe (1)
    Bois Fort (Nett Lake)
    Fond du Lac Band
    Grand Portage Band
    Leech Lake Band
    Mille Lac Band
    White Earth
  Lower Sioux Indian Community (Morton) (1)
  Prairie Island Indian Community (1)
  Shakopee Mdewakanton Sioux Community (Prior Lake) (1)
  Upper Sioux Indian Community (Granite Falls) (3)

MISSISSIPPI

Mississippi Band of Choctaw Indians (1) Washington Office

MONTANA

Blackfeet Tribe (1) Blackfeet Agency
Chippewa Cree Tribe of the Rocky Boy's Reservation (1) Rocky Boy's Agency
Crow Tribe of Indians (2) Crow Agency
Confederated Salish and Kootenai Tribes of the Flathead Reservation (1)
  Flathead Agency
Fort Belknap Indian Community (1) Fort Belknap Agency
Assiniboine and Sioux Tribes of the Fort Peck Reservation (2)
  Fort Peck Agency
Northern Cheyenne Tribe (1) Northern Cheyenne Agency

NEBRASKA

Oglala Sioux Tribe of the Pine Ridge Reservation (1) in South Dakota
  and Nebraska

Horton Agency
  Iowa Tribe (1) in Kansas and Nebraska
  Sac and Fox Tribe of Missouri (1) in Kansas and Nebraska

Winnebago Agency
  Omaha Tribe of Nebraska (1) in Nebraska and Iowa
  Santee-Sioux Tribe of Nebraska (1)
  Winnebago Tribe of Nebraska (1) in Nebraska and Iowa

NEVADA

Nevada Agency
  Confederated Tribes of the Goshute Reservation (1) (in Nevada & Utah)
  Duckwater Shoshone Tribe (1)
  Ely Indian Colony (1)
  Fort McDermitt Paiute and Shoshone Tribe (1) (in Nevada and Oregon)
  Las Vegas Tribe of Paiute Indians (1)
  Lovelock Paiute Tribe (1)
  Moapa Band of Paiute Indians (1)
  Paiute-Shoshone Tribe of the Fallon Reservation and Colony (2)

Pyramid Lake Paiute Tribe of Nevada (1)
Reno-Sparks Indian Colony of Nevada (1)
Ruby Valley (3)
Shoshone-Paiute Tribes of the Duck Valley Reservation (1) (Nevada & Idaho)
Summit Lake Paiute Tribe, Nevada (1)
Te-Moak Bands of Western Shoshone Indians (1) (Battle Mountain, Elko &
   S. Fork)
Walker River Paiute Tribe of Nevada (1)
Washoe Tribe of Nevada and California (1) Carson and Dresslerville
   Colonies, and Woodford's Community
Winnemucca Colony (3)
Yerington Paiute Tribe (Campbell Ranch) (1)
Yomba Shoshone Tribe (1)
Fort Mojave Tribe (1) in Arizona, Calif. & Nevada (Colorado River Agency)

NEW MEXICO

Apache Tribe of the Mescalero Reservation (1) Mescalero Agency
Jicarilla Apache Tribe (1) Jicarilla Agency
Navajo Nation (2) (Arizona, New Mexico, Utah)
Ute Mountain Ute Tribe (1) (in Colorado, New Mexico and Utah)
Zuni Tribe (1) Zuni Agency

Southern Pueblos Agency
   Acoma Pueblo (3)
   Cochiti Pueblo (3)
   Isleta Pueblo (1)
   Jemez Pueblo (3)
   Laguna Pueblo (1)
   San Felipe Pueblo (3)
   Sandia Pueblo (3)
   Santa Ana Pueblo (3)
   Santo Domingo Pueblo (3)
   Zia Pueblo (3)

Northern Pueblos Agency
   Nambe Pueblo (3)
   Picuris Pueblo (3)
   Pojoaque Pueblo (3)
   San Ildefonso Pueblo (3)
   San Juan Pueblo (3)
   Santa Clara Pueblo (1)
   Taos Pueblo (3)
   Tesuque Pueblo (3)

NEW YORK

Land cannot be disposed of without permission of Federal Government; some
   Federal services available.
Seneca Nation of Indians (3) (Allegany, Cattaraugus & Oil Springs Reservations)
Cayuga Nation (3) No reservation of its own—members live on Cattaraugus Res-
   ervation owned by Seneca Nation.
Oneida Nation of New York (3)

Onondaga Nation (3)
St. Regis Band of Mohawks (Akwesasne) (3)
Tonawanda Band of Seneca (3)
Tuscarora Nation (3)

NORTH CAROLINA

Eastern Band of Cherokee Indians (3) Cherokee Agency

NORTH DAKOTA

Devils Lake Sioux Tribe (2) Fort Totten Agency
Three Affiliated Tribes of the Fort Berthold Reservation (1)
    Fort Berthold Agency
Sisseton-Wahpeton Sioux Tribe (2) (North Dakota & South Dakota)
    Sisseton Agency
Standing Rock Sioux Tribe (North Dakota and South Dakota) (2)
    Standing Rock Agency
Turtle Mountain Band of Chippewa Indians (2) Turtle Mountain Agency

OKLAHOMA

Cheyenne-Arapaho Tribes of Oklahoma (1) Concho Agency
Chickasaw Nation of Oklahoma (3) Ardmore Agency
Choctaw Nation of Oklahoma (3) Talihina Agency
Osage Tribe of Indians (2) Osage Agency
Seminole Nation of Oklahoma (2) Wewoka Agency

Anadarko Agency
    Apache (Kiowa-Apache) (3)
    Caddo Indian Tribe of Oklahoma (1)
    Comanche Indian Tribe (2)
    Delaware Tribe of Indians of Western Oklahoma (2)
    Fort Sill Apache Tribe (3)
    Kiowa (2)
    Wichita Indian Tribe of Oklahoma (2)

Miami Agency
    Eastern Shawnee Tribe of Oklahoma (1)
    Miami Tribe of Oklahoma (1)
    Peoria Tribe of Indians of Oklahoma (1) (Termination pending)
    Quapaw Tribe of Indians (2)
    Seneca-Cayuga Tribe of Oklahoma (1)
    Wyandotte Tribe of Oklahoma (1) (Termination pending)

Okmulgee Agency
    Alabama-Quassarte Tribal Town (1)
    Creek Nation of Oklahoma (3)
    Kialegee Tribal Town (1)
    Thlopthlocco Tribal Town (1)

Pawnee Agency
    Kaw Indian Tribe of Oklahoma (2)
    Otoe-Missouria Tribe (3)
    Pawnee Indian Tribe of Oklahoma (1)

Ponca Tribe of Indians of Oklahoma (1)
Tonkawa Tribe of Indians of Oklahoma (1)

Shawnee Agency
  Absentee-Shawnee Tribe of Indians of Oklahoma (1)
  Citizen Band of Potawatomi Indians of Oklahoma (1)
  Iowa Tribe of Oklahoma (1)
  Kickapoo Tribe of Oklahoma (1)
  Sac and Fox Tribe of Indians of Oklahoma (1)

Tahlequah Agency
  Cherokee Nation of Oklahoma (3)
  United Keetoowah Band of Cherokee Indians of Oklahoma (1)
Scattered tribal and allotted tracts exist within Oklahoma—not indicated on map.

OREGON

Confederated Tribes of the Umatilla Indian Reservation (2)
Fort McDermitt Paiute and Shoshone Tribe (1) (in Nevada and Oregon) Nevada
  Agency

Warm Springs Agency
  Burns-Paiute Indian Colony (2)
  Confederated Tribes of the Warm Springs Reservation of Oregon (1)

SOUTH DAKOTA

Cheyenne River Sioux Tribe (1) Cheyenne River Agency
Flandreau Santee-Sioux Tribe (2) Flandreau School
Oglala Sioux Tribe of the Pine Ridge Reservation (1) (in South Dakota and
  Nebraska) Pine Ridge Agency
Rosebud Sioux Tribe (1) Rosebud Agency
Sisseton-Wahpeton Sioux Tribe (2) (in North Dakota and South Dakota) Sisseton
  Agency
Standing Rock Sioux Tribe (2) (in South Dakota and North Dakota) Standing
  Rock Agency
Yankton Sioux Tribe of Indians (2) Yankton Agency
Crow Creek Sioux Tribe of Fort Thompson (2)
Lower Brule Sioux Tribe of the Lower Brule Reservation (1)

UTAH

Ute Indian Tribe of Uintah and Ouray (1) Uintah & Ouray Agency
Skull Valley (3) Uintah & Ouray Agency
Ute Mountain Ute Tribe (1) in Colorado, New Mexico and Utah—Utah portion
  = scattered tracts occupied by the Allen Canyon Utes near Blanding, Utah.
Northwestern Band of Shoshone Indians (Washakie) (4) Fort Hall Agency
Confederated Tribes of the Goshute Reservation (1) (in Nevada & Utah)
Navajo Nation (2) (in Arizona, New Mexico & Utah)

WASHINGTON

Confederated Tribes of the Colville Reservation (2) Colville Agency
Kalispel Indian Community (1) Northern Idaho Agency

Spokane Tribe (2) Spokane Agency
Yakima Indian Nation (2) Yakima Agency

Western Washington Agency

Confederated Tribes of the Chehalis Reservation (2)
Hoh Indian Tribe (1)
Lower Elwha Tribal Community (1)
Lummi Tribe of Indians (2)
Makah Indian Tribe (1)
Muckleshoot Indian Tribe (1)
Nisqually Indian Community (1)
Port Gamble Indian Community (1)
Puyallup Tribe (1)
Quileute Tribe of Indians (1)
Quinault Tribe of Indians (2)
Shoalwater Bay Indian Tribal Organization (2)
Skokomish Indian Tribe (1)
Squaxin Island Tribe (1)
Suquamish Indian Tribe (1)
Swinomish Indian Tribal Community (1)
Tulalip Tribes (1)

XXX

Nooksack Indian Tribe (3)
Suak-Suiattle Indian Community of Public Domain Allottees (4)
Chinook Indians (5)
Cowlitz Indians (5)
Duamish Indians (5)
Jamestown Band of Clallam Indians (5)
Kikiallus Indians (5)
Lower Skagit (5)
Samish Tribe of Indians (5)
San Juan Indian Tribe (5)
Snohomish Indian Tribe (5)
Snoqualmie Indian Tribe (5)
Steilacoom Indian Tribe (5)
Stillaquamish Indian Tribe (5)
Upper Skagit Indians (5)

WISCONSIN

Great Lakes Agency

Bad River Band (Chippewa) (1)
Forest County Potawatomi Community (1)
Lac Courte Oreilles Band of Lake Superior Chippewa Indians (1)
Lac du Flambeau Band of Lake Superior Chippewa Indians (1)
Oneida Tribe of Indians of Wisconsin (1)
Red Cliff Band of Lake Superior Chippewa Indians (1)
Sokaogon Chippewa Community (Mole Lake) (1)
St. Croix Chippewa Indians of Wisconsin (1)

Stockbridge-Munsee Community (1)
Wisconsin Winnebago Tribe (1) (in Minn. & Wisconsin)

WYOMING

Northern Arapahoe (Wind River) (3) Wind River Agency
Shoshone (Wind River) (3) Wind River Agency

QUESTIONNAIRE: STUDY OF STATE ORGANIZATIONS FOR COORDINATION OF INDIAN AFFAIRS
(sent to all 50 States)

The GOVERNORS'
INTERSTATE INDIAN COUNCIL

ADDRESSEE   (Persons in State responsible for Indian coordination
(with copy to Governor. For States where we do not
(know of a special coordinator, send to Governor.)

Dear

    The Governors' Interstate Indian Council, with the help of the Bureau of Indian
Affairs and the National Council on Indian Opportunity, is developing a directory
of State organizations, officials, and activities concerned specifically with Indian
matters. Commissioner Bruce has asked Dr. Theodore W. Taylor, Assistant to the
Commissioner, to assist the Council in this study.

    The resulting handbook should be useful to Indian tribes and groups, State, and
Federal agencies. Its primary use would be as an information source on "who" is
responsible for "what" and therefore facilitate communication and responsive action
on important program matters and needs of Indians.

    I will greatly appreciate your cooperation in this endeavor by completing the
enclosed questionnaire and returning it to Dr. Taylor U. S. Dept. of Interior, Bureau
of Indian Affairs, Washington, D. C. 20242.

    If you have questions, please call me on AC 505–827–2763 or Dr. Taylor—Area
Code 202–343–5922.

Sincerely,

JOHN C. RAINER
Chairman
Villagra Building
Santa Fe, New Mexico   87501

STUDY OF STATE ORGANIZATIONS FOR COORDINATION OF INDIAN AFFAIRS

Various States have taken different approaches to working with their Indian citizens. Some have Indian advisory commissions, Indian coordinators with differing titles and functions (one even has a Commissioner of Indian Affairs), special personnel concerned with Indian matters in some of their functional departments (e.g., special Indian coordinators for Johnson O'Malley followup in State Departments of Education).

Because of the importance to the Indians of effective participation in policy formulation and execution by State and local governments, we are desirous of obtaining basic data on how States and their Indian citizens have approached this matter. We intend to publish the results of this study for use by all persons interested. All respondents will receive a copy.

QUESTIONNAIRE

1. *Identification.*

   a. Name of State reporting: _____

   b. Name and title of person completing questionnaire: _____

      (1) Mail Address: _____

      (2) Telephone: _____
                              (Area Code and Number)

2. *Demographic Data.*

   In this section we are indicating Bureau of Indian Affairs data for your State and requesting your comments as to their accuracy and consistency with any State studies.

   a, b, c and d on the enclosed sheet titled "Indian Population Data" indicate such data for all fifty States. The columns are:

   a. Indians on or near trust land eligible to receive services from the Federal Government as of March 1969.

   b. Total Indian population of States as indicated in the 1960 census.

   c. Urban centers estimated to have 1,000 or more Indians.

   d. Other Indian groups in your State.

   Please review the data indicated for your State and make any corrections here.

   _____

   _____

   _____

   e. From what source do you obtain demographic, income, and general level of living data concerning Indian people? _____

   _____

   f. What State officials are generally concerned with collecting and evaluating these data? (*Names and titles*)

   _____

   g. Please indicate titles of any State or other non-Federal publications containing demographic data on Indians for your State and include copies with your submission, if available.

   _____

   _____

3. *State organizational arrangements to facilitate resolution of Indian problems.*

   NOTE: Our understanding of your State's organizational arrangements may be facilitated by *inclusion of an organizational chart with your response*. It might be keyed in some way to the questions that follow. In any event, it would be helpful if an answer could be given to each of the following questions:

   a. Is there a part-time or full-time *individual* reporting to the Governor or the Legislature concerned specifically with Indian affairs? Yes ☐ No ☐ (If "No", skip to c.)

   b. If so, please indicate the following:

      (1) His title _____

      (2) Full-time ☐ Part-time ☐ Percentage of time on Indian affairs   %

      (3) His duties _____
                     (Use additional sheet to describe; if part-time, indicate other duties and approximate percentage of time on Indian affairs.)

      (4) Amount and source of salary (and other perquisites)—(Salary details will not be

identified by individual or State in the study; they will be used to compile statistical tables.)

(5) Name of present incumbent _____

(6) Is present incumbent Indian ☐   Non-Indian ☐

(7) Name, title, and organization of the person to whom he reports:

_____

(8) If there is a legislative authority for this position, please give citation

_____

(9) Please list on a separate sheet (identified as to this question) programs and projects worked on in the last two years.
Please include copies of annual and other reports and studies issued in the last two years. If none, check here ☐

(10) Please furnish the following budget information for the current fiscal year in support of this position (described in 3a. above):

Funds for personal services _____

Funds for other objects _____

Total Budget _____

Percentage of above spent on Indian matters _____ %

Please list staff, by title, included in the above budget:

_____

_____

_____

c. Is there an *advisory commission* or similar organization concerned with Indian matters? Ad hoc ☐   Permanent ☐   None ☐   If "None", skip to 4.

d. If "ad hoc" or "permanent", please indicate the following:

(1) What is the relationship (if any) to the commission of the person defined in 3(b) above?

_____

(2) Please *list on a separate sheet* names and titles of the members of the commission used in their regular work. Indicate who is chairman of the commission.

(3) Is chairman Indian ☐   Non-Indian ☐

(4) Name, title, and organization of person to whom the commission reports.

_____

(5) Description of the duties of the advisory commission, its subcommittees or its members. *Please use separate sheet or include copy of statute or executive order establishing commission, if pertinent.*

(6) Please list on separate sheet programs and projects worked on in the last two years. *Please include copies of annual and other reports and studies issued in the last two years with your answers.* If this question duplicates the answer to 3b. (9), check here. ☐

(7) Does the commission (or other State office) publish a newsletter or regular report other than the Annual Report referred to in 3d. (6)?
Yes ☐   No ☐   If so, *please enclose most recent issue.*

(8) Amount, type, and source of per diem, travel, or other remuneration for members of the commission.

_____

(9) If the budget and staff are not the same as in 3b. (10), please furnish the same breakdown of information for the current fiscal year in support of the commission on a separate sheet, keyed to this question.

(10) If there is legislative authority for this commission, please give citation if not included in 3b. (8) _____

4. *State policy concerning Indian citizens.*

a. Has the legislature adopted a policy statement concerning Indian citizens within the last five years? Yes ☐ No ☐
Any specific legislation (as distinct from a policy statement) within the last five years? Yes ☐ No ☐
Please enclose a copy of each such action under 4a with your submission.

b. Has the incumbent or previous Governor taken a stand on Indian policy, issued an Executive Order, or taken other action on Indian matters within the last five years? Yes ☐ No ☐

Please enclose a copy of each such action in line printed form, or indicate briefly the nature of such action if not available in printed form (separate sheet).

c. Have there been important court cases in the last five years concerning Indians and their relation to the State (e.g., fishing rights, water rights, welfare)? Yes ☐ No ☐ If "Yes", please give citations.

_____

_____

d. Insofar as available, name and title of each Indian now serving:

   (1) As Legislators or key staff or committee assistants. (*Names and titles*)

   _____

   (2) In the Executive branch—other than those already listed in previous answers. (*Names, titles and organizations*)

   _____

   (3) In the Judicial branch. (*Names and titles*)

   _____

   (4) On State Boards and Commissions. (*Names and titles*)

   _____

   (5) On Ad hoc State committees or other activities such as Constitutional Conventions during Calendar Year 1969. (*Names and titles*)

   _____

5. *State Assistance Programs for Indians.*

   Not all States will have programs or facilitating services for Indians as distinct from their other citizens. If this is the case in your State, check None ☐ and skip to 6.

   a. State programs for financial assistance to Indians:

      (1) Are there special financial aids to Indians (e.g., Indian preference for loans, lower interest rates, grants, special housing assistance, special guarantees, etc.) not available to others? Yes ☐ No ☐
      If "Yes", *please attach copy of statute or other authority or otherwise describe on a separate sheet of paper and key to this question.*

      (2) Is there a State official(s) charged with facilitating Indian use of financial assistance available either from private or public sources? Yes ☐ No ☐ If "Yes", please indicate his name(s), organizational location, title, and percentage of time spent on Indian affairs.

      _____

   b. State programs for increasing economic opportunity:

      (1) Are there special State incentives for economic development by Indians (or others in Indian communities) through such policies as Indian preference for State contracts, Indian preference for employment, other special Indian employment incentives, or tax incentives to industry? Yes ☐ No ☐ If "Yes", *describe on separate sheet.*

      (2) Is there a State official(s) charged with facilitating Indian awareness and encouraging Indians to take advantage of existing economic opportunities? Yes ☐ No ☐ If "Yes", please indicate their name(s), organizational location(s), title(s), and percentage of time spent on Indian matters:

      _____

      _____

   c. Other special services for Indians:

      (1) Are there any State programs or services especially modified or oriented to, or

especially for Indians in such areas as education, training, community development, employment placement services, welfare, etc?

Yes ☐ No ☐ If "Yes", *describe on separate sheet.*

(2) Is there a State official (or officials) charged with facilitating Indian awareness of education, training, and such other opportunities?

Yes ☐ No ☐ If "Yes", please indicate their name(s), organizational location, title, and percentage of time spent on Indian matters.

_____

_____

NOTE: Questions 5(a), (b), (c) are somewhat arbitrarily divided as to subject matter; you may wish to organize your answer in some other manner. We are interested in your description of State efforts to serve their Indian citizens and in helping them overcome cultural and economic barriers.

d. Does your State manage Indian-owned funds? Yes ☐ No ☐ If "Yes", please indicate the following:

(1) Amount of Indian-owned funds on deposit as of December 31, 1969; if for specific tribes and purposes, please indicate the amount for each.

_____

_____

(Use separate sheet if necessary)

(2) Amount of Indian funds spent during last State fiscal year by same specific tribes and purposes indicated under (d)(1) above:

_____

_____

(Use separate sheet if necessary)

6. *Please indicate universities or colleges within the State that have special Indian programs.*

_____

(Use separate sheet if necessary)

7. *Indian Organizations and State Representation.*

a. Please list the Statewide Indian organizations in your State (e.g., Affiliated Tribes of North Dakota): (*Names of organization, officers, and address of chairman*)

_____

_____

b. Does the State have Governor's representation on any groups concerned with interstate Indian matters? Yes ☐ No ☐ If so, please list by such interested group (e.g., Governor's Interstate Indian Council) and indicate name(s) of present State representative(s).

_____

_____

c. What interstate Indian groups do Indian tribes or groups in your State belong to? (e.g., such as the NCAI, Northwest Affiliated Tribes, American Indians United (Urban), and United Southeastern Tribes).

_____

_____

_____

(Use separate sheet if necessary)

8. *Please give any ideas or suggestions you have for facilitating Indian-State-Federal coordination on Indian matters; also, your thoughts on what might be desirable concerning State organizations for the coordination of Indian affairs.*

COMPILATION OF RESPONSES:
INDIAN ORGANIZATION QUESTIONNAIRE
(sent to chairmen of all federally
recognized Indian groups)

On April 2, 1971, this questionnaire was sent to 245 chairmen of Federally recognized Indian groups. The purpose was stated at the beginning of the questionnaire and the main points are included in the Introduction of this compilation.

The compilation was sent to all respondents April 2, 1971, requesting any comments or suggestions they might have. The letter stated: "After review of any comments and suggestions you may have it is planned to make the tabulation available to you, governmental officials, and others interested in Indian policy." No comments or responses suggesting changes were received.

In some instances respondents chose to remain anonymous and their request has been honored.

LIST OF RESPONDENTS

	Identification Used in Summary
Alaska	
Grand Camp Alaska Native Brotherhood/Sisterhood	ANB
Central Council of the Tlingit-Haida Indians of Alaska	Tlingit-Haida
Arizona	
Ak-Chin Indian Community	Ak-Chin
Havasupai Tribe	Havasupai
Hopi Tribe	Hopi
Kaibab-Paiute Indian Tribe	Kaibab-Paiute
Navajo Nation	Navajo
White Mountain Apache Tribe	White Mt. Apache
Yavapai Prescott Community Association	Yavapai
Cocopah Tribe	Cocopah
California	
Augustine Band of Mission Indians	Augustine
Barona Group of Captain Grande Band	Barona
Chemehuevi Indian Tribe	Chemeheuvi
Dry Creek Rancheria	Dry Creek
Manzanita Band of Mission Indians	Manzanita
Pit River Home and Agricultural Cooperative Association	Pit River
San Pasqual Band of Mission Indians	San Pasqual

251

	Identification Used in Summary
California (continued)	
Tule River Indian Tribe	Tule River
Anonymous	Anon
Florida	
Miccosukee Tribe of Indians of Florida	Miccosukee
Idaho	
Nez Perce Tribe of Idaho	Nez Perce
Kansas	
The Iowa Tribe of Kansas and Nebraska	Iowa
Louisiana	
Chitimacha Tribe of Louisiana	Chit
Michigan	
Keeweenaw Bay Indian Tribe	L'Anse
Minnesota	
Red Lake Tribe	Red Lake
Shakopee Mdwekanton Sioux Indian Community	S.M. Sioux
Upper Sioux Indian Community	Upper Sioux
Mississippi	
Mississippi Band of Choctaw Indians	Choctaw
Montana	
Anonymous	Anon
Northern Cheyenne Tribe	Northern Cheyenne
Confederated Salish and Kootenai Tribes	Salish and Kootenai
Nebraska	
Winnebago Tribe	Winnebago
Nevada	
Ely Indian Colony	Ely
Pyramid Lake Tribe	Pyramid Lake
New Mexico	
Pueblo of Acoma	Acoma
Jicarilla Apache Tribe	Jicarilla
Tesuque Pueblo	Tesuque
Pueblo of Zia	Zia
New York	
St. Regis Mohawk Tribe	St. Regis
North Dakota	
The Three Affiliated Tribes of the Ft. Berthold Reservation	Ft. Berthold
Oklahoma	
The Cherokee Nation of Oklahoma	Cherokee
Eastern Shawnee Tribe	E. Shawnee
Iowas of Oklahoma	Iowas
Kaw Indian Tribe	Kaw
Seminole Nation of Oklahoma	Seminole

Oklahoma (continued)

	Identification Used in Summary
Tonkawa Indian Tribe of Oklahoma	Tonkawa
Wyandotte Tribe of Oklahoma	Wyandotte

Oregon

Burns Paiute Colony	Burns Paiute
Confederated Tribes of the Umatilla Indian Reservation	Umatilla

South Dakota

Flandreau Santee Sioux Tribe	Flandreau
Cheyenne River Sioux Tribe	Cheyenne River
Oglala Sioux Tribe of the Pine Ridge Reservation	Oglala

Wisconsin

Great Lakes Inter-Tribal Council, Inc.	GLITC
Oneida Tribe of Indians of Wisconsin	Oneida
Forest County Potawatomi	Pot.
St. Croix Chippewas	S.C. Chip.
Lac Courte Oreilles Tribe	LCO

Wyoming

Shoshone and Arapaho Tribes	S & A

National Congress of American Indians   NCAI

Late—not included in tabulation:
Lone Pine Paiute-Shoshone Band

I. INTRODUCTION

A. Purpose

The Indian governments could be considered as a "fourth" government in our Federal system—the other three governments being local, State and Federal.

It was thought it would be useful for tribal leaders (and leaders of State and regional Indian organizations) to know how other tribes relate to local, State, and Federal services and be able to consider for local application the most successful arrangements worked out in various parts of the country.

The purpose of the questionnaire was to assess relationships of tribes (and State and regional organizations of tribes) to the various other governments for the following purposes:

1. Provide comparative information for the use of tribal leadership.
2. Obtain suggestions for the relocation of responsibilities from one governmental level to another if considered desirable.
3. Secure evaluation of present coordination between the various governments serving Indians and possible suggestions for improvement when appropriate.

In April 1970 the Governors' Interstate Indian Council forwarded a questionnaire to the 50 States asking them about State programs or activities that were special for Indians. Some of the responses indicated considerable activity on the part of the States. The activity of the Federal Government through the Bureau of Indian Affairs, Indian Health Service, Economic Development Administration, Small Business Administration, etc., is better documented than State and local activity. The tribes know the services of the neighboring localities better than anyone else. They were asked to report the nature of the relationship of their organization to these various governmental activities.

It was indicated to the tribes that their answers to the specific questions and any general comments they cared to make, especially on question 34 "Coordination of Indian Programs" would be most informative.

It was also stated that results of the questionnaire would be tabulated and each respondent organization would receive a copy. This tabulation carries out that commitment.

It was pointed out to the respondents that the tabulation would be most useful to tribal leaders and others concerned with Indian policy if the organizations and officials responding were identified with their comments in the tabulation. If any respondent preferred that his name or tribe (or other organization) not be related to any portion of the response or comments, this request would be honored. (Only two respondents preferred anonymity.)

A full response was encouraged.

B. Response

On April 2, 1971, questionnaires were mailed to tribal leaders of federally recognized Indian tribes and to statewide, regional and national Indian organizations. The response was:

Entity	Mailed	Returned	Percent
Tribal leaders	245	56	23
State-wide, regional and national Indian organizations	17	3	18
Totals	262	59	23

There are very few generalities that hold true for Indian groups, but one that most would agree to is that Indian groups are different and have different settings, resources, and opportunities. The responses came from a wide spectrum of varying Indian and native groups—from the Navajo, the largest with a considerable resource base, to a rancheria with only two members. Twenty-one (21) different States are included.

The five States with the largest Indian populations had the highest proportion of returns, except for Alaska:

State	No. of Indians or Natives	Respondents
Oklahoma	97,731	7
Arizona	95,812	8
California	91,018	9
New Mexico	72,788	4
Alaska	51,528	2
Totals	408,877	30

Other States [1] with over 10,000 Indians responded as follows:

State	No. of Indians	Respondents
North Carolina	43,487	0
Washington	33,386	0
South Dakota	32,365	3
New York	28,330	1
Montana	27,130	3
Minnesota	23,128	3
Wisconsin	18,924	5
Texas	18,132	0
Michigan	16,854	1
North Dakota	14,369	1
Oregon	13,510	2
Illinois	11,413	0
Utah	11,273	0
Totals	292,301	19

[1] North Carolina Cherokee was the only tribe receiving questionnaire in that State; Texas tribes received no questionnaires, as they are not recognized by the Federal Government; Illinois Indian population is mainly urban (Chicago).

The alphabetical list of States and number of responses follows:

Alaska	2	Nebraska	1
Arizona	8	Nevada	2
California	9	New Mexico	4
Florida	1	New York	1
Idaho	1	North Dakota	1
Kansas	1	Oklahoma	7
Louisiana	1	Oregon	2
Michigan	1	South Dakota	3
Mississippi	1	Wisconsin	5
Montana	3	Wyoming	1
			58
		NCAI	1
		Total	59

Identification of the individual tribes or groups responding will be found in the table under the analysis of question 14.

No questionnaires were sent to non-federally related Indian groups. They are now completely involved with their States and localities. The questions were designed for tribes who had the option of receiving special services from the Federal Government. If other tribal groups had been included, it is assumed that many of their responses might have been different, e.g., percent of time working with State and local governments. This is an area that should be explored. The author advocates the desirability of an Indian attitude survey, including in such a survey statistically valid samples of individual Indian attitudes from federally recognized Indian groups,

State rural Indian groups (non-federal), and urban groups (which would include both members of federally recognized tribes and non-federally recognized Indians).

It should be borne in mind that the responses reported here are generally by Tribal Chairmen or a member or members of the Tribal Council. The attitudes of these officials, because of their perspective, may not be the same as the attitudes of all members of their respective groups on such questions as: who should operate the schools, the value of employment assistance efforts to the individuals concerned, the placement of children in foster homes or the appropriate location of law and order responsibility. An individual attitude survey would help illuminate this area and be of great help to tribal leaders and others concerned with Indian policy.

II. GENERAL SUMMARY

A strong desire comes through in a majority of the responses for continued direct relationships with the Federal Government where that now exists, and some desired expanded relationships in specific areas such as law and order.

Underlying most responses—either specifically stated or by implication—is continued Federal or State funding where it now exists, and requests for increases in such funding. However, it is also clear from the analysis, that most groups responding consider such funding a transitional support for as long as they consider it necessary.

Most indicate a desire to build up individual and tribal competence, increase economic resources and payroll, and look to the day when they can support themselves and their governmental institutions. Many (93 percent) recognize that cooperation from the non-Indian community is needed for such economic development. Neighboring towns, county governments and State departments, as well as private consultants, were recognized as important because of geographical relationships and involvement in the general economy and because of expertise now lacking in many Indian communities. The Federal Government is considered the most important of the governmental levels by most of the respondents. Respondents were strongly supportive of health programs and indicated the need for additional funds for the Indian Health Service. But they also recognized that education, better housing, improvement of the economic base and more job opportunities were important to improved health.

Considering the responses related to Indian-State relations, the concensus seems to be that tribes and their members are inevitably involved with State and local institutions, even those tribes and their members with maximum direct Federal involvement. A few do not like the relationship, some do not trust the States, but many of these as well as the majority of the others indicated a positive (though watchful in some instances) attitude toward trying to work with all pertinent governments and other sources of help for bettering the Indian condition.

Education of Indian children is to a considerable extent (68 percent) under State law in local public schools. The responses indicated a desire for more tribal operation or involvement, but with continuing heavy emphasis on operation in accordance with or under State school regulations and policy. (BIA statistics indicate that in 1971 there were 232 public school districts with Indian membership on the school boards totaling 631 Indian board members. For example, the Tuba City elementary and high school boards both have an Indian majority as does the Whiteriver elementary school.) Most comments on direct tribal operation referred to taking over BIA operated schools. Two stressed quality of teaching and extra help for students that needed it with Federal funding to assist public schools.

Heavy use, with general satisfaction, is made of State employment services. Use is also made of the BIA Employment Assistance Program, especially by the larger Federal tribes.

States and counties are heavily involved in foster home placement of Indian children and in judicial, prevention and enforcement services for Indians.

Complaints against present serving agencies (local, State, or Federal) seem to be generally based on what the respondents consider unsatisfactory performance. (Similar favorable and unfavorable reactions to Tribal Governments would probably be discovered in sample survey of individual Indian opinion.)

The responses indicate an interest in increased Indian involvement either through direct operation of activities that affect their lives (e.g., schools, law and order) or effective participation in cooperation with others in such operation. Several respondents reported the value of State Indian commissions and some wanted this activity strengthened in their States.

No "assimilation" philosophy is generally expressed; rather recognition of the validity of Indian groups and governments (when large enough to have them) is stressed, with the additional recognition that such Indian groups, their neighbors (county and city or town groups), the State and Federal Governments must work effectively together to resolve the problems of the Indian communities concerned.

The majority of the respondents, especially the larger groups, seem to see no unresolvable problem in the four systems of Government working together to resolve problems as they arise.

III. SUMMARY OF RESPONSES TO EACH QUESTION

Not all respondents answered or commented on each question. Therefore, the number of responses to each question is indicated. Percentages relate to the total number of answers for the specific question. An effort has been made to group written comments in rough categories for summary purposes. All responses that could relate to the State and Federal Governments and their services are included (58). NCAI's response, along with the other 58, was considered in the *General Summary*.[2]

1. *Identification of tribe or group*—not summarized

2. *Geographical coverage*—not summarized other than as described in the Introduction.

3. *Is working with the State one of the objectives of the tribe or organization?*

    Responses: 56 *Yes*   34   61%
                        No   22   39%

What is the percentage of your organization's time spent with local, State, and Federal Governments and private organizations?

    Responses: 46 Local 10%
                      State 11%
                      Federal 71%
                      Private 4.5%

---

[2] Not all responses totaled 100 percent; the percentages in the responses were added and divided by the number responding.

4. *With which Federal Government agencies, other than BIA and IHS, do you have important working relations and in what city is your major contact located?*
Separate analysis is being made.

5. *The lack of funds for continuity of a tribal administrative staff has hindered many tribes from providing needed services to their members. Some tribes and groups use a sales tax (e.g., Zuni, Eastern Cherokee, Alaska Villages); the Oglala Sioux Tribe receives a return of a portion of the State sales tax collected on the reservation; some tribes have considerable tribal income from tribal resources and tribal activities; other tribes may have other solutions.*
What do you recommend should be done to achieve a long-term solution to the problem?

Thirty-two of the 42 respondents that commented on this question indicated by direct statement or implication that the tribe should develop resources and income to provide for tribal administrative staffs if they were not already doing so; six said such funds should come from the Federal Government; nine indicated that Federal funding should be supplied if tribal funds were not available. For example, Hopi reported a three percent sales tax used to support administrative staff, but also indicated that Federal funding should be provided if local funds are not adequate.

The 32 responses indicating that funding of tribal administrative staff should be a tribal responsibility suggested various ways of achieving the necessary income: set up tribal enterprises (boat launch, tribal business) develop tribal resources (recreation, timber, industrial parks, lease land); long range planning; receipt of portion of sales and other taxes collected; family assessment; make tribal government and operations more efficient to reduce costs; local fuel tax; train tribal members; bring in industry to make jobs more available; tribes receiving awards should invest a substantial percentage and use income to support affairs of tribe; education the long-term solution; establish an occupation tax; water charges; grazing fees, fishing and hunting fees.

For those tribes in this group that do not have the necessary jobs and resources on the reservation at the present time to achieve income to support tribal administrative costs Tesuque made a comment that sums up the challenge: "Until our people become adequately trained and employable, and jobs become available on our reservation there is no point in contemplating taxation or other forms of revenue generation for a jobless people. Emphasis should be placed in developing tribal economies. Our tribe is attempting to generate funds through long-term leasing." As an example of a tribe with income, the Cherokee Tribe, reported that it pays all administrative costs of Cherokee programs. Revenues come from invested funds, rentals, sales at arts and crafts centers, the Cherokee Restaurant, and tourism generally.

Other suggestions made were: State should fund programs along with the Federal Government (1); change Federal laws requiring 10 percent matching funds so that tribal economic development could be improved (1); the complete change in councilmen every two years most disrupting thing in tribal government (1); need funds, didn't indicate where such funds should come from (1).

6. *What should be the procedure for settling disputes involving protests of tribal elections:*

Responses: 56 [3]

a. Tribal appeal board or other tribal body or individual	37	66%
b. Impartial person or persons appointed by State or regional Indian organization (e.g., United Tribes of North Dakota, Northwest Affiliated Tribes).	5	9%
c. State Indian Commission	2	4%
d. A respected justice-of-the-peace, judge, or election official or board of the county or nearby community	3	5%
e. Other (Specify)	12	21%

Many of the tribes who checked "(e) Other" described a tribal type solution e.g., such as the tribal council, in their comments. The general sentiment is summed up in the statement made by Tlingit-Haida: "We should work to develop the machinery to assure justice by utilizing talent within our society. If we cannot unite sufficiently to do that, then other facets of our efforts are headed for difficult times." Most of the tribes checking "b c or d" are small and/or under State law and order and are either too small to have a full fledged tribal government or are used to non-Indian institutions.

Economic Development

7. *Do you feel that more cooperation is needed from the non-Indian community to help reservation Economic Development?*

Responses: 54

Yes	50	93%
No	4	7%

If "Yes" from:

a. Neighboring towns?	28	56%
b. County government(s)?	29	58%
c. State departments?	36	72%
d. Federal agencies?	43	86%
e. State, regional or national Indian organizations (e.g., Northwest Affiliated Tribes, NCAI)	25	50%

COMMENTS: (If "Yes" to a, b, c, d, or e, give details why you said "Yes" and if more than one of the above is checked, indicate the governmental level or organization which is or could be most important in helping reservation economic development.)

In the comments the importance of the Federal Government was mentioned in 21 responses, frequently along with a comment that cooperation with other governments was important, too. Where towns, counties, States or Indian organizations were specifically mentioned or a statement that cooperation with all was important, the following counts are recorded: towns 12; counties 11; States 14, and Indian organizations 6.

Two examples of comments follow.

Navajo: "Presently federal agencies assistance in most necessary. We believe development must, additionally, be considered in relation to localities adjacent to the reservation so that the total area will benefit."

Fort Berthold: "Most important are the neighboring towns and county govern-

---

[3] Some respondents checked more than one item; only "yes" answers tabulated for simplification of summary.

ments. A larger area than just the reservation is needed for sound economic development. The counties are also planning so that the two should be coordinated."

8. *Do you believe more cooperation from the non-Indian community would help in:*

    a. Planning?   35   66%
    b. Advertising?   33   62%
    c. Negotiating with industry?   35   66%
    d. Financing?   30   57%
    e. Training labor force?   32   **60%**
    f. Providing services and amenities for employees of industry 31   58%
       (schools, recreation, roads, police and fire protection, etc.)?

Responses: 53

In general, those commenting indicated the need for cooperation between the
Indian and non-Indian community to achieve maximum economic development. Red
Lake, for example, had the following comment: "b. sale of local products; c. establish
new enterprises, new markets and new products; d. local area banks show more
interest in reservation expansion; e. more job opportunities and union participation;
f. road building."

Several tribes pointed out that at present their members do not have the education
and training that is obtainable from the non-Indian community which can help
in economic development. One tribe checked "No" on all items.

9. *Do you invite non-Indian participation—*

    a. In your discussions?   41   73%
    b. In your official meetings?   37   66%
    c. As consultants?   45   80%
    d. In some other manner?   22   39%

Responses: 56

COMMENTS: (If "Yes" on any of the above, please describe, indicating who
the invitees are: organization, governmental level or firm they represent; and type
of help sought.)

Representatives of Federal agencies drew the most frequent mention (13), followed
by private organizations or individuals (11). Private types mentioned were architects,
civic groups, chambers of commerce, environmental consultant, university consultants,
bank, and movie industry. State departments were next in line (8), with specific
references to such activities as employment services and health and education departments. Local government (counties and towns) and attorneys were each mentioned six (6) times, with mayors, county commissioners, planning commission,
sheriff, health, welfare, weed inspectors and judges being specifically referred to.
Local school boards (3), soil conservation district (1) and Indian interest organizations (1) were also mentioned.

10. *Does your organization (reservation, State, regional or national) have an Industrial Development Committee?* Yes_____ No_____

Responses: 55

                Yes   27   49%
                No   28   51%

If "yes"

    a. Does it work with local and State industrial development 20   74%
       people to develop or attract local industry
    b. With BIA, EDA, OEO, SBA, or other Federal Agencies?   26   96%

c. With other Indian groups (e.g., NCAI)?   18   67%

COMMENTS: (If "Yes" on any of the above, please describe.) Of three tribes checking "No," two indicated that the full council acted as a committee for this purpose, and one had two designated representatives who apparently were not considered a committee.

Sometimes the "Yes" indicated a different device than a committee. For example, the Cherokee Development Co., Inc. (principal officers and board members Cherokee) performs this function for the tribe. Some comments were: Tlingit-Haida: "We develop proposals consistent with our development planning program and seek funding and the expertise." The Hopi committee "works with the Arizona Department of Economic Development, the Northeastern Arizona Development Board, the Winslow Industrial Development Endeavor Board, the federal agencies listed and IDDA (Indian Development District of Arizona)." "A committee of the Navajo Tribal Council, supported by our staff, regularly works with industrial development prospects and with agencies involved in the promotion of reservation based and other tribally supported industry." Red Lake: "a. We work with all agencies, state and federal; b. To aid in getting industry on the reservation; c. NCIO." Another tribe: "Our activity has been very good. I hope it continues. All above agencies have been involved and we now have 3 industries going—meaning 160 to 180 new jobs."

Several tribes indicated that they were working with State-wide or regional groups. Specifically mentioned were IDDA, Nebraska Indian Intertribal Development Corporation, United Sioux Tribes of South Dakota, and the United South-Eastern Tribes.

Education

11. *The number of Indian children in your jurisdiction (e.g., reservation, State, region) attending—*
    a. Public schools?   Approximate number of children _____
    b. Federal schools? (e.g.,   Approximate number of children _____
       BIA)
    c. Other?   Approximate number of children _____

Responses: 52

Some tribes did not have information available for all items; and there was a variety of information presented under "other," such as college students, pre-school, etc. Rather than giving the approximate information in the responses, statistics for fiscal year 1970 are presented for the 22 States for which BIA reports educational statistics.

Indian children 5–18 years of age		
Public schools	127,596	68%
Federal schools	47,922	26%
Others (mission, private)	10,942	6%
Total	186,460	

(NOTE: There are five communities operating schools under direct contract with BIA with an approximate total enrollment (for the five schools) of 760 students as of the end of the 1970–71 school years.)

12. *Is there compulsory attendance up to a certain age or level of schooling?* Yes_____ No_____ *If so, what authority (tribe, locality, State) enforces attendance?*

Responses: 53

Yes	46	87%
No	7	13%

Tribal and State statutes were the general source of compulsory attendance authority cited. There were a few references to the county or other local government. Enforcement is generally by State school authorities for public schools and tribal authorities for BIA schools according to the few who commented on this aspect of the question. One said BIA enforces attendance. Some tribes said there was no compulsory attendance when others from the same State said there was.

13. *Who should operate schools for Indian children—*

    a. The Tribe?   18   33%

    b. The community under public school laws of the State?   35   65%

    c. The Federal Government?   12   22%

    d. Other?   5   9%

Responses: 55

"Other" included parochial schools. One tribe who checked "Other" said: "Indians in supervisory positions." Two tribes indicated they were having referenda on how schools should be operated.

Other comments were: stop public schools from discriminating; Federal Government should assist in achieving public school operation when possible; public schools should be used if Indians have control of the school board in the public district; "competent, dedicated folks!"; tribe should have some authority or jurisdiction over Federal schools even though they are operated by BIA.

The following table indicates the present situation and that desired by the respondents.

	No. of [1] Respondents	Present Operation (1970 figures)			Proposed Operation				Comments
	Tribe [2] a	Pub. Sch. b	BIA c	Other d	Tribe a	Pub. b	BIA c	Other d	
Alaska	2	13,212	7,245	411	2				
Arizona	8	354	19,747	17,824	3,957	3	3	1	1	
Calif.	9		All Public			2	4	2	1	2 blank; 2 checked more than one column
Florida	1	40	258	84	–	1	1			one respondent; 2 columns checked
Idaho	1		1,569	73	58	1	1			one respondent; 2 columns checked
Kansas	1		1,196	44	–		1	1		one respondent; 2 columns checked
Louisiana	1		Mostly Public	44	?			1		one respondent; 2 columns checked
Michigan	1		Mostly Public	143	?	1	1			one respondent; 2 columns checked
Minnesota	3		2,995	23	207		3		1	one checked (b) and (d) parochial
Miss.	1		263	1,193	14	1				
Montana	3		8,274	769	939	1	2			
Nebraska	1		737	44	92	1				
Nevada	2		1,675	125	20	2				

	No. of [1] Respondents	Present Operation (1970 figures)				Proposed Operation				Comments
		Tribe [2] a	Pub. Sch. b	BIA c	Other d	Tribe a	Pub. b	BIA c	Other d	
New Mex.	4	167	20,377	8,733	1,855	1	3	2	1	one checked 3 columns; one checked 2 columns
New York	1		All Public				1			
No. Dak.	1		3,409	3,459	1,119	1				
Oklahoma	7		35,278	1,102	89	2	4	3		two checked 2 columns
Oregon	2		1,200	55	47	1	1			one blank; other checked 2 columns
So. Dak.	3	200	5,167	4,347	1,553	1		1	1	
Wisconsin	5		1,804	–	–	2	3	1		one blank; 2 checked 2 columns
Wyoming	1		1,041	80	183	1	1			checked 2 columns
	58					18	35	12	5	

[1] The specific responses of each tribe can be found in table under question 14.
[2] 1971 estimates of students in Blackwater and Rough Rock (Ariz.), Raman (N.M.), Miccosukee (Fla.), and Stefan (S.D.) operated by tribes under contract with BIA.

The significance of the responses to 13 would seem to be a swing toward more tribal operation or involvement, but with continuing heavy emphasis on operation in accordance with or under State school regulations or policy. Alaska is headed for public school operation. California, which now has public school operation, has some tribes who want more tribal and Federal involvement. The larger groups in Oklahoma (Cherokee and Seminole) checked public schools, while the smaller groups divided between public schools and tribal and Federal emphasis. Since several tribes checked more than one column, a review of the detailed table under question 14 is necessary to ascertain as closely as possible each tribe's position.

14. *If in question 13 you indicate the desirability of a change from the present situation, e.g., from BIA Federal schools to tribal or public schools or vice versa—*
   a. *What time schedule for making the change would be feasible in your judgment?*
   b. *Who should pay the cost under your suggested or preferred arrangement?*
   c. *If "Other" in 13 above is checked, please explain:*

To obtain the best understanding of the desires of the various tribes, their recommended operation (responses to question 13) and comments on question 14 must be considered together. Following is a table presenting in detail the responses to these two questions:

Indian Organization Questionnaire—Responses to Questions 13 and 14

State Tribe	13. Who Should Operate?					14. If Change Desired		
	Tribe (a)	Pub. Sch. (b)	Fed. Sch. (c)	Other (d)	Comment	Time Scheduled (a)	Who Pay (b)	Other and General Comments (c)
Alaska								
ANB	x				—	Gradual phase out in progress	Share equally by State and Federal Gov't.	
Tlingit-Haida		x			The Fed Gov't but should assist in achieving (b)		Federal then State	Essential to a successful change is the sincerity of the Federal Gov't's effort to assist tribal groups in preparing to participate in the development and administration of the schools.
Arizona								
Ak-Chin	x				—	Right away	BIA & Tribe if possible	We were hoping to start a formal kindergarten with BIA backing and that we could set up our own school board.
Havasupai	x				—	Community decide poss. 5 years	Fed.	a. The Havasupai school should continue to be federally funded and administered by the community according to State public school standards.
Hopi	x				H.S. Ref. April 9	Start FY 72	BIA	a. A tentative timetable for turnover of the five elementary schools to the Tribe has been prepared, starting in FY 1972.
Kaibab-Paiute			x		—	—	Fed.	
Navajo				x	See 14	10 years	Fed. & State	a b & c: The Tribe has generally supported the Bureau operated schools. Policy is flexible, providing for expression of local wishes for public schools and contracts with the Bureau to operate present schools. Consultations to provide information on organization and management are most desirable—supporting the efforts of local Navajo school boards and the planning for a Navajo Department of Education.
White Mt. Apache		x			—	1973	State & Fed.	Federal Governments—c.—(blank)
Yavapai		x			—	—		No choice. Walking distance to schools.
Cocopah		x			—	(Blank on 14)		
California								
Augustine					(Blank)			
Barona	x		x		—	(14 Blank)		This reservation has no children

Location			(d) Parochial Schools	(14 Blank)	
Chemehuevi	x				
Dry Creek		x	—	As soon as possible	Fed.
Manzanita		x	—	—	Fed.
Pit River	x	?	No	No Indian school in area	
San Pasqual	x	x	Stop public schools from discriminating	Sooner the better	
Tule River			(Blank)	(Blank)	
Anon.	x		—	"	
Florida					
Miccosukee	x	x	—	At least 2 yrs	BIA
Idaho					
Nez Perce	x	x	—		
Kansas—Iowa	x	x	—	—	
Louisiana				—	(Blank)
Chitimacha	x		—		
Michigan					"
L'anse	x	x			
Minnesota			(d) Parochial Schools		
Red Lake	x	x	—	—	State & Fed.
S.M. Sioux	x		—	—	
Upper Sioux	x		—	—	

—Indians pay taxes, Gov't. owns reservations. Public utilities use reservation without paying on this reservation.

All schools should have an American Indian qualified teacher.

a. What time schedule for making the change would be feasible in your judgment?

May I state that to have solid education we must have started proper from the beginning to the last year in high school. Special teachers should be available to students that are slow to learn and should not be allowed to continue with poor grades where eventually the student begins to find excuses to drop out—why?, Because he has fallen back in grade.

b. Who should pay the cost under your suggested or preferred arrangement?

The Johnson O'Malley should finance the salary for such a teacher. I realize this will present another problem where parents will assume that their children must be senile or purile to be segregated from other students. If this be so then there should be no complaint about the Johnson O'Malley Funds, being used only for the convenience of the non-Indians. In all nationalities there are students that grasp knowledge quicker than other students. Not because the student is dumb NO. Just slow in learning.

I do not favor change

(d) Good private schools should be subsidized by Federal and State aid.

No change indicated.

(Blank)

State Tribe	13. Who Should Operate?					14. If Change Desired		
	a Tribe	b Pub. Sch.	c Fed. Sch.	d Other	Comment	a Time Scheduled	b Who Pay	c Other and General Comments
Mississippi								
Choctaw	x				—	2 years	Fed.	a. The Tribal takeover of the educational responsibilities of Indian children needs to be coordinated with the budgeting procedures of BIA, preferably within 2 years.
Montana								
Anon		x					(Blank)	
Northern Cheyenne	x				Negot. with BIA	July 1, 1971	BIA	Target date for takeover of Busby School (only Fed. operated school in Montana)
Salish & Kootenai		x				There now.	Fed. & State	
Nebraska	x				If Indians had control School Board in public district	—	State & Fed.	(a) If a crisis situation can be properly set up, then the change in the school board could be arranged before the next school board election by calling for a special election. Then progressive changes in education could be made. (b) These changes should be financed by the present agencies, and it is important that this money is spent wisely. Presently JOM and Title I money is not spent as intended by the Acts intent.
Nevada								
Ely		x			—		(Blank)	
Pyramid Lake		x			—		(Blank) ʺ	
New Mexico								
Acoma	x	x	x		—	10 years from BIA to Tribe	Fed.	(No qualified administrators at the present time). Possible contract with the Un. of N.M. to operate school.
Jicarilla		x			—	(Blank)		
Tesuque				x	Competent, dedicated folks!	—	—	It appears there are many people concerned about who can educate the Indian best. We make the observation tht Indians are no different from other folks and if people are willing to accept us on those basis and if these folks understand our cultural backgrounds and

Location			Recommendation	Time schedule	Jurisdiction	Comments
Zia	x	x	BIA schools on reservation (with local school board)	At least 5 years	Fed. & State	are willing to relate formal education around such differences and build on our cultural strengths and not degrade our difference we can learn. But as indicated in "13" above—we need more than folks interested in job security, $, status, etc.—preferably folks who have a missionary zeal for helping others to help themselves. a. It is the desire of the tribe to keep the BIA elementary school. The tribe is not ready to take over the school and will not be for at least 5 years. The public school is also used from grades K-12, b. In the present setup funds should be made available under the same funding system.
New York St. Regis	x		—	—	—	The State pays complete education costs through high school. Better communication on both local and State level is needed. We (as of June 70) have two school board members and the legal right to vote in school board elections. We had to fight for this right.
North Dakota Ft. Berthold	x		—	—	Fed. & State	14a. A partnership arrangement between the school districts and the BIA now exists with local persons serving on the school boards. Immediate steps should be taken to turn the operation over to school districts if they so desire. 14b. The school districts on the reservation receive no revenue. The local school boards should contract with the BIA for financing with the school board operation of the school.
Oklahoma Cherokee	x		We feel that the Tribe should have some authority or jurisdiction over BIA schools even tho BIA operates the schools	—	Local State Fed.	We are not indicating a time schedule for making any change in management and supervision of the Federal Indian Boarding Schools, but strongly recommend that the Tribe have some authority or jurisdiction for improving the Federal Schools in which Indian children enrolled in the tribal area. Public Schools through strong, constructive representation on School Boards may be improved. b. Who should pay the cost under your suggested or preferred arrangement? As long as the school systems, both Federal and State, continue under present plans, costs should remain under the same jurisdictions . . . Local, State and Federal.
E. Shawnee	x	x	— —	No change	— —	
Iowas		x				
Kaw	x	x	— —	(Blank)		We do not have enough children here to make any substantial comments.
Seminole	x	x		"		

State Tribe	13. Who Should Operate?					14. If Change Desired		
	a Tribe	b Pub. Sch.	c Fed. Sch.	d Other	Comment	a Time Scheduled	b Who Pay	c Other and General Comments
Tonkawa	x				—	(Blank)		
Wyandotte		x			—	"		
Oregon								
Burns-Paiute					(Blank)	(Blank)		
Umatilla	x	x			—	—	Fed.	
South Dakota								
Flandreau				x	Indians in supervisory position	—	Fed.	Buy Indian contract.
Cheyenne River			x		—	No change	Fed.	I do not believe there should be any change from BIA schools to any other type of management. The Federal Government should run these schools because the majority of tribes do not have sufficient money or expertise to manage these schools.
Oglala	x				—	Whenever people decide to take over	Fed.	
Wisconsin								
GLITC	x	x			—	(Blank)	Fed.	—
Oneida	x				—	Feasibility study not made		—
Potawatomie					(Blank)	(Blank)		
S.C. Chippewa								
LCO		x	x		—	Continue as is "	State & Fed.	The Federal Government should continue to help the reservation until we decide to go our own way.
Wyoming								
S & A	x	x			—	(Blank)		

A review of the table supports the general statements under 13. Some observations on those checking "(a) tribal operations."

Ak-Chin is thinking of a tribal operation for K–3 under a BIA contract. (The other grades will continue in public school.) Havasupai wants Federal funding through a BIA contract but administration "by the community according to state public school standards." Dry Creek and San Pasqual are small California groups. Miccosukee has already contracted to operate the former Federal school. Most of the Nez Perce children are in public school, and although Nez Perce checked both (a) and (b), they do not seem to be making a pitch against continued State operation, but presenting a strong case for a qualified Indian teacher in each school with Indian children and the Federal Government should finance the salary for such a teacher. This seems to be a plea for culturally adjusted compensatory educational backup for slow learners. L'Anse checked both (a) and (b) with no explanation. Probably means continued State operation with more tribal input and influence.

Mississippi Choctaw is undoubtedly thinking of tribal (not State) operation because of the situation in the surrounding communities.

Northern Cheyenne is apparently referring to Busby, the only federally operated school in the State. Although Northern Cheyenne only checked (a) they only discussed Busby and gave no evidence of wanting to change existing public and private school operations. Acoma checked (a), (b), and (c) and is thinking of transferring operation of BIA schools to the tribe. No mention is made of change for those children now attending public school.

The Iowas and Tonkowas are small Oklahoma groups. Umatilla checked both (a) and (b) without further explanation of the relationship. The Oglala Sioux at Pine Ridge sound as if they are contemplating tribal operation for their children now in Federal schools at such time as the "people" decide to take over.

GLITC checked both (a) and (b). Oneida checked (a) only but indicated a feasibility study had not been made. The Shoshone and Arapaho in Wyoming checked both (a) and (b) without any further explanation.

In summary, many of those checking (a) seem to mean either Indian run schools under BIA contract using State standards, taking over present BIA operation but leaving present Indian children in public schools unchanged, or continued public school operation with greater input and influence by the Indian community.

The net result is perhaps a heavier emphasis on public schools than the column totals in question 13 indicate.

These comments deserve special attention. Navajo is supportive of what the local community on the reservation desires—they have public, Federal, and Navajo community operated schools.

Nez Perce and Tesuque stress the quality of education, dedication of school personnel, and compensatory education rather than who operates the schools.

15. *Are State employment services used by Indians in your jurisdiction?* Yes_____ No_____

Responses: 54

Yes	47	87%
No	3	6%

Please check services used:
a. Counseling	40	74%
b. Testing	38	70%
c. Placement	46	85%

d. Service to veterans	40	74%
e. Occupational analysis	31	57%
f. Labor area information	36	67%
g. Industrial development	20	37%

Favorable outweighed unfavorable comments. Navajo: "Full State Employment Services are available in all areas of the reservation. There is cooperation with Bureau and Tribal personnel." Pit River: "An Indian works this field for the State Department of Human Resources Development." Nez Perce: "This area is serviced well in this category of employment. But we still have chronically unemployed members. Reason for this could be that automation has come on us so fast that it had caught members that never had strenuous training on demanded skills of today." L'Anse: "We should have 10% of the jobs available in the community . . . We are 10% of the population."

Red Lake reports receiving full services. The S.M. Sioux (Minnesota) say: "The assistance received has not generally led to improvement in the employment picture." Ely: "We use all of the services of the Nevada Employment Agency with very good results." Acoma: "In the past very little assistance of this type was received. Services in 1970 were greatly improved." Tesuque: "Services such as actual job placement of Indians appears poor—maybe, due to lack of experience, training, etc. Of course, this is almost standard answer."

St. Regis: "We have an Indian representative who is very active in this field. She does an excellent job." Ft. Berthold: "The State has established a State Employment Office conveniently located to the reservation to render all assistance possible. Itinerant service is furnished at various points on the reservation." Kaw and Wyandotte indicate that the Oklahoma Employment Service helps with counseling and obtaining jobs. Cheyenne River: "We have a Job Developer who is financed by OEO who does counseling, testing, services to veterans, labor area information, and industrial development." The Great Lakes Intertribal Council indicated that the employment service "cooperated well with the tribes but their first survey of the tribes' labor force was not complete in Wisconsin." Oneida, however, stated: "The Intertribal Apprenticeship Center does a far better job in all above facets."

16. *Is the BIA Employment Assistance Program (relocation and adult vocational training) used by Indians in your jurisdiction?* Yes____ No____

Responses: 58

Yes	48	83%
No	10	17%

The tribes reporting that they do not use the Employment Assistance Program are four small groups in California, Miccosukee in Florida, Chitimacha in Louisiana, S.M. Sioux in Minnesota, the Ely Colony in Nevada, and St. Regis in New York. Nez Perce checked both columns. All of the above are relatively small and one of the California groups said: "Very few live upon reservation, mostly aged." St. Regis reported: "We have not actively asked for employment assistance, federal level. So few want to work away from home."

The comments by users fall into the following categories: important program to tribal members; emphasis should be changed to training and placement on or near reservation; and program not very important. Examples indicating importance to tribe are: Iowa tribe: "We have an adult vocational training center located in Kansas City, Mo., operated by Indians, doing very well." Montana Anonymous: "Real active useage in all areas." Ft. Berthold: "The BIA Assistance Program is one of the highest used in this area. The chief complaint has been the sending of participants such a great distance from the reservation to receive training. The adjustment from country to city life is not easily made; consequently, many of the participants fail to complete their courses." Cherokee "The Employment Assistance Program is federally funded and tribally administered and working well." Kaw: "The Vocational Training Service is of vital importance to our Indians—they use this service and we need it very much." Cheyenne River: "This service is used quite extensively by our people." Cheyenne and Arapaho: "Successful program on the reservation."

Ft. Berthold cited above indicated the complaint of sending trainees too far from home and the difficulty of adjusting to the urban environment. This was echoed by Ak-Chin, Acoma, and Northern Cheyenne.

Several suggested revising the emphasis to provide training and employment nearer the reservation and stop the drain on reservation manpower resources. The Confederated Salish and Kootenai Tribes: "The program should be restructed to train and secure employment applicable to the reservation to stop the drain on our manpower resources." Northern Cheyenne stated 90 percent of the trainees had returned to the reservation: "The council feels that the funds for the program should be given to the Northern Cheyenne Tribe for our use in our own training programs." Winnebago said: "They have the money, but their program is not at all geared to the relevant needs of the reservation." Tesuque: "Some of our people have taken advantage of Employment Assistance but it appears that only the more potentially successful go. This, in our minds is a 'brain drain' since many of these folks could be pointed to as successes when counseling with delinquents of all ages. Also these folks could very (possibly) help as councilmen, etc., for the benefit of the tribe." Umatilla: "Need more concern for training of tribal members to fill available jobs in local market."

Indications that program was less important to some tribes are: Yavapai: "Use vocational training but not relocation." The Upper Sioux have the same reaction. Pit River "Very limited." Nez Perce: "BIA—very little." L'Anse: "We haven't had an Employment Assistance here in the area for about one year." Red Lake "as much as funding allows." GLITC "Understaffed." Oneida: "so! so!" S.C. Chippewa (Wisconsin): "Several have taken training, but no jobs were available."

17. *What other employment assistance do Indians receive (e.g., other Federal or private agencies)?*

Other Federal agencies cited were: OEO (CAP, NYC, Job Corps); Park Service; Labor (CEP, Manpower Development Training Job 70 Program, MDTA, Operation Mainstream, etc.); Federal Civil Service; and interagency job placement.

State agencies other than State employment services cited were: State Civil Service and Oklahoma Department of Institutional, Social and Rehabilitation Services.

Private assistance cited: Fred Harvey Company, cattle ranches, IDDA, Navajo Tribe Job Development Program, Green Thumb (Minnesota), private employers, local Iron Workers Union, farms, Okmulgee Technical School, United Sioux Employment Center (cited by Oglala Sioux), Great Lakes Inter-Tribal Apprenticeship Center, and apprenticeships.

18. *Who checks periodically with employers within commuting distance of where Indians live to determine future job openings and skills and training required to fill them?*

a. Tribal officials	25	56%
b. Bureau of Indian Affairs employees	25	56%
c. State Employment Service	30	67%

Responses: 45

Many respondents made no comments. Six that did comment said "No one or nobody checks." Others said there were occasional checks.

19. *Who follows up on information indicated in 18 above to see that Indians have an opportunity for appropriate training and know about job opportunities well in advance?*

a.	Tribal officials	24	55%
b.	Bureau of Indian Affairs employees	31	70%
c.	State Employment Service	18	41%
d.	State or county welfare	6	14%

Responses: 44

It is interesting that BIA received more checks on this than they did on 18.

Health

20. *What rules and regulations to control communicable diseases apply in your jurisdiction—please check as appropriate:*

a.	Tribal?	18	33%
b.	Local or State?	41	75%
c.	Federal?	29	53%

Responses: 55

Comments on this question: Havasupai: "The Tribal Court has authority to order and compel the medical examination and treatment of any person found with communicable disease." Navajo: "The Tribe has passed resolutions supporting federal regulation. IHS reports morbidity to State in areas not covered by local health jurisdiction." Yavapai: "Public Health Service and County." Chemehuevi: "Public Law 280." Dry Creek: "USPHS of Sacramento promised to install better water and sewer facilities to some of the families in this rancheria, but up to now we don't have any result." Pit River: "State laws." San Pasquel: "Public School." Miccosukee: "IHS." Nez Perce: "PHS . . . authorizes any health assistance with the Contract Doctors." Red Lake: "a) Tribe code, b) IHS." Choctaw (Miss): "State and Federal communicable disease investigators are located in Meridian and Jackson. There are no local investigators in this area for immediate follow-up. Tabulation and reporting of communicable disease are done through Arizona rather than through the State Department of Health which causes a delay in follow-ups." Northern Cheyenne: ". . . recently established a Board of Health . . ." which "is in the process of developing rules and regulations that will apply to our reservation." Confederated Salish and Kootenai: "Indian Public Health Service works with local county officials with concurrent jurisdiction over Indians." Winnebago (Nebraska): "We use IHS." Acoma: "PHS, county Health." Tesuque: "Because it involves the general welfare of all tribal members, the Tribal Council enforces all regulations whether they may be state or federally requested." St. Regis: "State health clinic Doctor and Nurse, also County programs. Also recent mental health program and drug and alcohol program." Ft. Berthold: "No tribal laws exist so state laws are applicable." Cherokee: "The Cherokee Tribe has a Health and Sanitation Committee, an Advisory Board to the United States Public Health Hospitals, and through constituted representation works closely with all available health resources." Wyandotte: "Federal and State laws apply to us as citizens of U.S." GLITC: "Tribal health committees—10." LCO: "CAP, State, BIA," Cheyenne and Arapaho (Wyoming): "IHS."

21. *What suggestions do you have for improving the health of Indians in your jurisdiction?*

The main thrust of the majority of the comments is—more money for IHS, more and better facilities, decentralization of facilities, and additional health personnel. Tesuque points out that their present hospital (Santa Fe) just lost its accreditation and asks "Are you going to do something?" Education, better housing, better living conditions, and improvement of the economic base through such efforts as developing more industries and job opportunities are also indicated as important to improving health.

Several indicated they were served well under present arrangements (e.g., Ak-Chin and Yavapai). Several stressed preventive public health education programs. Nez Perce commented: "Tribe has Community Health Representatives in two areas. This position will have to stress more on health than being a taxicab for tribal members. We should be showing films on the prevention of various diseases. Go out and give ways of good health." There were several comments on the need for a nursing home or an aged facility.

Kaw pointed to the need for personal responsibility: "I feel our Indians should have regular check-ups, this they neglect. They should follow the instructions of the doctor, again this they are neglective."

Orientation of doctors assigned to IHS hospitals was stressed by Cheyenne River: ". . . so that they can better communicate and help the Indian people without creating harsh feelings between the two cultures."

Roads

22. *Do you have problems with the maintenance of roads or local airports which are—*

a. Federally maintained?	Yes	21	43%	No	17	35%
b. State maintained?	Yes	15	31%	No	17	35%
c. County maintained?	Yes	26	53%	No	15	31%

Responses: 49

Most comments were concerned with poor maintenance. Many recognized that the limited maintenance provided was due to limited funds. Nevertheless, two groups in Wisconsin indicated that Indian roads were the last to get attention and are less maintained. Cheyenne River pointed out that State and county "officials feel since the Indian does not pay taxes (property Tax), they will not obtain tax dollars to maintain roads that cross trust land. They, too, are short of funds to properly maintain roads, if they are willing to do so."

Welfare

23. *What court exercises authority on the reservation over placement of Indian children away from their own home?*

a. Tribal court	18	35%
b. Local or State court	32	62%
c. Combination of above (Please explain under COMMENTS)	4	8%

COMMENTS: *(What changes, if any, would you recommend?)*

Responses: 52

Most did not have any comments. Mississippi Choctaw explained checking (c) by "Tribal Court of Indian Offenses (Juvenile Court)" and Cheyenne River explained their check of (c) "I believe the Tribal Court should maintain jurisdiction, but the State Courts should lend comity to the Tribal Court's decisions." The other two respondents checking (c) made no comments.

The most frequent other comment was that the Tribe would like a voice in helping place children (Barona, Tule River, Winnebago, Acoma, GLITC). L'Anse felt that Indian children should be placed with Indian families.

Many of those making no comments may be satisfied as is Northern Cheyenne: "Our Tribal Court seems to be handling this situation very well and we do not recommend any changes at this time." Other small groups may not be faced with this problem very often as indicated by Ely Indian Colony.

24. *What agency actually places Indian children in foster homes under court authority?*

Responses: 56

a. State or local welfare offices	41	73%
b. Bureau of Indian Affairs	22	39%
c. Private agency	2	4%
d. Combination of above (Please explain under COMMENTS)	8	14%

COMMENTS: *(What change, if any, would you recommend?)*

Comments of those checking (d). Ak-Chin: "It should be strictly tribal affairs backed by federal funding." White Mt. Apache: "Tribal Court refers cases to BIA Branch of Social Services which refers to State Welfare for child placement and supervision." Chemehuevi and the Iowas of Kansas checked (a) (b) and (d) and made no comment. Mississippi Choctaws checked (d) only with no comment. Jicarilla said: "Tribal and State." Tesuque reported: "Mostly when Tribal Court or Council is unaware, adoption, placement, etc. occurs through other than Tribal Court." Ft. Berthold says: "Tribal court, county welfare, state courts, and the BIA work together to place Indian children in foster homes when needed. The tribe is in the process of establishing a juvenile home on the reservation for the rehabilitation of the youth."

Yavapai checked only (b) but said: "Local welfare, public school, and BIA." Others checking (b) that commented are: Northern Cheyenne checked both (a) and (b): "The Tribal Council has expressed their desire to see all our Cheyenne children, who are abandoned and left to shift on their own, be placed in foster homes on the reservation, rather than be placed in homes off the reservation. It is hoped that a remedy to this type of situation can be worked out in the near future." Winnebago (also (a) and (b)): "We want them to work with the Council." Acoma (b) only): "Tribal council should have more control." Zia (both (a) and (b)): "Both BIA and state depending on which agency is working with the family." Cherokee checked (a) (b) and (c) and said: "All of the above agencies cooperate and work together in child placement."

Four groups checking (a) only want closer involvement of the tribal councils and keep children on reservation if possible. GLITC suggests (a) "An advisory committee to the Welfare Department." St. Regis (a): "Only children's court and welfare—local clergyman and chiefs help."

25. *Who pays for foster home care or institutional care for Indian children from the reservations?*

a. State or local welfare offices	32	64%
b. Bureau of Indian Affairs	25	50%
c. Private agency	--	--

   d. Other (Explain under **COMMENTS**)   3   6%

   e. Combination of above (Explain under **COMMENTS**)   3   6%

   COMMENTS: *(What change, if any, would you recommend?)*

Responses: 50

Comments for those checking (d) and (e) follow: Tule River: "Parents are supposed to pay part of cost. Sometimes money for child is taken out of his per capita payment for this purpose." Nez Perce: "Individual income through BIA" Jicarilla: "Payment made by tribal or personal funds. Would like to see state take responsibility for payment of services." Ft. Berthold: "If Indian children are residents of the reservation, the BIA will pay for the cost unless they are residents receiving public assistance, the county then pays for the care."

The only other comments were: Winnebago: "That a program be set up to assist Indian families in becoming foster parents." St. Regis: "N. Y. State pays all." Cherokee checked both (a) and (b): "(b) BIA boarding schools." Seminole and Wyandotte in Oklahoma pointed out that there are no reservations in Oklahoma. Seminole went on to state: "Indian children treated as non-Indians in institutional care, except for certain BIA facilities and assistance." GLITC suggested" "Enlargement of BIA Social Services."

26. *What is your working relationship with county and State welfare departments?*

    a. Attend each other's meetings   15   29%

    b. Work on projects together   20   39%

    c. Informal talks   34   67%

    d. Other   9   18%

    (Please explain under **COMMENTS**)

Responses: 51

Those checking (d) commented as follows: White Mt. Apache: "Frequent telephone and written communication conferences in DPW and BIA offices." Calif. Anon.: "ITC (Inter Tribal Council) works with our Health Board." Winnebago: "On occasion as the *crisis* indicates, we get together with them and try to help them spend their money in a manner relevant to the needs of our Indians." Acoma: "Communication improving." Tesuque: "Usually individuals handle their own cases and unless T C is requested to assist we have no involvement. Our relationship remains cordial." Cheyenne River: "We work jointly on all welfare problems with regard to child welfare, adoption, etc." GLITC: "Very poor relation in regard to county boards, a bettering relation with state and county welfare departments."

Other comments were: Ak-Chin: "Due to small population base, hardly anyone relies on welfare here at this community." Cocopah: "Their visits to our reservation are very few and far between." Barona: "People who are on welfare work with the county welfare office." Pit River: "Need for more involvement by Indian community. It appears to be an individual affair of members of Band." Tule River: "We don't have that much of a working relationship with each other so this could be improved." Miccosukee checked (c) and said "About one a month." Red Lake (c) "Tribe offers assistance when needed." S.M. Sioux (c) "This working relationship stood up well under recent use." Northern Cheyenne (c) "There should definitely be better working relations between the Tribal Council, BIA, State and County Welfare agencies, since we are all working with the same people and towards the same goal." Jicarilla (c) "A very good relationship exists between Tribal, BIA and State departments." St. Regis: "We have very good cooperation with welfare department. The county administers and the state pays for this service." Ft. Berthold (a) and (b):

"We have tribal committees that coordinate the BIA and tribal programs. Also, some Indian members serve on welfare boards for the county." Cherokee (a) (b) (c): "This working relationship is excellent." Wyandotte (a) and (b): "Any Indian in Oklahoma is entitled to all assistance that any other person is entitled to."

27. *What is your working relationship with the Bureau of Indian Affairs Social Services Program?*

a.	Attend each other's meetings	20	42%
b.	Work on projects together	27	56%
c.	Informal talks	30	63%
d.	Other (Please explain under COMMENTS)	12	25%

Responses: 48

Small and isolated tribes, such as Ak-Chin (Ariz), L'Anse (Mich). S.M. Sioux and Upper Sioux (Minn.), and rancherias in California don't have much need or are too far away from a BIA office for effective service. St. Regis in New York is served by the State; no BIA social worker available. However, the Iowas, a small tribe in Kansas, say the BIA services are good.

Navajo, as a larger tribe with BIA services, states: "There is a close relationship between the BIA and Tribal Social Services Program. Problems are shared, joint projects are undertaken, careful mutual review insures that duplication of services does not exist."

Red Lake in Minnesota has a Bureau office and works with BIA on such programs as surplus commodities and planning child care facilities, and emergencies. Jicarilla checked (a) and (b) and commented "Excellent" while Tesuque reports "working relationship is average." Ft. Berthold: "Tribal committees coordinate BIA and tribal programs." Cherokee states: "There is always room for improvement on both sides of the coin." Cheyenne River indicates "working relationship is good" and Oglala says they "maintain a welfare contract."

In summary, where BIA services are readily available, as with the larger federally recognized tribes, working relationships on the whole seem to be good. Some smaller groups are well serviced by BIA but many are not, especially when BIA offices are not available.

28. *Does your organization have a committee or other official group which concerns itself with welfare problems?* Yes_____ No_____

Responses: 55

Yes	25	45%
No	30	55%

If "Yes" please describe: (Also indicate your organization's thoughts or policy on how welfare should be handled in the future)

Thirty respondents made no comments or stated they had no recommended changes. Most of those commenting described or identified the committee or group working on such problems and indicated no desire for change. Hopi, however, did say they "Need a Tribal Welfare Committee."

The types of committees or groups identified by the respondents were: local community action program; Health, Alcoholism and Welfare Committee; Human Resources Committee; Welfare Committee; Health Education and Welfare Sub-Committee; Emergency Food and Medical Aid; Community Services Committee; Law and Order and Recreation Committees; Health, Sanitation and Welfare Committee; Vista; and the entire council acting as a welfare committee.

Judicial, Prevention, and Enforcement Services

29. *Who operates Judicial, Prevention, and Enforcement Services for your jurisdiction?*

a. Tribe (or Tribes)	11	20%
b. Locality or State	34	61%
c. Bureau of Indian Affairs	13	23%
d. Combination of above	16	29%

(Include explanation of "d" if checked)

Responses: 56

The comments of those checking (d) follow: Havasupai: "BIA appoints the Judge and policemen with Tribal Council recommendation." Navajo: "The Tribe supports a Police Force and Judicial System which handles crimes (excluding those reserved to Federal authorities) among Indians on the Reservation. Bureau program pays for prevention and enforcement services involving 10 major crimes. State and local government pay for some services in the portion of the reservation (checkerboarded) where land status is not clearly defined." Yavapai: "BIA contracts county law enforcement." San Pasquel: "Does not matter who is applied to. None reply." Red Lake: "Police and criminal investigator under BIA. Tribal Judge under Buy-Indian contract." Northern Cheyenne, under a memorandum of agreement with BIA the Tribe ". . . handles the judicial system and pays the salary of the Chief Judge, Court Clerk, Associate Judge and all police officers. The Bureau handles the hiring and firing of the Police. They also handle the maintenance of the Municipal Center." Confederated Salish and Kootenai: "State has concurrent jurisdiction over Indians." Jicarilla: "Tribe has own police department and Law and Order Code: a state patrolman is stationed at Dulce; BIA has Agency Criminal Investigator." Tesuque: "Tribe for tribal members or other Indians on reservation and assist county and state through cross deputization of tribal policemen. BIA cooperates and assists as well as state." Ft. Berthold: "The tribe established a law and order code which the BIA enforces. Through a Buy-Indian contract, the tribe hires about half of the police officers." Cheyenne River: "BIA furnishes a Special Officer to assist Tribal law enforcement against the twelve major crimes. The Tribe pays for the services of their judicial personnel." GLITC: "Three counties have tribal members as full time Deputy Sheriffs . . . ."

Comments from those checking (a) (b) or (c) and not (d) are: Kaibab-Paiute (c): indicated that the BIA, State highway and county officers "work hand in hand on most problems that come up." Chemehuevi (b): "State has not provided adequately." Pit River: "P.L. 280—State." St. Regis (a) and (b): "Chiefs handle all land cases, probate wills and minor civil disputes. N. Y. State courts and county on all criminal cases. State troopers enforce. County sheriffs assist. We have two deputies." Oglala (a) and (c): "Tribe maintains contract on Law and Order."

30. *Who pays for these services?*

a. Tribe (or Tribes)	10	19%
b. Locality or State	31	58%
c. Bureau of Indian Affairs	21	40%
d. Combination of above	5	9%

(Include explanation of "d" if checked)

Responses: 53

Some of the responses under question 29 indicated the sources of financial support. They will not be repeated here. Other comments were: Red Lake: "Tribal income is insufficient to Tribal Law and Order system. Tribe has no desire or intent to assume enforcement obligation. Buy-Indian contract." Salish and Kootenai: "Each pays his own efforts in Law and Order." Pyramid Lake (a) said: "No funds." Jicarilla: "Each agency supports its own." Tesuque (d) "Tribe-non paid except expenses. State, BIA." St. Regis (b): "Tribe does not contribute." Ft. Berthold (d): "Some of the costs of the staff are defrayed by court fines and fees collected by the tribal court." Iowas (Okla.)" "Sometimes the individuals themselves." Oglala: "BIA and tribe pay the bills." GLITC: "Assisted in bringing counties, tribes and state together to program through LEEA."

31. *Do you consider it desirable to have uniform judicial, prevention, and enforce-ment services in your jurisdiction?* Yes_____ No_____

Responses: 47

Yes	45	96%
No	2	4%

If "Yes" who should operate:

a. Tribe	26	58%
b. Locality or State	19	42%
c. Bureau of Indian Affairs	13	29%
d. Other	2	4%

(If you indicate the desirability of a change from the present situation, e.g., from BIA and tribe to locality and State or vice versa, what time schedule for making the change would be feasible in your judgment? Who should pay the cost under your suggested or preferred arrangement? If "Other" is checked, please explain.)

The respondents endorsed the desirability of uniform judicial, prevention, and enforcement services but did not see the necessity for it to be administered by one authority. Many checked "Yes" and two or more in the (a), (b), (c) and (d) columns.

It is obvious that several tribes have indicated increased tribal participation in the administration of law and order as desirable when the responses to question 29 and 31 are compared. However, only seven tribes checked (a) alone, whereas 15 others checked (a) and (b) or (c) or all three on question 31. On question 29, only four tribes checked (a) alone, indicating exclusive tribal administration at the present time (others in the same position may have also checked (c) as the Federal government is involved in specified major crimes).

Federal funds should continue and the tribe should administer (Havasupai and L'Anse); Chemehuevi, Havasupai, Miccosukee, L'Anse and Umatilla wanted the tribe to take over, all but Umatilla indicating the change should be made immediately.

Nine tribes checked (b) alone, almost as many as checked (a). The reactions apparently reflect the tribes' experience to some extent. California, which has had State law and order, had four tribes checking (a) (3 (a) only and one (a) and (c)) and only one checked (b) only. Oklahoma, on the other hand, had five tribes checking (b)—with one adding an (a) and another a (c). So the reactions in the respondents in these two States were quite different. Most of those with present tribal-BIA combinations preferred to continue the arrangement, some suggesting all operation by tribe with only funding support from BIA.

Red Lake and Navajo are examples of the last point. Red Lake: "Tribe does not have funds for Law and Order and does not wish to take it by Buy-Indian Contract. State could not furnish adequate enforcement due to tax base structure and tribe does not wish to relinquish any of its treaty rights of self-government."

Navapo: "The Tribe currently supports a well trained, well organized police force and an excellent court system providing judicial, prevention and enforcement services for Indians on the Reservation. Financial assistance to continue the operation has been requested from BIA x x x We would have major problems relating to the crimes presently handled by BIA and crimes among non-Indians residing on the reservation. The tribe does not see fit to transfer jurisdiction to the several states in which the reservation is located."

Mississippi Choctaw stated: "It is desirable that all policemen are Federal officers."

Several tribes mentioned continued law and order jurisdiction and "tribal sovereignty"—Red Lake above, Cheyenne River, and Oneida. The Salish and Kootenai tribes point to the lack of complete sovereignty: "The non-Indian can take an Indian to their court for any violation. Indian must take a non-Indian to Federal court. State and Federal courts do not give satisfaction. If the offense is on the reservation the non-Indian should go to Tribal Court."

Some under State jurisdiction want out. Umatilla: "It is the desire of my tribe to be released from the clutches of P.L. 280 and returned to Federal and Tribal law enforcement. In the beginning it should be funded by the Federal Government until the tribe is economically able to pay their way." Barona (Calif.): "Get away from state."

St. Regis (New York): "Except for the need of an Indian Justice of the Peace and funding of our own officers, system is working."

Jicarilla, who checked (a) (b) and (c): "The cooperation of the three agencies seems very desirable and has worked satisfactorily for our tribe; improvements are always in order and we work toward a better prevention system at all times."

Realty Services

32. *Reservation or restricted land is supervised by either the Federal or State Governments. Should the present situation continue in your jurisdiction?* Yes____ No____

(If "No" please describe your proposal)

Responses: 51

Yes	48	94%
No	3	6%

The comments of those checking "No" are: Upper Sioux (Minnesota): "Should be handled by local tribal government." S. C. Chippewa (Wisc): "Let the tribe make their own decisions." Barona checked "No" but apparently wanted Federal trust to continue as their comment was "Federal Government."

There were few other comments. Cheyenne River was one: "Because under Federal statutes and treaties, the Federal Government has the trust relationship with individual tribes to guard these trust and interest lands from State encroachment." St. Regis: "Our problem is treaty granted land on which non-Indians reside. We need help in resolving this problem."

33. *Coordination of Indian Programs*

In April 1970 a questionnaire was forwarded to the 50 States by the Governor's Interstate Indian Council to find out about State programs for Indians. One of the items was:

"Please give any ideas or suggestions you have for facilitating Indian-State-Federal coordination on Indian matters; also, your thoughts on what might be desirable concerning State organizations for the coordination of Indian affairs."

The States have had an opportunity to comment on the above. Your comments or suggestions on this subject would be appreciated.

Responses: 37

Nine tribes stressed cooperation of all groups—Indian, local, State, and Federal—as the best way to assist Indians: L'Anse: "We would like to have assistance by these agencies, but not to set any policies unless approved by the tribal councils." Upper Sioux: "It is my personal feeling we need the help and advice of non-Indians, who are interested and concerned, to assist in all our tribal matters. Indian people lack education and cannot properly work and cooperate together." Choctaw (Miss.): "A dire need exists in planning development and coordination of various services available from all sources. Funds are needed from other sources to establish an agency or an office within the tribe to fill the need." St. Regis: "We hope that the Federal government through BIA can assist us where the State cannot or will not. Our administration of our problems has been haphazard, but we seem to be getting along. But we need help in business programs, banking and related services." Cherokee: "We feel the better coordination of tribal programs with local county, state and Federal programs, the better opportunities for raising the social and economic status of the Cherokees." Iowas (Okla.): "I think or suggest that a more closely related or more intimate coordination between these agencies would enlighten each other better on Indian problems or any other matter." Seminole (Okla.): "The Indian Affairs Commission should work more closely with BIA and with tribal governments to coordinate Indian affairs and services to our Indian people." Cheyenne River: "By having the three-agency coordination, I can see the benefit which would be derived by the Indian, but we must guard against what is his inherent right of the tribal group which cannot be encroached upon by the State or local government or vice versa. By cooperation, we could have the necessary expertise of the three-agency group, thereby any and all plans, and all Indian matters would be more beneficial to the Indian population of each state. Also, an interesting side benefit would be the gradual disappearance of any discrimination or hostility that may now exist between the two cultures and between the three governments." GLITC: "The tribes must present their ideas and plans for the reservation and what they may see as a gain by state involvement. And always be aware of the need to maintain their tribal lands."

Eight tribes endorsed their State Indian commissions or said there should be a State office working on Indian matters. ANB: "Each state should have an Indian affairs agency to coordinate state and federal programs re Indians and their various problems with a view of adequate solutions." Pit River: "Desperately need a state advisory commission on Indian affairs." Red Lake: "We work through the State Indian Affairs Commission." S.M. Sioux: "We are now becoming more active in relation to the State Indian Commission and see this as a good development." Winnebago (Nebr.): "It would be to our advantage to have federal funds to the reservation by different agencies coordinated. But to give control to the States is not good considering their inability to respond to Indian needs in the past. We would want this in the State Indian Commission." Ft. Berthold: "For more efficient coordination of Indian affairs between the State and the reservation, it would be recommended that an Indian desk be established at the state capitol. Although the State has an Indian Commissioner, his office cannot administer all the Indian business. We feel an additional Indian office at the State level would provide a source to keep the Indian as well as the State better informed on Indian affairs in the state." Cherokee: "The State of Oklahoma has a Commission on Indian Affairs which is working effectively." Seminole: "Oklahoma has an Indian Affairs Commission which should work more closely with BIA and tribal governments."

In the foregoing there have been references to need for maintaining Indian land and some questions about giving control to the State (e.g., Winnebago). Four tribes flatly state their distrust of the States. Nez Perce: "State's goal is to try and have all trust properties as deeded property. State is also desirous of repealing the Fishing and Hunting Rights of American Indians which is guaranteed by Federal Treaties. Now if the State of Idaho were given this authority all privileges that are available to American Indians would soon be erased." Pyramid Lake: "We would rather not— under State." Acoma: "PL 280 off books." Oneida: "As long as the Indian has land— the state and its personnel will work with an ulterior motive."

Four other tribes are in the same general posture, but state it as their preference to deal directly with the Federal Government. Hopi: "The Hopi Tribe receives better service by dealing directly with Federal agencies." Barona: "Go back under Federal Government on Civil Law." Montana (Anon): "We desire *direct* relationship with the federal system—*do not* desire *state* involvement on services or program implementation." Salish and Kootenai: "The programs for Indians should be administered directly by the Federal government. When the state becomes involved it is only occasionally, when their conscience bothers them, or when year end funds begin to pile up threatening next year's allocation do they filter the funds down to the Indians."

Two tribes approach this same area from another viewpoint, that State governments should recognize tribes as separate entities. Chemehuevi: "The state governments should recognize tribal organizations as separate entities enjoying sovereign immunities." Tesuque: "In our case, let New Mexico respect its constitution—re waiver of jurisdiction on Indian lands, and require all state departments, offices, etc., to respect the wishes of Indians in observing such waivers in dealing with Tribal governments."

Nine States presented general comments, description of coordination activities, or were non-committal. Havasupai: "The Havasupai Community Action Program is funded by OEO to coordinate the tribal activities with those of other agencies in solving mutual problems and this should be continued. The State Economic Opportunity Office in Phoenix is also set up to give assistance to the community." Cocopah: "Listen to Indian leaders rather than the Anglo so-called 'Indian Expert'." Chitimacha: "In areas or states without Indians in large numbers, the state or area not adjacent to the reservation usually takes pride in the fact there are Indians there. Surrounding the reservation, people usually avoid the Indian and the Indian community. Yet we do the same to them." Jicarilla: "A more flexible program of conditions with more local authority for the execution of the program once granted provided the conditions are met to the satisfaction of the program. More Indian involvement." Wyandotte: "More help and better service from the Claims Commission —closer relationship between the tribe and commission. Broader information and more financial assistance to the Indian people in Oklahoma for education." Oglala: "Organization such as United Sioux Tribes of South Dakota is essential."

And the more non-committal: Navajo: "Since we have not had an opportunity to review the April 1970 questionnaire and the replies, we would not care to comment. The Tribe is always interested in cooperative programs creating opportunities for mutual use of human and natural resources whenever such programs are mutually beneficial." White Mountain Apache: "State organization and programs just now developing. Appear to be desirable, but more time required to study and experience." Northern Cheyenne: "No comments until I see what the state of Montana comes up with."

Yavapai had a kind word: "Have appreciated Arizona State Employment Service, Indian Department."

And two California groups suggested BIA action; Dry Creek: "I would suggest that BIA officers should come visit the rancherias or reservations often to discuss the problems and improvements of the community. They should give decent jobs for rancheria residents if qualified." Tule River: "If there is going to be a BIA they should be the ones to coordinate the efforts between the state, federal and Indian tribes. This may supposed to be true already but it sure isn't here on this reservation."

SELECTED BIBLIOGRAPHY

There are many references in the footnotes throughout the text that will be of interest to those who wish to do further research in depth. Following is a limited list of works covering a broad range which will be helpful to the general reader.

Answers to Your Questions About American Indians. Washington, D.C. U.S. Department of the Interior, Bureau of Indian Affairs, 1970.

Presents answers to the most frequently asked questions about Indian culture, legal status, citizenship, the Bureau of Indian Affairs, Indian land, economic status of Indians, Indian education, law and order on reservations, and Indian health. Also presents selected reading lists. May be obtained from the Bureau of Indian Affairs in Washington or the Superintendent of Documents.

Are You Listening Neighbor? Olympia: State of Washington. Report of the Indian Affairs Task Force, 1971.

This report was prepared by a joint task force of the Governor's Advisory Council on Urban Affairs and the Governor's Indian Advisory Committee and deals primarily with the reservation Indian. The chairman and vice-chairman as well as a majority of the task force were Indian. Indian, State, and Federal relationships and services are discussed.

BROPHY, WILLIAM A. and ABERLE, SOPHIE D. *The Indian, America's Unfinished Business, Report of the Commission on the Rights, Liberties, and Responsibilities of the American Indian.* Norman, Okla.: University of Oklahoma Press, 1966.

A very informative discussion of American Indian values, government, and assimilation, and the meaning of reservation, the role of the BIA, Indian law, economic development. Contains recommendations.

Note: An earlier summary report by the same Commission *A Program for Indian Citizens,* was published in January 1961, Fund for the Republic. Members of the Commission were: W. W. Keeler, Principal Chief of the Cherokee Tribe and then Executive Vice President of Phillips Petroleum; Karl N. Llewellyn, Professor of Jurisprudence, University of Chicago; A. M. Schlesinger, Professor of History, Harvard; Charles A. Sprague, The Oregon Statesman; and O. Meredith Wilson, Chairman, President of the University of Minnesota. William A. Brophy, former Commissioner of Indian Affairs (1945–48), was the first Executive Director of the Commission. Dr. Sophie D. Aberle (Mrs. Brophy) succeeded Mr. Brophy in this position. From 1935 to 1944 she served as Superintendent of the United Pueblos Agency, Bureau of Indian Affairs.

COLLIER, JOHN. *Indians of the Americas.* New York: W. W. Norton, 1947.

Collier was Commissioner of Indian Affairs longer than any other Commissioner, and was the leading force behind the Indian Reorganization Act of 1934. His book describes the evolution of Indian tribes from pre-history to the New Deal period.

CUSHMAN, DAN. *Stay Away, Joe.* 4th ed. Great Falls, Mont.: Stay Away Joe Publishers, 1968.

A fictional account of an extended Indian family showing various stages of acculturation among the different members. There are several other excellent fictional accounts cited in the text (by Harry James, Hal Glen Borland, Thomas Berger, and Alan Fry) but this one presents the broadest view of the acculturation drama and pathos. All of these stories, though labeled fiction, are written by keen observers and give a flavor based on real life which will be helpful to readers who have not had first hand experience in Indian communities. Momaday, N. Scott. *House Made of Dawn.* New York: Harper and Row, 1968, is a Pulitzer Prize winning novel that describes the trauma an Indian faces when he leaves reservation life. Mr. Momaday is a Kiowa–Cherokee Indian.

DELORIA, VINE, Jr. *Custer Died for Your Sins.* New York: The Macmillan Co., 1969. This is a "biting" and "witty" analysis of the causes for and present condition of the American Indian as interpreted by a Sioux Indian. He discusses the problem of Indian leadership, predicts that urban Indians will become the leaders of the Indian movement, and presents a "redefinition" of Indian affairs.

DRIVER, HAROLD E. *Indians of North America.* Chicago: The University of Chicago Press, 1961.

Presents a comparative description and interpretation of native American cultures from the Arctic to Panama. Has maps showing distribution of particular culture traits.

Federal Indian Law. Washington, D. C.: U. S. Department of the Interior, 1958.

A revision and updating of Felix Cohen's *Handbook of Federal Indian Law.* An authoritative reference for the complex field of Indian law.

HAGAN, WILLIAM T. *American Indians.* Chicago: The University of Chicago Press, 1961.

This is a brief (190 pp.) , readable, and perceptive history of the relations between the Indians and the United States, indicating the clash of cultures, and relating this clash to the mainstream of American history. For the general reader this book is an excellent introduction.

A more recent general history by Angie Debo, *A History of the Indians of the United States,* Norman, Okla.: University of Oklahoma Press, 1971; describes in more detail than Hagan Oklahoma and Alaskan Native problems and opportunities.

Handbook of American Indians North of Mexico. Edited by Frederick Webb Hodge. 2 vols.; Washington, D. C.: Smithsonian Institution, Bureau of Ethnology, 1907 2nd printing, 1912) , Bulletin 30.

The Handbook contains a descriptive list of the stocks, confederacies, tribes, tribal divisions, and settlements north of Mexico; the names by which these have been known; biographies of Indians of note; sketches of the history, archeology, manners, arts, customs, and institutions of various groups; and aboriginal words incorporated into the English language.

The Smithsonian Institution is working on a new "Handbook of North American Indians," of 20 volumes, scheduled for publication in 1976.

Handbook on Wisconsin Indians. Madison, Wis.: Governor's Commission on Human Rights, 1966.
Compiled and written by Joyce M. Erdman, this presents an informative description of "Who is an Indian?" It presents a history of Wisconsin tribes and a description of education, resources, health and housing for Indians. The relationships of the various State departments to Wisconsin Indians are described as well as the changing status of the Indians and the Federal Government.

Indians in Minnesota. St. Paul, Minn.: League of Women Voters of Minnesota, 1971.
This is an excellent review of Minnesota Indian needs and their relationship to government—tribal, Federal, State and local. The appendix contains the major treaties and a brief listing of major Federal and State laws, and details of Indian tribal government. A previous edition was published in 1962.

JOSEPHY, ALVIN M., Jr. *The Indian Heritage of America.* New York: Alfred A. Knopf, 1968.
Presents the archeology, ethnology, and history of the tribes and cultures of the Indians of North and South America from prehistoric times to the present day.

KROEBER, ALFRED L. *Cultural and Natural Areas of Native North America.* Berkeley: University of California Press, 1947.
A scholarly account of the relationship of Indian tribes to their physical environment.

MILLER, GEORGE FREDERICK. *A Wild Indian.* Washington, D. C.: The Daylion Co., 1942 (Printed by Mt. Vernon Publishing Co., Washington, D. C.)
Published anonymously. Miller was one of seven supervisors of Indian education in 1929. His novel reflects the Indian-Agent relationship, a description of Indian school operations, the vagaries of policy changes and directives from Washington, and the frustration of the field personnel with the Washington attempts to upgrade services. Many parallels can be seen between this description of the 1920's and 1930's and today.

The Problem of Indian Administration. Edited by Lewis Meriam. Baltimore: The Johns Hopkins Press, Institute for Government Research, 1928.
A landmark study involving a survey of the economic, social, educational, health and other conditions of the American Indians. The objective of the survey was "to look to the future and insofar as possible to indicate what remains to be done to adjust the Indians to the prevailing civilization so that they may maintain themselves in the presence of that civilization according at least to a minimum standard of health and decency." Many descriptions and recommendations are still applicable today. Of particular interest are his comments on relationships between tthe Indians and the States, and his proposals for the evolution of these relationships. Meriam was the director of a staff of eight who were specialists in various fields. This study was requested of the Institute for Government Research by Secretary of the Interior Hubert Work, in 1926.

Report of the Committee on Indian Affairs. Washington, D. C.: Commission on Organization of the Executive Branch of the Government (Hoover Commission) (mimeograph) October 1948.
This is a 345 page study by Charles J. Rhoads, John R. Nichols, Gilbert Darlington, and George A. Graham, Chairman, on which the majority report of the Hoover Commission based its conclusions. It is a thorough review of Indian programs and discusses the relationships of Indian tribes, States, and the Federal Government.

Social Security, Education, Indian Affairs, A Report to the Congress. Washington, D. C.: Commission on Organization of the Executive Branch of the Government (Hoover Commission), March 1949.

This includes the Commission's recommendation on Indian policy, including their recommendations for transfer of responsibilities to the States, and minority reports. It presents the diverse views often posed in Indian policy consideration.

SORKIN, ALAN L. *American Indians and Federal Aid.* Washington, D. C. Brookings Institution, 1971.

This is a first rate presentation of Federal programs and an analysis of their effectiveness. Education, health, agricultural development, industrial development, manpower development, property and income management, and welfare services are described and evaluated. The author's recommendations for improvement are included. This is the best of several recent books on this subject.

STEINER, STAN. *The New Indians.* New York, Evanston, London: Harper and Row, 1968.

As the dust cover states this book is a "report of the gathering 'Red Power' movement . . . a revolt against the white man's culture and its debasement of the tribal way."

SWANTON, JOHN R. *The Indian Tribes of North America.* Washington, D. C.: Smithsonian Institution, Bureau of American Ethnology, 1952, Bulletin 145.

A description of the tribes and groups about 1650. Discussion organized on the boundaries of the present States. Very convenient for those wanting information of early Indian groups in any particular State, Caribbean island, or Central American country.

UNDERHILL, RUTH M. *Red Man's America.* Chicago: The University of Chicago Press, 1953.

Discusses the Indian's varied origins, backgrounds, and customs.

WISSLER, CLARK. *Indians of the United States.* Garden City, N.Y.: Doubleday and Company, Inc. Revised Edition, 1966.

A historical review of Indians of the United States, grouping them by language families. Wissler was Dean of the Scientific Staff, American Museum of Natural History.

INDEX

287

State commissions on Indian affairs and
coordinators (continued)
funding, 158, 205
GIIC, 186
list of states with commissions and
staffs, 176
Nevada, 97
New Mexico, 101
North Dakota, 101, 102
Oklahoma, 92
relation to trust land, 79
twenty states have special organi-
zation, 89, 90
State correctional institutions, 74
State education subsidies, 85
State employment services, 103, 150, 158
State enabling acts, 151
State government
House Select Committee, 1944, 192
Indian acceptance of, 132
(See also State responsibility; Trans-
fer of functions to states)
State Indian role, 131
State initiative, 41
State involvement of Indians, 105
State judicial and institutional services,
103
State and federal responsibilities, 46
State or local court, 74
State philosophy and objectives con-
cerning Indian citizens, 90, 91, 202
State reservations, list of, with acreage
and population, 226
State responsibility
acceptance of changing responsibilities, 43
importance of state departments to
Indians, 103
Indians not on federal reservation, 19
insecurity of Indians re funds through
states, 141
process through which responsibility
acquired, 28, 29
responsiveness, 158
seeds go back to beginning, 27
services to Indians, 74, 190, 203, 206,
209, 210, 219
Edward P. Smith, 13
state and local responsibilities for
their citizens, 54, 139, 140
(See also, subject matter headings,
e.g., Education, Law and Order.

Transfer of federal programs
and responsibilities to states)
State shortcomings, 131–132
State status for Delaware Indians, 7
State trust Land, table for all states
acreage and population, 176, 226
State work with Indian leaders, 91
States as operating arm of the federal
system, 132
States derelict, 42
States with 10,000 or more Indians, 76
States with 50,000 or more Indians, 76
States without special organizational
arrangements but which do have
programs or services for Indians,
213
Stockbridge-Munsee, 217
Student guidance, 184
Subsidy for planning, 171
Subsistence economy, 123
Subsistence farming, 20
Superintendent, origin of, 17
Support for federally recognized In-
dians, 172
Supreme Court, 116
Surplus population, 57
Sustained yield management, 189

Taholah, 188, 189
Takeover of supervision of BIA agency
personnel, 163
legislation, 166
Zuni, 142
Tamiami Trail, 103
Taos Pueblo, 147, 156
Taxation
perparation of Indian to pay taxes,
19
tax exempt land, 3, 31
taxable value of trust land, 57
(See also Indian Organization Ques-
tionnaire, compilation of re-
sponses to)
Tennessee, 176, 206
Terminated tribes and groups, list of,
with acreage and membership, 231
Termination
Bosone resolution, 56
California and Oregon Indians, 58
GIIC, 44, 186
House report 2503, 1952, 56
incorporation proposals, 52, 189